PERFORMANCE
MANAGEMENT

PERFORMANCE MANAGEMENT

Herman Aguinis

The Business School
University of Colorado at Denver and Health Sciences Center

Upper Saddle River, New Jersey 07458

Library of Congress Cataloging-in-Publication Data

Aguinis, Herman,
   Performance management / Herman Aguinis.
     p. cm.
   Includes bibliographical references and index.
   ISBN 0-13-186615-X
   1. Employees—Rating of.   2. Performance—Management.   I. Title.

   HF5549.5.R3A38 2005
   658.3'125—dc22

                                         2005054977

VP/Editorial Director: Jeff Shelstad
Senior Acquisitions Editor: Jennifer Simon
Assistant Editor: Rich Gomes
Editorial Assistant: Stephanie Kamens
Marketing Manager: Anne Howard
Associate Director: Judy Leale
Managing Editor: Renata Butera
Production Editor: Suzanne Grappi
Permissions Coordinator: Charles Morris
Manufacturing Buyer: Indira Gutierrez
Production Manager, Manufacturing: Arnold Vila
Cover Design Manager: Jayne Conte
Full-Service Project Management: Progressive Publishing Alternatives
Typeface: 10/12 Times

Credits and acknowledgments borrowed from other sources and reproduced, with permission, in this textbook appear on appropriate page within text.

Pearson Prentice Hall™ is Pearson Education, Inc.
Pearson® is a registered trademark of Pearson plc
Prentice Hall® is a registered trademark of Pearson Education, Inc.

Pearson Education LTD.   Pearson Education Australia PTY, Limited
Pearson Education Singapore, Pte. Ltd   Pearson Education North Asia Ltd
Pearson Education, Canada, Ltd   Pearson Educación de Mexico, S.A. de C.V.
Pearson Education–Japan   Pearson Education Malaysia, Pte. Ltd

10 9 8 7 6 5 4 3
ISBN 0-13-186615-X

**To my wife, Heidi,
the best coach I've ever had**

BRIEF CONTENTS

CONTENTS

ACKNOWLEDGMENTS

Several individuals were extremely instrumental in allowing me to produce this book. I am indebted to Graeme Martin for encouraging me to start this project. Wendy O'Connell helped me gather numerous examples and illustrations that I used throughout. Christine Henle allowed me to use her extremely useful lecture notes. Barbara Stephens, Bonnie Davis, Debra Lammers, and Ray Zammuto gave me excellent and detailed comments that allowed me to improve each of the chapters. Numerous undergraduate, master's, and doctoral students at the University of Colorado at Denver and Health Sciences Center, Instituto de Empresa (Madrid, Spain), and Université Jean Moulin Lyon 3 (Lyon, France) allowed me to beta-test the book and gave me very useful feedback. I thank each of you for your time and intellectual investment in this project. Your coaching and feedback certainly helped improve my performance!

INTRODUCTION

In today's globalized world, it is relatively easy to gain access to the competition's technology and products. Thanks to the Internet and the accompanying high speed of communications, technological and product differentiation is no longer a key competitive advantage in most industries. For example, most banks offer the same types of products (e.g., different types of savings accounts and investment opportunities). If a particular bank decides to offer a new product or service (e.g., online banking), it will not be long until the competitors offer precisely the same product.

So, what makes some businesses more successful than others? What is today's key competitive advantage? The answer is people. Organizations with motivated and talented employees offering outstanding service to customers are likely to pull ahead of the competition, even if the products offered are similar to those offered by the competitors. Customers want to get the right answer at the right time and they want to receive their products or services promptly and accurately. Only people can make these things happen. Only people can produce a sustainable competitive advantage. And, performance management systems are the key tools to transform people's talent and motivation into a strategic business advantage.

Performance management is a continuous process of identifying, measuring, and developing the performance of individuals and teams and aligning performance with the strategic goals of the organization. Performance management is critical to small and large organizations, for-profit and not-for-profit, domestic and global, and to all industries. After all, the performance of an organization depends on the performance of its people, regardless of the organization's size, purpose, and other characteristics. As noted by Siemens CEO Heinrich von Pierer, "whether a company measures its workforce in hundreds or hundreds of thousands, its success relies solely on individual performance."

Unfortunately, however, if they have one, few organizations use their existing performance management systems in productive ways. Performance management is usually vilified as an "HR department requirement." In many organizations, performance management means that managers must comply with their HR department's request and fill out tedious, and often useless, evaluation forms. These evaluation forms are often completed because it is a requirement from the "HR cops." And, unfortunately, the only tangible consequence of the evaluation process is that the manager had to spend time away from his or her "real" job duties.

PLAN FOR THE BOOK

This book is about the design and implementation of successful performance management systems. In other words, it focuses on research-based findings and up-to-date applications that help increase an organization's human capital. Performance management is ongoing and cyclical. But, for pedagogical reasons, the book needs to follow a linear structure. Because performance observation, evaluation, and improvement are ongoing processes, some concepts and practices may be introduced early on in a cursory manner first but receive more detailed treatment in later sections. Also, this book focuses on best practices and describes the necessary steps to create a top-notch performance management system. However, due to practical constraints and lack of knowledge about system implementation, many organizations cut corners and do not implement systems following best practices due to environment and political issues (e.g., goals of raters may not be aligned with goals of the organization). Because the way in which systems are implemented in practice is often not close to the ideal system, the book includes numerous examples from actual organizations to illustrate how systems are implemented given actual situational constraints.

Part I includes Chapters 1 through 3 and addresses general as well as strategic considerations regarding performance management. Chapter 1 includes a discussion of the advantages of implementing a successful performance management system, as well as the negative outcomes associated with deficient systems, including lowered employee motivation and perceptions of unfairness; this chapter also includes what can be described as the features of an ideal system. Chapter 2 describes the performance management process starting with what should be done before a system is implemented, and ending with the performance renewal and recontracting phases. Chapter 3 links performance management systems with reward systems and an organization's strategic plan. This chapter makes it clear that a good performance management system is a critical component of the successful implementation of an organization's strategy.

Part II, including Chapters 4 through 7, addresses the details of system implementation. The discussion is sufficiently general, yet detailed, so that all managers, not just HR managers, will benefit from this material. Chapters 4 and 5 describe some of the technical aspects associated with the assessment of performance and how to identify and measure both behaviors and results. Chapter 6 discusses appraisal forms, various types of rating schemes, and discusses advantages and disadvantages of using various sources of performance information (e.g., supervisor, peers, customers). Finally, Chapter 7 describes the steps involved in implementing a performance management system, including a communication plan and pilot testing of the system before it is implemented.

Part III addresses employee development issues. Chapter 8 includes a description of employee developmental plans and the advantages of using 360-degree systems for developmental purposes. Chapter 9 addresses the skills needed of supervisors to observe and assess performance, as well as those needed to provide constructive feedback.

Part IV is about the relationship between performance management, rewards, the law, and teams. Chapter 10 includes a discussion of traditional and contingent pay plans, pay structures, and their links to performance management. In addition, this chapter provides a discussion of legal issues to consider when implementing a performance management system. Finally, Chapter 11 addresses the timely topic of how to design and implement performance management systems dealing with team performance.

Each of the chapters includes a list of its learning objectives as well as summary points and cases for discussion. I hope this additional material will allow you to have an enjoyable and productive learning experience that will enhance your own individual human capital.

Herman Aguinis

Denver, Colorado

ABOUT THE AUTHOR

Dr. Herman Aguinis (http://www.cudenver.edu/~haguinis) is the Mehalchin Term Professor of Management in the Business School at the University of Colorado at Denver and Health Sciences Center. He has been a visiting scholar at universities in the People's Republic of China (Beijing and Hong Kong), Malaysia, Singapore, Australia, Argentina, France, and Spain. His teaching, research, and consulting activities are in the areas of human resources management, organizational behavior, and research methodology.

Dr. Aguinis is the author of *Applied Psychology in Human Resource Management* (with Wayne F. Cascio, 6th ed., 2005, Prentice Hall), the author of *Regression Analysis for Categorical Moderators* (2004), and the editor of *Test-Score Banding in Human Resource Selection* (2004). In addition, he has written over 50 refereed journal articles in *Academy of Management Journal*, *Academy of Management Review*, *Journal of Applied Psychology*, *Personnel Psychology*, *Organizational Behavior and Human Decision Processes*, and elsewhere. Dr. Aguinis served as Division Chair for the Research Methods Division of the Academy of Management (2003–2004) and currently serves as editor-in-chief for the journal *Organizational Research Methods*. He has delivered over 100 presentations at professional conferences and consulted with organizations in the United States, Europe, and South America.

C H A P T E R

1

Performance Management and Reward Systems in Context

A manager is responsible for the application and performance of knowledge.
—PETER F. DRUCKER

Learning Objectives

By the end of this chapter, you will be able to do the following:

■ Explain the concept of performance management.

■ Distinguish performance management from performance appraisal.

■ Explain the many advantages and make a business case for implementing a well-designed performance management system.

■ Recognize the multiple negative consequences that can arise from the poor design and implementation of a performance management system. These negative consequences affect all the parties involved: employees, supervisors, and the organization as a whole.

■ Understand the concept of a reward system and its relationship to a performance management system.

■ Distinguish among the various types of employee rewards, including compensation, benefits, and relational returns.

■ Describe the multiple purposes of a performance management system including strategic, administrative, informational, developmental, organizational maintenance, and documentational purposes.

■ Describe and explain the key features of an ideal performance management system.

■ Create a presentation providing persuasive arguments in support of the reasons that an organization should implement a performance management system, including the purposes that performance management systems serve and the dangers of a poorly implemented system.

■ Note the relationship and links between a performance management system and other HR functions, including recruitment and selection, training and development, workforce planning, and compensation.

1.1 DEFINITION OF PERFORMANCE MANAGEMENT (PM)

Consider the following scenario:

> Sally is a sales manager at a large pharmaceutical company. The fiscal year will end in one week. She is overwhelmed with end-of-the year tasks, including reviewing the budget she is likely to be allocated for the following year, responding to customers' phone calls, and supervising a group of 10 salespeople. It's a very hectic time, probably the most hectic time of the year. She receives a phone call from the human resources (HR) department: "Sally, we have not received your performance reviews for your 10 employees; they are due by the end of the fiscal year." Sally thinks, "Oh, those performance reviews. . . . What a waste of my time!" From Sally's point of view, there is no value in filling out those seemingly meaningless forms. She does not see her subordinates in action because they are in the field visiting customers most of the time. All that she knows about their performance is based on sales figures, which depend more on the products offered and geographic territory covered than the individual effort and motivation of each salesperson. And, nothing happens in terms of rewards, regardless of her ratings. These are lean times in her organization, and salary adjustments are based on seniority rather than on merit. She has less than three days to turn in her forms. What will she do? She decides to follow the path of least resistance: to please her employees and give everyone the maximum possible rating. In this way, Sally believes the employees will be happy with their ratings and she will not have to deal with complaints or follow-up meetings. Sally fills out the forms in less than 20 minutes and gets back to her "real job."

There is something very wrong with this picture, which unfortunately happens all too frequently in many organizations. Although Sally's HR department calls this process "performance management," it is not.

Performance management is a *continuous process of identifying, measuring, and developing the performance of individuals and teams and aligning performance with the strategic goals of the organization.* Let's consider each of the definition's two main components:

1. *Continuous process.* Performance management is ongoing. It involves a never-ending process of setting goals and objectives, observing performance, and giving and receiving ongoing coaching and feedback.[1]
2. *Alignment with strategic goals.* Performance management requires that managers ensure that employees' activities and outputs are congruent with the

organization's goals and, consequently, help the organization gain a competitive advantage. Performance management therefore creates a direct link between employee performance and organizational goals and makes the employees' contribution to the organization explicit.

Note that many organizations have what is labeled a "performance management" system. However, we must distinguish between performance management and performance appraisal. A system that involves employee evaluations once a year without an ongoing effort to provide feedback and coaching so that performance can be improved is not a true performance management system. Instead, this is only a performance appraisal system. Performance appraisal is the systematic description of an employee's strengths and weaknesses. Thus, performance appraisal is an important component of performance management, but it is just a part of a bigger whole.

As an illustration, consider how Merrill Lynch has transitioned from a performance appraisal system to a performance management system. Merrill Lynch is one of the world's leading financial management and advisory companies, with offices in 36 countries and private client assets of approximately US$1.1 trillion (http://www.ml.com/). As an investment bank, it is a leading global underwriter of debt and equity securities and strategic adviser to corporations, governments, institutions, and individuals worldwide. Recently, Merrill Lynch started the transition from giving employees one performance appraisal per year to focusing on one of the important principles of performance management: the conversation between managers and employees in which feedback is exchanged and coaching is given if needed. In January, employees and managers set employee objectives. Mid-year reviews assess what progress has been made toward the goals and how personal development plans are faring. Finally, the end of the year review incorporates feedback from several sources, evaluates progress toward objectives, and identifies areas that need improvement. Managers also get extensive training on how to set objectives and conduct reviews. In addition, there is a Web site that managers can access with information on all aspects of the performance management system. In sharp contrast to their old performance appraisal system, Merrill Lynch's goal for its newly implemented performance management program is worded as follows: "This is what is expected of you, this is how we're going to help you in your development, and this is how you'll be judged relative to compensation."[2]

As a second example, consider the performance management system for managers at Germany-based Siemens, which provides mobile phones, computer networks, and wireless technology by employing 400,000 people in 190 countries. At Siemens, the performance management system is based on three pillars: setting clear and measurable goals, implementing concrete actions, and imposing rigorous consequences. The performance management at Siemens has helped change people's mindset, and the organization is now truly performance oriented. Every manager understands that performance is a critical aspect of working at Siemens, and this guiding philosophy is communicated in many ways throughout the organization.[3]

Performance management systems that do not make explicit the employee contribution to the organizational goals are not true performance management systems. Making an explicit link between an employee's performance objectives and the organizational goals also serves the purpose of establishing a shared understanding about what's to be achieved and how it is to be achieved. This is painfully clear in Sally's case described earlier: from her point of view, the performance review forms did not provide any useful information regarding the contribution of each of her subordinates to the organization.

In subsequent chapters, we describe best practices on how to design and implement performance management systems. For now, however, let's say that well-designed and implemented performance management systems make substantial contributions to the organization. Let's describe these contributions in detail.

1.2 THE PERFORMANCE MANAGEMENT CONTRIBUTION

There are many advantages associated with the implementation of a performance management system. A performance management system can make the following important contributions:[4]

1. *Motivation to perform is increased.* Receiving feedback about one's performance increases the motivation for future performance. Knowledge about how one is doing and recognition about one's past successes provide the fuel for future accomplishments.

2. *Self-esteem is increased.* Receiving feedback about one's performance fulfills a basic human need to be recognized and valued at work. This, in turn, is likely to increase employees' self-esteem.

3. *Managers gain insight about subordinates.* Direct supervisors and other managers in charge of the appraisal gain new insights into the person being appraised. The importance of knowing your employees is highlighted by the fact that the Management Standards Center, the Government recognized organization in the United Kingdom for setting standards for the management and leadership areas, has recognized that developing productive relationships with colleagues is a key competency for managers (www.management-standards.com, Unit 19). Gaining new insights into a person's performance and personality will help the manager build a better relationship with that person. Also, supervisors gain a better understanding of each individual's contribution to the organization. This can be useful for direct supervisors, as well as for supervisors once removed.

4. *The definitions of job and criteria are clarified.* The job of the person being appraised may be clarified and defined more clearly. In other words, employees gain a better understanding of the behaviors and results required of their specific position. Employees also gain a better understanding of what it takes to be a successful performer (i.e., what are the specific criteria that define job success).

5. *Self-insight and development are enhanced.* The participants in the system are likely to develop a better understanding of themselves and of the kind of development activities that are of value to them as they progress through the organization. Participants in the system also gain a better understanding of their particular strengths and weaknesses that can help them better define future career paths.

6. *Administrative actions are more fair and appropriate.*   Performance management systems provide valid information about performance that can be used for administrative actions such as merit increases, promotions, and transfers, as well as terminations. In general, a performance management system helps ensure that rewards are distributed on a fair and credible basis. In turn, such decisions based on a sound performance management system lead to improved interpersonal relationships and enhanced supervisor-subordinate trust.[5]

7. *Organizational goals are made clear.*   The goals of the unit and the organization are made clear and the employee understands the link between what she does and organizational success. This is a contribution to the communication of what the unit and the organization are all about and how organizational goals cascade down to the unit and the individual employee. Performance management systems can help improve employee acceptance of these wider goals (i.e., organizational and unit level).

8. *Employees become more competent.*   An obvious contribution is that employee performance is improved. In addition, there is a solid foundation for helping employees become more successful by establishing developmental plans.

9. *There is better protection from lawsuits.*   Data collected through performance management systems can help document compliance with regulations (e.g., equal treatment of all employees regardless of sex or ethnic background). When performance management systems are not in place, arbitrary performance evaluations are more likely, resulting in an increased exposure to litigation for the organization.

10. *Better and more timely differentiation between good and poor performers.* Performance management systems allow for a quicker identification of good and poor performers. Also, they force supervisors to face up to and address performance problems on a timely basis (i.e., before the problem becomes so entrenched that it cannot be easily remedied).

11. *Supervisors' views of performance are communicated more clearly.*   Performance management systems allow managers to communicate to their subordinates their judgments regarding performance. Thus, there is greater accountability in how managers discuss performance expectations and provide feedback. Both assessing and monitoring the performance of others are listed as key competencies for managers by the Management Standards Center (www.management-standards.com, Unit 26 & 27). When managers possess these competencies, subordinates receive useful information about how their performance is seen by their supervisor.

12. *Organizational change is facilitated.*   Performance management systems can be a useful tool to drive organizational change. For example, assume an organization decides to change its culture to give top priority to product quality and customer service. Once this new organizational direction is established, performance management is used to align the organizational culture with the goals and objectives of the organization to make change possible. Employees are provided training in the necessary skills and are also rewarded for improved performance so that they have both the knowledge and motivation to improve product quality and customer service. This is

precisely what IBM did in the 1980s when it wanted to switch focus to customer satisfaction: the performance evaluation of every member in the organization was based, to some extent, on customer satisfaction ratings regardless of function (i.e., accounting, programming, manufacturing, etc.).[6] For IBM, as well as numerous other organizations, performance management provides tools and motivation for individuals to change, which, in turn, helps drive organizational change. In short, performance management systems are likely to produce changes in the culture of the organization and, therefore, the consequences of such cultural changes should be considered carefully before implementing the system.[7] As noted by Randy Pennington, president of Pennington Performance Group, "The truth is that the culture change is driven by a change in performance. An organization's culture cannot be installed. It can be guided and influenced by policies, practices, skills, and procedures that are implemented and reinforced. The only way to change the culture is to change the way individuals perform on a daily basis."[8]

Table 1.1 lists the 11 contributions made by performance management systems. Recall Sally's situation earlier in the chapter. Which of the contributions included in Table 1.1 result from the system implemented at Sally's organization? For example, are Sally's employees more motivated to perform as a consequence of implementing their "performance management" system? Is their self-esteem increased? What about Sally's insight and understanding of her employees' contributions to the organization? Is Sally's organization now better protected in the face of potential litigation? Unfortunately, the system implemented at Sally's organization is not a true performance management system, but simply an administrative nuisance. Consequently, many, if not most, of the potential contributions of the performance management system are not realized. In fact, poorly implemented systems, as in the case of Sally's organization, not only do not make positive contributions but can also be very dangerous and lead to several negative outcomes.

BOX 1.1

What CEOs Say About the Contribution of Performance Management Systems

A study conducted by Development Dimensions International (DDI), a global human resources consulting firm specializing in leadership and selection, found that performance management systems are a key tool that organizations use to translate business strategy into business results. Specifically, performance management systems influence "financial performance, productivity, product or service quality, customer satisfaction, and employee job satisfaction." In addition, 79% of the CEOs surveyed say that the performance management system implemented in their organizations drives the "cultural strategies that maximize human assets."[9]

TABLE 1.1   Contributions of Performance Management Systems
Motivation to perform is increased.
Self-esteem is increased.
Managers gain insight about subordinates.
The definitions of job and criteria are clarified.
Self-insight and development are enhanced.
Administrative actions are more fair and appropriate.
Organizational goals are made clear.
Employees become more competent.
There is better protection from lawsuits.
There is better and more timely differentiation between good and poor performers.
Supervisors' views of performance are communicated more clearly.
Organizational change is facilitated.

1.3 DISADVANTAGES/DANGERS OF POORLY IMPLEMENTED PM SYSTEMS

What happens when performance management systems do not work as intended, as in the case of Sally's organization? What are some of the negative consequences associated with low-quality and poorly implemented systems? Consider the following list:

1. *Increased turnover.* If the process is not seen as fair, employees may become upset and leave the organization. They can leave physically (i.e., quit) or withdraw psychologically (i.e., minimize their effort until they are able to find a job elsewhere).

2. *Use of misleading information.* If a standardized system is not in place, there are multiple opportunities for fabricating information about an employee's performance.

3. *Lowered self-esteem.* Self-esteem may be lowered if feedback is provided in an inappropriate and inaccurate way. This, in turn, can create employee resentment.

4. *Wasted time and money.* Performance management systems cost money and quite a bit of time. These resources are wasted when systems are poorly designed and implemented.

5. *Damaged relationships.* As a consequence of a deficient system, the relationship among the individuals involved may be damaged, often permanently.

6. *Decreased motivation to perform.* Motivation may be lowered for many reasons, including the feeling that superior performance is not translated into meaningful tangible (e.g., pay increase) or intangible (e.g., personal recognition) rewards.

7. *Employee burnout and job dissatisfaction.* When the performance assessment instrument is not seen as valid and the system is not perceived as fair, employees are likely to feel increased levels of job burnout and job dissatisfaction. As a consequence, employees are likely to become increasingly irritated.[10]

BOX 1.2

What Happens When Performance Management Is Implemented Poorly?

One example of a poorly implemented performance management system resulted in a $1.2 million lawsuit. A female employee was promoted several times and succeeded in the construction industry until she started working under the supervision of a new manager. She stated in her lawsuit that once she was promoted and reported to the new manager, that boss ignored her and did not give her the same support or opportunities for training that her male colleagues received. After eight months of receiving no feedback from her manager, she was called into his office, where the manager told her that she was failing, resulting in a demotion and a $20,000 reduction in her annual salary. When she won her sex discrimination lawsuit, a jury awarded her $1.2 million in emotional distress and economic damages.[11]

---

8. *Increased risk of litigation.*   Expensive lawsuits may be filed by individuals who feel they have been appraised unfairly.
9. *Unjustified demands on managers' resources.*   Poorly implemented systems do not provide the benefits that well implemented systems provide, yet they still take up managers' time. Such systems will be resisted because of competing obligations and allocation of resources (e.g., time). What is sometimes worse, managers may simply choose to avoid the system altogether.
10. *Varying and unfair standards and ratings.*   Both standards and individual ratings may vary across and within units and also be unfair.
11. *Emerging biases.*   Personal values, biases, and relationships are likely to replace organizational standards.
12. *Unclear ratings system.*   Because of poor communication, employees may not know how their ratings are generated, and how the ratings are translated into rewards.

Table 1.2 summarizes the list of disadvantages and negative consequences resulting from the careless design and implementation of a performance management system. Once again, consider Sally's organization. What are some of the consequences of the system implemented by her company? Let's consider each of the consequences listed in Table 1.2. For example, is it likely that the performance information used is false and misleading? How about the risk for litigation? How about the time and money invested in collecting, compiling, and reporting the data? Unfortunately, an analysis of Sally's situation, taken with the positive and negative consequences listed in Table 1.1 and Table 1.2, leads to the conclusion that this particular system is more likely to do harm than good. Now think about the system implemented at your current organization, or at the organization you have worked for most recently. Take a look at Tables 1.1 and 1.2. Where does the system fit best? Is the system more closely aligned with some of the positive consequences listed in Table 1.1 or more closely aligned with some of the negative consequences listed in Table 1.2?

TABLE 1.2   Disadvantages/Danger of Poorly Implemented Performance Management Systems
Increased turnover
Use of false or misleading information
Lowered self-esteem
Wasted time and money
Damaged relationships
Decreased motivation to perform
Employee job burnout and job dissatisfaction
Increased risk of litigation
Unjustified demands on managers' resources
Varying and unfair standards and ratings
Emerging biases
Unclear ratings system

One of the purposes of a performance management system is to make decisions about employees' compensation (e.g., pay raises). For many employees, this is perhaps one of the most meaningful consequences of a performance management system. Chapter 10 provides a detailed discussion of how a performance management system is used to allocate rewards. However, here we will discuss some basic features of reward systems and the extent to which the allocation of various types of rewards are dependent on the performance management system.

1.4 DEFINITION OF REWARD SYSTEMS

An employee's compensation, usually referred to as *tangible returns*, includes cash compensation (i.e., base pay, cost-of-living and merit pay, short-term incentives, and long-term incentives) and benefits (i.e., income protection, work/life focus, tuition reimbursement, and allowances). However, employees also receive intangible returns, also referred to as *relational returns*, which include recognition and status, employment security, challenging work, and learning opportunities. A reward system is the set of mechanisms for distributing both tangible and intangible returns as part of an employment relationship.

It should be noted that not all types of returns are directly related to performance management systems. This is the case because not all types of returns are allocated based on performance. For example, some allocations are based on seniority as opposed to performance. The various types of returns are defined next.[12]

1.4.1 Base Pay

Base pay is given to employees in exchange for work performed. The base pay, which usually includes a range of values, focuses on the position and duties performed rather than an individual's contribution. Thus, the base pay is usually the same for all employees performing similar duties and ignores differences across employees. However, differences within the base pay range may exist based on such variables as experience and differential performance. In some countries (e.g., United States), there is a difference between wage and salary. Salary is base cash compensation received by employees who are exempt from regulations of the Fair Labor Standards Act and, in most cases, cannot receive overtime pay. Employees in most professional and managerial jobs (also called salaried employees) are exempt employees. On the other hand, nonexempt employees receive their pay calculated on an hourly wage.

1.4.2 Cost-of-Living Adjustments and Contingent Pay

Cost-of-living adjustments (COLA) imply the same percentage increase for all employees regardless of their individual performance. Cost-of-living adjustments are given to combat the effects of inflation in an attempt to preserve the employees' buying power. For example, in 2003 in the United States, organizations that implemented a COLA used a 2.1% pay increase. In 2001, this same percentage was only 1.4%. Year-by-year COLA percentages can be obtained from such agencies as the Social Security Administration in the United States (http://www.ssa.gov/OACT/COLA/colaseries.html).

Contingent pay, sometimes refer to as *merit pay*, is given as an addition to the base pay based on past performance. Chapter 10 describes the topic of contingent pay in detail. But, in a nutshell, contingent pay means that the amount of additional compensation depends on an employee's level of performance. So, for example, the top 20% of employees in the performance score distribution may receive a 10% annual increase, whereas employees in the middle 70% of the distribution may receive a 4% increase, and employees in the bottom 10% may receive no increase at all.

1.4.3 Short-Term Incentives

Similar to contingent pay, incentives are allocated based on past performance. However, incentives are not added to the base pay and are only temporary pay adjustments based on the review period (e.g., quarterly or annual). So incentives are one-time payments and this is why they are also referred to as *variable pay*.

A second difference between incentives and contingent pay is that incentives are known in advance. For example, a salesperson in a pharmaceutical company knows that if she meets her sales quota, she will receive a $3,000 bonus at the end of the quarter. She also knows that if she exceeds her sales quota by 10%, her bonus will be $6,000. In contrast, in the case of contingent pay, in most cases, the specific value of the reward is not known in advance.

1.4.4 Long-Term incentives

Whereas short-term incentives usually involve an attempt to motivate performance in the short term (i.e., quarter, year) and involve cash bonuses or specific prizes (e.g., two extra days off), long-term incentives attempt to influence future performance over a longer period of time. Typically, they involve stock ownership or options to buy stocks at a preestablished and profitable price. The rationale for long-term incentives is that employees will be personally invested in the organization's success, and this investment is expected to translate into a sustained high level of performance.

Both short-term and long-term incentives are quite popular. Take, for example, the public sector in the United States. A survey administered in late 1998 to 25 state and 400 local governments employing more than 6 people showed that all but one of the state governments and 242 (i.e., 85%) of the local governments used some type of incentive.[13]

1.4.5 Income Protection

Income protection programs serve as a backup to employees' salaries in the event that an employee is sick, disabled, or no longer able to work. Some countries mandate income protection programs by law. For example, Canadian organizations pay into a fund that provides income protection in the case of a disability. Take, for instance, the University of Alberta, which offers a monthly income of 70% of salary to employees who become severely disabled (http://www.hrs.ualberta.ca/Benefits/index.aspx?Page=467). In the United States, employers pay 50% of an employee's total contribution to Social Security so that income is protected in case of death, a disability that prevents the employee from doing substantial work for one year, and when an employee reaches retirement age. For example, 40-year-old employee earning an annual salary of $90,000, and expected to continue to earn that salary until retirement age, would receive about $1,400 a month if he decides to retire at age 62, about $2,000 a month if he retires at age 67, and about $2,500 if he retires at age 70.

Other types of benefits under the income protection rubric include medical insurance, pension plans, and savings plans. These are optional benefits that organizations provide, but they are becoming increasingly important and often guide an applicant's decision to accept a job offer. In fact, a recent survey including both employees in general and HR professionals in particular showed that health care/medical insurance is the most important benefit, followed by paid time off and retirement benefits.[14]

1.4.6 Work/Life Focus

Benefits related to work/life focus include programs that help employees achieve a better balance between work and nonwork activities. These include time away from work (e.g., vacation time), services to meet specific needs (e.g., counseling, financial planning, on-site fitness program), and flexible work schedules (e.g., telecommuting, nonpaid time off). For example, Sun Microsystems actively promotes an equal balance between work and home life and closes its Broomfield, Colorado, campus from late December through early January every year. This benefit (i.e., vacation time for all employees in addition to individual yearly vacation time) is part of Sun's culture. Sun believes in a work hard–play hard attitude, as is evident by CEO Scott McNealy's motto: "Kick butt and have fun".[15]

1.4.7 Allowances

Benefits in some countries and organizations include allowances covering housing and transportation. These kinds of allowances are typical for expatriate personnel and are also popular for high-level managers throughout the world. In South Africa, for example, it is common for a transportation allowance to include one of the following choices:[16]

- The employer provides a car and the employee has the right to use it both privately and for business.
- The employer provides a car allowance, more correctly referred to as a *travel allowance*, which means reimbursing the employee for the business use of the employee's personal car.

1.4.8 Relational Returns

Relational returns are intangible in nature. They include recognition and status, employment security, challenging work, opportunities to learn, and opportunities to form personal relationships at work (including friendships and romances).[17] For example, Sun Microsystems allows employees to enroll in SunU, which is Sun's own online education tool. SunU encapsulates a mix of traditional classroom courses with online classes that can be accessed anywhere in the world at any time.[18] Sun offers its employees enormous scope for development and career progression, and there is a commitment to ensuring that all employees are given the opportunity to develop professionally. The new knowledge and skills acquired by employees can help them not only to further their careers within Sun, but they can also take this knowledge with them if they seek employment elsewhere. Thus, some types of relational returns can be long lasting.

Table 1.3 includes a list of the various returns, together with their degree of dependency on the performance management system. As an example of the low end of the dependency continuum, cost-of-living adjustment has a low degree of dependency on the performance management system, meaning that the system has no impact on this type of return. In other words, all employees receive this type of return regardless of past performance. On the other end, short-term incentives have a high degree of dependency, meaning that the performance management system dictates who receives these incentives and who does not. Long-term incentives (e.g., profit sharing and stock options, which are discussed in more detail in Chapter 10) also have a high degree of dependency; although this type of incentive is not specifically tied to individual performance, it does depend on performance measured at the team, unit, or even organizational levels. Between the high and low end, we find some returns with a moderate degree of dependency on the performance management system such as base pay, a type of return that may or may not be influenced by the system.

Think about the performance management system of your current employer, the system used by your most recent employer, or the system in place at an organization

TABLE 1.3	Returns and Their Degree of Dependency on the Performance Management System
Return	*Degree of Dependency*
Cost-of-living adjustment	Low
Income protection	Low
Work/life focus	Moderate
Allowances	Moderate
Relational returns	Moderate
Base pay	Moderate
Contingent pay	High
Short-term incentives	High
Long-term incentives	High

where someone you know is employed at present. Based on Table 1.3, try to think about the various types of tangible and intangible returns allocated in this organization. To what extent is each of these returns dependent on the organization's performance management system?

1.5 AIMS AND ROLE OF PM SYSTEMS

The information collected by a performance management system is most frequently used for salary administration, performance feedback, and the identification of employee strengths and weaknesses. In general, however, performance management systems can serve the following six purposes:[19] strategic, administrative, informational, developmental, organizational maintenance, and documentational purposes. Let's consider each of these purposes in turn.

1.5.1 Strategic Purpose

The first purpose of performance management systems is to help top management achieve strategic business objectives. By linking the organization's goals with individual goals, the performance management system reinforces behaviors consistent with the attainment of organizational goals. Moreover, even if for some reason individual goals are not achieved, linking individual goals with organizational goals serves as a way to communicate what are the most crucial business strategic initiatives.

1.5.2 Administrative Purpose

A second function of performance management systems is to furnish valid and useful information for making administrative decisions about employees. Such administrative decisions include salary adjustments, promotions, employee retention or termination, recognition of superior individual performance, identification of poor performers, layoffs, and merit increases. Therefore, the implementation of reward systems based on information provided by the performance management system falls within the administrative purpose.

1.5.3 Informational Purpose

Performance management systems serve as an important communication device. First, they inform employees about how they are doing and provide them with information on specific areas that may need improvement. Second, related to the strategic purpose, they provide information regarding the organization's and the supervisor's expectations and what aspects of work the supervisor believes are most important.

1.5.4 Developmental Purpose

As noted earlier, feedback is an important component of a well-implemented performance management system. This feedback can be used in a developmental manner. Managers can use feedback to coach employees and improve performance on an ongoing basis. This feedback allows for the identification of strengths and weaknesses as well as the causes for performance deficiencies (which could be due to individual, group, or contextual factors). Of course, feedback is useful only to the extent that remedial action is taken and concrete steps are implemented to remedy any deficiencies. Feedback is useful only when employees are willing to receive it. Organizations should strive to create a "feedback culture" that reflects support for feedback, including feedback that is nonthreatening and is focused on behaviors and coaching to help interpret the feedback provided.[20]

Another aspect of the developmental purpose is that employees receive information about themselves that can help them individualize their career paths. Thus, the developmental purpose refers to both short-term and long-term aspects of development.

1.5.5 Organizational Maintenance Purpose

A fifth purpose of performance management systems is to provide information to be used in workforce planning. Workplace planning is a set of systems that allows organizations to anticipate and respond to needs emerging within and outside the organization, to determine priorities, and to allocate human resources where they can do the most good.[21] An important component of any workforce planning effort is the talent inventory, which is information on current resources (e.g., skills, abilities, promotional potential, and assignment histories of current employees). Performance management systems are the primary means through which accurate talent inventories can be assembled.

Other organizational maintenance purposes served by performance management systems include assessing future training needs, evaluating performance achievements at the organizational level, and evaluating the effectiveness of HR interventions (e.g., whether employees perform at higher levels after participating in a training program). These activities cannot be conducted effectively in the absence of a good performance management system.

1.5.6 Documentational Purpose

Finally, performance management systems allow organizations to collect useful information that can be used for several documentation purposes. First, performance data can be used to validate newly proposed selection instruments. For example, a newly developed test of computer literacy can be administered to all administrative personnel. Then, scores on the test can be paired with scores collected through the performance management system. If scores on the test and on the performance measure are correlated, then the test can be used with future applicants for the administrative positions. Second, performance management systems allow for the documentation of important administrative decisions. This information can be especially useful in the case of litigation.

Several companies implement performance management systems that allow them to accomplish the multiple objectives described earlier. For an example of one such company, consider the case of SELCO Credit Union (http://selco.org/) in Eugene, Oregon, a not-for-profit consumer cooperative that was established in 1936.[22] SELCO's eight branches serve nearly 60,000 members. SELCO offers many of the same services offered by other banks, including personal checking and savings accounts, loans, and credit cards. However, being a member of the credit union allows individual members a say in how the credit union is run, something a traditional bank does not permit. Recently, SELCO scrapped an old performance appraisal system and replaced it with a new multipurpose and more effective performance management system. First, the timing of the new system is now aligned with the business cycle, instead of the employee's date of hire, to ensure that business needs are aligned with individual goals. This alignment serves both strategic and informational purposes. Second, managers are given a pool of money that they can work with to award bonuses and raises as needed, which is more effective than the complex set of matrices that had been in place to calculate bonuses. This improved the way the system is used for allocating rewards and therefore serves the administrative purpose. Third, managers are required to sit down and have regular conversations with their employees about their performance and make note of any problems that arise. This gives the employees a clear sense of areas in which they need improvement and also provides documentation if disciplinary action is needed. This component serves both the informational and documentational purposes. Finally, the time that was previously spent filling out complicated matrices and forms is now spent talking with the employees about how they can improve their performance, allowing for progress on an ongoing basis. This serves the developmental purpose.

Although multiple purposes are possible, a survey of industrial and organizational psychologists working in human resources departments in over 100 different organizations reported that the two most frequent purposes are administrative (i.e., salary decisions) and developmental (i.e., to identify employees' weaknesses and strengths). Overall, in the organizations that participated in this study, performance management served at least two of the purposes mentioned earlier.[23] As will be discussed in Chapter 9, these purposes place conflicting demands on the raters because they must be both judges (i.e., make salary decisions) and coaches (i.e., provide useful feedback for performance improvement) at the same time.

Now, think about the performance management system implemented in your organization or the last organization you worked for. Table 1.4 summarizes the various purposes served by a performance management system. Which of these purposes are being served by the system you are considering?

TABLE 1.4   Purposes Served by a Performance Management System

Strategic: To help top management achieve strategic business objectives

Administrative: To furnish valid and useful information for making administrative decisions about employees

Informational: To inform employees about how they are doing and about the organization's and the supervisor's expectations

Developmental: To allow managers to provide coaching to their employees

Organizational maintenance: To provide information to be used in workplace planning and allocation of human resources

Documentational: To collect useful information that can be used for various purposes (e.g., test development, administrative decisions)

1.6 CHARACTERISTICS OF AN IDEAL PM SYSTEM

So far, we have defined performance management, described the advantages of implementing good performance management systems, discussed some of the dangers of not doing a good job with the design and implementation of the system, and described the various purposes achieved by a good system. But what does a good system look like? The following is a set of characteristics that is likely to allow a performance management system to be successful. Practical constraints may not allow for the implementation of all these features. The reality is that performance management systems are seldom implemented in an ideal way.[24] For example, there may not be sufficient funds to deliver training to all people involved, supervisors may have biases in how they provide performance ratings, or people may be just too busy to pay attention to a new organizational initiative that requires their time and attention. However, we should strive to place a check mark next to each of these characteristics, as the more features that are checked, the more likely it will be that the system will live up to its promise.

- *Strategic congruence.*   The system should be congruent with the unit and organization's strategy. In other words, individual goals must be aligned with unit and organizational goals.
- *Thoroughness.*   The system should be thorough regarding four dimensions. First, all employees should be evaluated (including managers). Second, all major job responsibilities should be evaluated (including behaviors and results; a detailed discussion of this topic is presented in Chapter 5). Third, the evaluation should include performance spanning the entire review period, and not just the few weeks or months before the review. Finally, feedback should be given on positive performance aspects as well as those that are in need of improvement.
- *Practicality.*   Systems that are too expensive, time-consuming, and convoluted will obviously not be effective. Good systems that are easy to use (e.g., performance data are entered using user-friendly software) are available for managers to use to make decisions. Finally, the benefits of using the system (e.g., increased performance and job satisfaction) must be seen as outweighing the costs (e.g., time, effort, money).
- *Meaningfulness.*   The system must be meaningful in several ways. First, the standards and evaluations conducted for each job function must be considered important and relevant. Second, performance assessment must emphasize only those functions that are under the control of the employee. For example, there is no point in letting an employee know she needs to increase the speed of service delivery when the supplier does not get the product to her on time. Third, evaluations must take place at regular intervals and at appropriate moments. Just one formal evaluation per year is usually not sufficient, so informal quarterly reviews are recommended. Fourth, the system should provide for the continuing skill development of evaluators. Finally, the results should be used for important administrative decisions. People will not pay attention to a system that has no consequences in terms of outcomes that they value.

- *Specificity.* A good system should be specific: it should provide detailed and concrete guidance to employees about what is expected of them and how they can meet these expectations.
- *Identification of effective and ineffective performance.* The performance management system should provide information that allows for the identification of effective and ineffective performance. That is, the system should allow for distinguishing between effective and ineffective behaviors and results, thereby also allowing for the identification of employees displaying various levels of performance effectiveness. In terms of decision making, a system that classifies or ranks all levels of performance, and all employees, similarly is useless.
- *Reliability.* A good system should include measures of performance that are consistent and free of error. For example, if two supervisors provided ratings of the same employee and performance dimensions, ratings should be similar.
- *Validity.* The measures of performance should also be valid. In this context, validity refers to the fact that the measures include all relevant performance facets and do not include irrelevant performance facets. In other words, measures are relevant (i.e., include all critical performance facets), not deficient (i.e., do not leave any important aspects out), and are not contaminated (i.e., do not include factors outside of the control of the employee). In short, measures include what is important and do not assess what is not important and outside of the control of the employee.
- *Acceptability and fairness.* A good system is acceptable and perceived as fair by all participants. Perceptions of fairness are subjective and the only way to know if a system is seen as fair is to ask the participants. We can ask about distributive justice, which includes perceptions of the performance evaluation received relative to the work performed, and perceptions of the rewards received relative to the evaluation received. If a discrepancy is perceived between work and evaluation or between evaluation and rewards, then the system is likely to be seen as unfair.[25] In addition, we can ask about procedural justice, which includes perceptions of the procedures used to determine the ratings as well as the procedures used to link ratings with rewards. Because a good system is inherently discriminatory, some employees will receive ratings that are lower than those received by other employees. However, we should strive to develop systems that are seen as fair from both a distributive and procedural perspective. This is because each type of justice perception leads to different outcomes. For example, a perception that the system is not fair from a distributive point of view is likely to lead to a poor relationship between employee and supervisor and lowered satisfaction of the employee with the supervisor. On the other hand, a perception that the system is unfair from a procedural point of view is likely to lead to decreased employee commitment toward the organization and intentions to leave.[26] One way to improve both distributive and procedural justice is to set clear rules that are applied consistently by all supervisors.
- *Inclusiveness.* Good systems include input from multiple sources on an ongoing basis. First, the evaluation process must represent the concerns of

all the people who will be affected by the outcome. Consequently, employees must participate in the process of creating the system by providing input regarding what behaviors or results will be measured and how. Second, input about employee performance should be gathered from the employees themselves before the appraisal meeting.[27]

- *Openness.* Good systems have no secrets. First, performance is evaluated frequently and performance feedback is provided on an ongoing basis. Therefore, employees are continually informed of the quality of their performance. Second, the appraisal meeting consists of a two-way communication process where information is exchanged, and not delivered from the supervisor to the employee without his or her input. Third, standards should be clear and communicated on an ongoing basis. Finally, communications are factual, open, and honest.

- *Correctability.* The process of assigning ratings should minimize subjective aspects. However, it is virtually impossible to create a system that is completely objective because human judgment is an important component of the evaluation process. When employees perceive an error has been made, there should be a mechanism through which this error can be corrected. Establishing an appeals process, through which employees can challenge what may be unjust decisions, is an important aspect of a good performance management system.

- *Standardization.* As noted earlier, good systems are standardized. This means that performance is evaluated consistently across people and time. To achieve this goal, the ongoing training of the individuals in charge of appraisals, usually managers, is a must.

- *Ethicality.* Good systems comply with ethical standards. This means that the supervisor suppresses her personal self-interest in providing evaluations. In addition, the supervisor evaluates only performance dimensions for which she has sufficient information and the privacy of the employee is respected.[28]

Table 1.5 lists the characteristics of an ideal performance management system. Think about the performance management system implemented in your organization or the last organization you worked for. Which of the features listed in Table 1.5 are included in the system you are considering? How far is your system from the ideal?

BOX 1.3

Good Performance Management Implementation Pays Off

Implementing a performance management system that includes the characteristics just described will pay off. A study conducted for Mercer, a global diversified consulting company, revealed that the 1,200 workers surveyed stated that they could improve their productivity by an average of 26% if they were not held back by a lack of "direction, support, training and equipment." Successfully implementing a performance management system can give workers the direction and support that they need to improve their productivity.[29]

TABLE 1.5   Characteristics of an Ideal Performance Management System
Strategic congruence
Thoroughness
Practicality
Meaningfulness
Specificity
Identification of effective and ineffective performance
Reliability
Validity
Acceptability and fairness
Inclusiveness
Openness
Correctability
Standardization
Ethicality

1.7 INTEGRATION WITH OTHER HUMAN RESOURCES AND DEVELOPMENT ACTIVITIES

Performance management systems serve as important "feeders" to other human resources and development activities. For example, consider the relationship between performance management and *training*. Performance management provides information on developmental needs for employees. In the absence of a good performance management system, it is not clear that organizations will use their training resources in the most efficient way (i.e., to train those who must need it in the most critical areas).

Performance management also provides key information for *workforce planning*. Specifically, an organization's talent inventory is based on information collected through the performance management system. Development plans provide information on what skills will be acquired in the near future. This information is also used in making *recruitment and hiring* decisions. Knowledge of an organization's current and future talent is important when deciding what types of skills need to be acquired externally and what types of skills can be found within the organization.

Finally, there is an obvious relationship between performance management and compensation systems. Compensation and reward decisions are likely to be arbitrary in the absence of a good performance management system.

In short, performance management is a key component of talent management in organizations. It allows for assessing the current talent and making predictions about future needs both at the individual and organizational levels. Implementing a successful performance management system is a requirement for the successful implementation of other HR functions, including training, workforce planning, recruitment and selection, and compensation.

SUMMARY POINTS

- Performance management is a continuous process of identifying, measuring, and developing the performance of individuals and teams and aligning performance with the strategic goals of the organization.

- Although many organizations have systems labeled "performance management," they usually are only performance *appraisal* systems. Performance appraisal emphasizes the assessment of an employee's strengths and weakness and does not include strategic business considerations. Also, performance appraisal systems usually do not include extensive and ongoing feedback that an employee can use to improve her performance in the future. Finally, performance appraisal is a once-a-year event that is often driven by the HR department, whereas performance management is a year-round way of managing business that is driven by managers.

- Implementing a well-designed performance management system has many advantages. From the perspective of employees, a good system increases motivation and self-esteem, helps improve performance, clarifies job tasks and duties, provides self-insight and development opportunities, and clarifies supervisors' expectations. From the perspective of managers, good systems allow them to gain insight into employees activities and goals, allow for more fair and appropriate administrative actions, allow them to communicate organizational goals more clearly, let them differentiate good and poor performers, and help drive organizational change. Finally, from the perspective of the HR function, a good system provides protection from litigation.

- Poorly designed and implemented performance management systems can

have disastrous consequences for all involved. For example, employees may quit, those who stay may be less motivated, and relationships (e.g., supervisor-subordinate) can suffer irreparable damage. Also, poorly designed systems can be biased, resulting in costly lawsuits and wasted time and resources. In the end, low-quality and poorly implemented systems can be a source of enormous frustration and cynicism for all involved.

- Reward systems include all mechanisms for determining and distributing tangible and intangible returns as part of an employment relationship. Tangible returns are collectively referred to as *compensation* and include both cash and benefits. Intangible returns, also referred to as *relational returns*, include recognition and status, employment security, challenging work, and learning opportunities. Not all types of returns are directly related to performance management systems because not all types of returns are allocated based on past performance.

- Performance management systems serve multiple purposes. First, they serve a strategic purpose because they help link employee activities with the organization's mission and goals, they identify results and behaviors needed to carry out strategy, and they maximize the extent to which employees exhibit the desired behaviors and produce the desired results. Second, they serve an administrative purpose in that they produce information used by the reward system and other HR decision making (e.g., promotions, termination, disciplinary actions). Third, they serve an information purpose because they are where employees learn about their performance in relation to the organization's expectations. Fourth, they serve a developmental purpose in that performance feedback allows individuals to learn about their strengths and weaknesses, to identify training needs, and to make better decisions regarding job assignments. Fifth, performance management systems serve an organizational maintenance purpose because they provide useful information for workforce planning and for evaluating the effectiveness of other HR systems (e.g., comparing performance before and after an expensive training program to see if training made a difference). Finally, performance management systems also serve a documentation purpose; for example, to support HR decisions and help meet legal requirements.

- Ideal performance management systems are rare. Such ideal systems are

  - congruent with strategy (i.e., there is a clear link among individual, unit, and organizational goals)
  - thorough (e.g., they include all relevant performance dimensions)
  - practical (e.g., they do not require excessive time and resources)
  - meaningful (e.g., they have important consequences)
  - specific (e.g., they provide a concrete employee improvement agenda)
  - able to identify effective and ineffective performance (e.g., they help distinguish employees at different performance levels)
  - reliable (e.g., the measurement of performance is consistent)
  - valid (e.g., the measures of performance are not contaminated or deficient)
  - fair (e.g., people participating in the system believe the processes and outcomes are just)
  - inclusive (i.e., they include input from multiple sources on an ongoing basis)

  - open (i.e., they are transparent and there are no secrets)
  - correctable (i.e., they include mechanisms so that errors can be corrected)
  - standardized (i.e., performance is evaluated consistently across people and time)
  - ethical (i.e., they comply with ethical standards)

Many trade-offs take place in the real-world implementation of performance management systems. However, the closer the system is to the ideal characteristics, the greater the return will be for the employees, supervisors, and the organization as a whole.

- A performance management system is the key factor determining whether an organization can manage its human resources and talent effectively. Performance management provides information on who should be trained and in what areas, which employees should be rewarded, and what type of skills are lacking at the organization or unit level. Therefore, performance management also provides information on the type of employees that should be hired. When implemented well, performance management systems provide critical information that allows organizations to make sound decisions regarding their people resources.

As should be evident by now, implementing an ideal performance management system requires a substantial amount of work. However, this does not start when the system is put into place. The process starts much earlier because, unless specific conditions are present before the system is implemented, the system will not achieve its multiple purposes. Chapter 2 provides a description of the entire performance management process.

Case Study 1.1 Reality Check: Ideal versus Actual Performance Management System

The table here summarizes the key characteristics of an ideal performance management system as discussed in Chapter 1. Think about a performance management system you know. This could be the one implemented at your current (or most recent) job. If you don't have information about such a system, talk to a friend or acquaintance who is currently working and gather information about the system used in his or her organization. Use the Y/N column in the table to indicate whether each of the features is present (Y: yes) or not (N: no) in the system you are considering. In some cases, some elements may be present to a matter of degree and may require that you include some additional information in the Comments column.

Next, prepare a brief report addressing the following issues:

1. How many of the 14 characteristics of an ideal system are present in the system you are evaluating?
2. Identify two characteristics that are not present at all, or barely present, in your system. Discuss the implications that the lack of these characteristics has on the effectiveness of the system.
3. Identify one characteristic that is clearly present in your system. Discuss the implications of the presence of this characteristic on the effectiveness of the system.
4. Identify the characteristic in your system that is furthest from the ideal. What can be done to produce a better alignment between your system and the ideal? Who should be responsible for doing what so that your system becomes "ideal" regarding this characteristic? ■

Characteristics	Y/N	Definition	Comments
Strategic congruence		Individual goals are aligned with unit and organizational goals.	
Thoroughness		All employees are evaluated.	
		Evaluations include performance spanning the entire review period.	
		All major job responsibilities are evaluated.	
		Feedback is provided on both positive and negative performance.	
Practicality		It is readily available for use.	
		It is easy to use.	
		It is acceptable to those who use it for decisions.	
		Benefits of the system outweigh the costs.	

Meaningfulness	Standards and evaluations for each job function are important and relevant.	
	Only the functions that are under the control of the employee are measured.	
	Evaluations take place at regular intervals and at appropriate moments.	
	System provides for continuing skill development of evaluators.	
	Results are used for important administrative decisions.	
Specificity	Detailed guidance is provided to employees about what is expected of them and how they can meet these expectations.	
Identification of effective and ineffective performance	The system distinguishes between effective and ineffective behaviors and results, thereby also identifying employees displaying various levels of performance effectiveness.	
Reliability	Measures of performance are consistent.	
	Measures of performance are free of error.	
Validity	Measures include all critical performance facets.	
	Measures do not leave out any important performance facets.	
	Measures do not include factors outside employee control.	
Acceptability and fairness	Employees perceive the performance evaluation and rewards received relative to the work performed as fair (distributive justice).	
	Employees perceive the procedures used to determine the ratings and subsequent rewards as fair (procedural justice).	
Inclusiveness	Employee input about their performance is gathered from the employees before the appraisal meeting.	
	Employees participate in the process of creating the system by providing input on how performance should be measured.	
Openness	Performance is evaluated frequently and feedback is provided on an ongoing basis.	
	Appraisal meeting is a two-way communication process and not one-way communication delivered from the supervisor to the employee.	
	Standards are clear and communicated on an ongoing basis.	
	Communications are factual, open, and honest.	
Correctability	There is an appeals process, through which employees can challenge unjust or incorrect decisions.	
Standardization	Performance is evaluated consistently across people and time.	
Ethicality	Supervisors suppress their personal self-interest in providing evaluations.	
	Supervisors evaluate performance dimensions for which they have sufficient information only.	
	Employee privacy is respected.	

Case Study 1.2 Performance Management at Network Solutions, Inc.

Network Solutions, Inc.,[1] is a worldwide leader in hardware, software, and services essential to computer networking. Until recently, Network Solutions, Inc., had over 50 different systems with which to measure performance within the company, many employees did not receive a review, fewer than 5% of all employees received the lowest category of rating, and there was not recognition program in place to reward high achievers. Overall, there was recognition that performance problems were not being addressed and tough pressure from competitors increased the costs of ineffectively managing human performance. In addition, quality initiatives were driving change in several areas of the business, and Network Solutions decided that these initiatives should also apply to "people quality." Finally, Network Solutions wanted to improve its ability to meet its organizational goals, and one way of doing this would be to ensure they were linked to each employee's goals.

Given this situation, in 2001 Network Solutions' CEO announced that he wanted to implement a forced distribution performance management system in which a set percentage of employees was classified in each of several categories (e.g., rating of 1 to the top 20% performers; rating of 2 to the middle 70% performers; and rating of 3 to the bottom 10% performers). A global cross-divisional HR team was put in place to design and implement the new system. The first task for the design team was to build a business case of the new system by showing that if organizational strategy was carried down to team contributions and team contributions were translated into individual goals, then business goals would be met. Initially the program was rolled out as a year round people management system that raises the bar on performance management at Network Solutions by aligning individual performance objectives with organizational goals by focusing on development of all employees. The desired outcomes of the new system included raising the performance level of all employees, identifying and retaining top talent, and identifying low performers and improving their performance. Network Solutions also wanted the performance expectations for all employees to be clear.

Before rolling out the program, the design team received the support of senior leadership. They did this by communicating that the performance management system was the future of Network Solutions and by encouraging all senior leaders to ensure that those reporting directly to them understood the process and also accepted it. In addition, they encouraged senior leaders to use the system with all of their direct subordinates, and to demand and utilize output from the new system. Next, the design team encouraged the senior leaders to stop the development and use of any other performance management system and pushed for standardization of performance management across all divisions. Finally, the team had senior leaders emphasize the new program by involving employees in training of talent management, and assessing any needs in their divisions that the new system would not address.

---

[1]This case study is based, in part, on actual information. Network Solutions, Inc., is a pseudonym to protect the identity of the actual company in question.

The Network Solutions global performance management cycle consisted of the following process:

1. Goal cascading and team building
2. Performance planning
3. Development planning
4. Ongoing discussions and updates between managers and employees
5. Annual performance summary

Training resources were made available on Network Solutions' intranet for managers and individual contributors, including access to all necessary forms. In addition to the training available on the intranet, 1- to 2-hour conference calls took place before each phase of the program was begun.

Today, part of the training associated with the performance management system revolves around the idea that the development planning phase of the system is the joint year-round responsibility of managers and employees. Managers are responsible for scheduling meetings, guiding employees on preparing for meetings, and finalizing all development plans. Individual contributors are responsible for documenting the developmental plans. Both managers and employees are responsible for preparing for the meeting, filling out the development planning preparation forms, and attending the meeting.

With forced distribution systems, there is a set number of employees that have to fall into set rating classifications. As noted, in the Network Solutions system employees are given a rating of 1, 2, or 3. Individual ratings are determined by the execution of annual objectives and job requirements as well as by a comparison rating of others at a similar level at Network Solutions. Employees receiving a 3, the lowest rating, have a specified time period to improve their performance. If their performance does improve, then they are released from the plan, but they are not eligible for stock options or salary increases. If performance does not improve, they can take a severance package and leave the company or they can start on a performance improvement plan, which has more rigorous expectations and time lines than did the original action plan. If performance does not improve after the second period, then they are terminated without a severance package. Individuals with a rating of 2 receive average to high salary increases, stock options, and bonuses. Individuals receiving the highest rating of 1 receive the highest salary increases, stock options, and bonuses. These individuals are also treated as "high potential" employees and given extra development opportunities by their managers. The company also makes significant efforts to retain all individuals receiving a rating of 1.

Looking to the future, Network Solutions plans to continue reinforcing the needed cultural change to support forced distribution ratings. HR Centers of Expertise of Network Solutions continue to educate employees on the system to ensure that they understand that Network Solutions still rewards good performance; they are just measuring it in a different way than in the past. There is also a plan to monitor for and correct any unproductive practices and implement correcting policies and practices. To do this, Network Solutions plans on continued checks with all stakeholders to ensure that the performance management system is serving its intended purpose.

Consider Network Solutions' performance management system in light of what we discussed as an ideal system. Then answer the following questions:

1. Overall, what is the overlap between Network Solutions' system and an ideal system?
2. What are the features of the system implemented at Network Solutions that correspond to what was described in the chapter as ideal characteristics? Which of

the ideal characteristics are missing? For which of the ideal characteristics do we need additional information to evaluate whether they are part of the system at Network Solutions?

3. Based on the description of the system at Network Solutions, what do you anticipate will be

some advantages and positive outcomes resulting from the implementation of the system?

4. Based on the description of the system at Network Solutions, what do you anticipate will be some disadvantages and negative outcomes resulting from the implementation of the system? ■

End Notes

1. DeNisi, A. S., & Kluger, A. N. (2000). Feedback effectiveness: Can 360-degree appraisals be improved? *Academy of Management Executive, 14,* 129–139.
2. Fandray, D. (2001, May). Managing performance the Merrill Lynch way. *Workforce Online.* http://www.workforce.com/arch ive/feature/22/28/68/223512.php Retrieval date: August 1, 2005.
3. Bisoux, T. (2004). Man, one business. *BizEd, 3*(4), 18–25.
4. Thomas, S. L., & Bretz, R. D. (1994). Research and practice in performance appraisal: Evaluating employee performance in America's largest companies. *SAM Advanced Management Journal, 59*(2), 28–34.
5. Keeping, L. M., & Levy, P. E. (2000). Performance appraisal reactions: Measurement, modeling, and method bias. *Journal of Applied Psychology, 85,* 708–723.
6. Peters, T. (1987). *The new masters of excellence.* Niles, IL: Nightingale Conant Corp.
7. Bititci, U. S., Memdibil, K., Nudurupati, S., Turner, T., & Garengo, P. (2004). The interplay between performance measurement, organizational culture and management styles. *Measuring Business Excellence, 8,* 28–41.
8. Pennington, R. G. (2003). Change performance to change the culture. *Industrial and Commercial Training, 35,* 251.
9. Sumlin, R. *Performance management: Impacts and trends.* DDI white paper. http://www.ddi.com/pdf/OCWP06.pdf Retrieval date: August 1, 2005.
10. Gabris, G. T., & Ihrke, D. M. (2001). Does performance appraisal contribute to heightened levels of employee burnout? The results of one study. *Public Personnel Management, 30,* 157–172.
11. FMI Corporation. (2000, November 15). *Using performance reviews to improve employee retention: Contractor's business management report,* 2, Denver, CO.
12. The following discussion is based in large part on Chapter 1 from G. T. Milcovich and J. M. Newman, *Compensation Management,* 7th ed. (New York: McGraw-Hill, 2002).
13. Lewin, D. (2002, January). *Incentive compensation in the U.S. public sector: A study of usage, perceptions, and preferences.* Paper presented at the annual meeting of the Industrial Relations Research Association, Atlanta, GA.
14. Esen, E. (2003). *Job benefits survey.* Alexandria, VA: Society for Human Resource Management.
15. *Why choose sun?* http://au.sun.com/employment/student/whysun.html Retrieval date: August 1, 2005.
16. *Company car or allowance?* http://www.buyingacar.co.za/company.htm Retrieval date: August 1, 2005.
17. Pierce, C. A., Aguinis, H., & Adams, S. K. R. (2000). Effects of a dissolved workplace romance and rater characteristics on responses to a sexual harassment accusation. *Academy of Management Journal, 43,* 869–880.
18. *Why choose sun?* http://au.sun.com/employment/student/whysun.html Retrieval date: August 1, 2005.
19. Cleveland, J. N, & Murphy, R. E. (1989). Multiple uses of performance appraisal: Prevalence and correlates. *Journal of Applied Psychology, 74,* 130–135.
20. London, M., & Smither, J. W. (2002). Feedback orientation, feedback culture, and the longitudinal performance management

process. *Human Resource Management Review, 12,* 81–100.

21. Cascio, W. F., & Aguinis, H. (2005). *Applied psychology in human resources management* (6th ed.). Upper Saddle River, NJ: Prentice Hall.

22. Fandray, D. (2001, May). The new thinking in performance appraisals. *Workforce Online.* http://www.workforce.com/archive/feature/ 22/28/68/index.php Retrieval date: August 1, 2005.

23. Cleveland, J. N, & Murphy, R. E. (1989). Multiple uses of performance appraisal: Prevalence and correlates. *Journal of Applied Psychology, 74,* 130–135.

24. McAdam, R., Hazlett, S., & Casey, C. (2005). Performance management in the UK public sector: Addressing multiple stakeholder complexity. *International Journal of Public Sector Management, 18,* 256–273.

25. Taylor, M. S., Masterson, S. S., Renard, M. K., & Tracy, K. B. (1998). Managers' reactions to procedurally just performance management systems. *Academy of Management Journal, 41,* 568–579.

26. Erdogan, B. (2002). Antecedents and consequences of justice perceptions in performance appraisals. *Human Resource Management Review, 12,* 555–578.

27. Cawley, B. D., Keeping, L. M., & Levy, P. E. (1998). Participation in the performance appraisal process and employee reactions: A meta-analytic review of field investigations. *Journal of Applied Psychology, 83,* 615–633.

28. Eddy, E. R., Stone, D. L., & Stone-Romero, E. F. (1999). The effects of information management policies on reactions to human resource information systems: An integration of privacy and procedural justice perspectives. *Personnel Psychology, 52,* 335–358.

29. Sumlin, R. Performance management: impacts and trends. DDI white paper. http://www.ddi.com/pdf/OCWP06.pdf Retrieval date: August 1, 2005.

2

Performance
Management Process

In theory, the Performance Review process can be thought of as a positive interaction between a "coach" and an employee, working together to achieve maximum performance. In reality, it's more like finding a dead squirrel in your backyard and realizing the best solution is to fling it onto your neighbor's roof.

—SCOTT ADAMS (THE DILBERT PRINCIPLE)

Learning Objectives

By the end of this chapter, you will be able to do the following:

■ Understand that performance management is an ongoing process that includes the interrelated components of prerequisites, performance planning, performance execution, performance assessment, performance review, and performance renewal and recontracting.

■ Conduct a job analysis to determine the job duties, knowledge, skills, and abilities (KSAs), and working conditions of a particular job.

■ Write a job description that incorporates the KSAs of the job and information on the organization and unit mission and strategic goals.

■ Understand that the poor implementation of any of the performance management process components has a negative impact on the system as a whole.

■ Understand that a dysfunctional or disrupted link between any of the performance management process components has a negative impact on the system as a whole.

■ Understand important prerequisites needed before a performance management system is implemented, including knowledge of the organization's mission and strategic goals and knowledge of the job in question.

■ Distinguish results from behaviors and understand the need to consider both in performance management systems.

■ Describe the employee's role in performance execution and distinguish areas over which the employee has primary responsibility from areas over which the manager has primary responsibility.

∎ Understand the employee's and the manager's responsibility in the performance assessment phase.

∎ Understand that the appraisal meeting involves the past, the present, and the future.

∎ Understand the similarities between performance planning and performance renewal and recontracting.

∎ Create results- and behavior-oriented performance standards.

As described in Chapter 1, performance management is an ongoing process. Performance management does not take place just once a year. Performance management is a continuous process including several components.[1] These components are closely related to each other and the poor implementation of any of them has a negative impact on the performance management system as a whole. The components in the performance management process are shown in Figure 2.1. This chapter provides a brief description of each of these components. Subsequent chapters address each of the components in greater detail. Let's start with the prerequisites.

2.1 PREREQUISITES

There are two important prerequisites that are required before a performance management system is implemented: (1) knowledge of the organization's mission and strategic goals, and (2) knowledge of the job in question. As described in detail in Chapter 3, knowledge of the organization's mission and strategic goals is a result of strategic planning (also discussed in detail in Chapter 3, the strategic planning process may take place *after* the mission and vision statements are created; thus, there is a constant interplay between mission and vision and strategic planning). Strategic planning allows an organization to clearly define its purpose or reason for existing, where it wants to be in the future, the goals it wants to achieve, and the strategies it will use to attain these goals. Once the goals for the entire organization have been established, similar goals cascade downward, with departments setting objectives to support the organization's overall mission and objectives. The cascading continues downward until each employee has a set of goals compatible with those of the organization.

Unfortunately, it is often the case that many organizational units are not in tune with the organization's strategic direction. However, there seems to be a trend in the positive direction. For example, a study including public sector organizations in Queensland, Australia, showed a fairly high level of strategic integration of the human resources (HR) function. Specifically, approximately 80% of the organizations that participated in the study were categorized as having achieved the highest level of strategic integration. This level is characterized by a dynamic and multifaceted linkage based on an "integrative relationship between people management and strategic management process."[2] Recall that an important objective of any performance management system is to enhance each employee's contribution to the goals of the organization. If there is a lack of clarity regarding where the organization wants to go, or the relationship between the organization's mission and strategies and the unit's mission and strategies is not clear, there will be a lack of clarity regarding what each employee needs to do and achieve to help the organization get there.

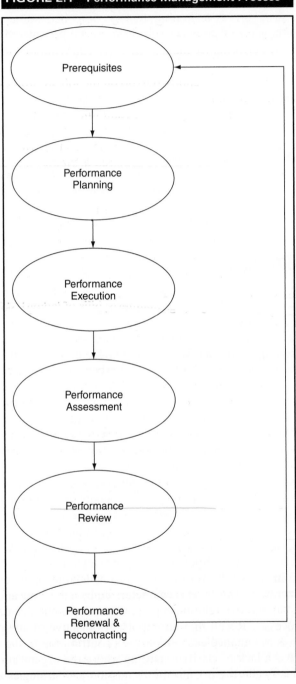

FIGURE 2.1 Performance Management Process

- Prerequisites
- Performance Planning
- Performance Execution
- Performance Assessment
- Performance Review
- Performance Renewal & Recontracting

The second important prerequisite before a performance management system is implemented is to understand the job in question. This is done through job analysis. Job analysis is a process of determining the key components of a particular job, including activities, tasks, products, services, and processes. A job analysis is a fundamental prerequisite of any performance management system. Without a job analysis, it is difficult to understand what constitutes the required duties for a particular job. If we don't know what an employee is supposed to do on the job, we won't know what needs to be evaluated and how to do so.

As a result of a job analysis, we obtain information regarding the tasks carried out and the knowledge, skills, and abilities (KSAs) required of a particular job. Knowledge includes having the information needed to perform the work, but not necessarily having done it. Skills refer to required attributes that are usually acquired by having done the work in the past. Ability refers to having the physical, emotional, intellectual, and psychological aptitude to perform the work but neither having done it nor having been trained to do the work is required.[3]

The tasks and KSAs needed for the various jobs are typically presented in the form of a job description, which summarizes the job duties, needed KSAs, and working conditions for a particular job. As an illustration, see the box "Job Description for Trailer Truck Driver." This job description includes information about what tasks are performed (e.g., operation of a specific type of truck). It also includes information about the needed knowledge (e.g., manifests, bills of lading), skills (e.g., keeping truck and trailer under control, particularly in difficult weather conditions), and abilities (e.g., physical and spatial abilities needed to turn narrow corners).

Job analysis can be conducted using observation, off-the-shelf questionnaires, or interviews. Data are collected from job incumbents (i.e., those doing the job at present) and their supervisors. Alternatively, if the job is yet to be created, data can be gathered from the individual(s) responsible for creating the new position and those who will supervise individuals in the new position. Observation methods include job analysts watching incumbents do the job, or even trying to do the work themselves, and then producing a description of what they have observed. This method can be subject to biases

---

BOX 2.1

Job Description for Trailer Truck Driver:
Civilian Personnel Management Service, U.S. Department of Defense

Operates gasoline or diesel powered truck or truck tractor equipped with two or more driving wheels and with four or more forward speed transmissions, which may include two or more gear ranges. These vehicles are coupled to a trailer or semi-trailer by use of a turntable (fifth wheel) or pintle (pivot) hook. Drives over public roads to transport materials, merchandise, or equipment. Performs difficult driving tasks such as backing truck to loading platform, turning narrow corners, negotiating narrow passageways, and keeping truck and trailer under control, particularly on wet or icy highways. May assist in loading and unloading truck. May also handle manifest, bills of lading, expense accounts, and other papers pertinent to the shipment.

because job analysts may not be able to distinguish important from unimportant tasks. Such analysis may not be suitable for many jobs. For example, a job analyst could not do the work of a police officer for safety reasons, or the work of a software programmer for lack of knowledge and skills do to the work. Off-the-shelf methods involve distributing questionnaires, including a common lists of tasks or KSAs and asking individuals to fill them out, indicating the extent to which each task or KSA is required for a particular job in question. These generic off-the-shelf tools can be practical, but may not allow capturing the nuances and idiosyncrasies of jobs out of the mainstream.

Interviews are a very popular job analysis method. During a job analysis interview, the job analyst asks the interviewee to describe what he or she does (or what individuals in the position do) during a typical day at the job from start to finish (i.e., in chronological order). Alternatively, the job analyst can also ask the interviewee to describe the major duties involved in the job and then have him or her break down these duties into specific tasks. Once a list of tasks has been compiled, all incumbents should have an opportunity to review the information and rate each task in terms of frequency and criticality. The frequency and criticality scales may be the following:[4]

Frequency	*Criticality*
0: not performed	0: not critical
1: every few months to yearly	1: low level of criticality
2: every few weeks to monthly	2: below average level of criticality
3: every few days to weekly	3: average level of criticality
4: every few hours to daily	4: above average level of criticality
5: hourly to many times each hour	5: extremely critical

Rating both frequency and criticality is needed because some tasks may be performed regularly (i.e., make coffee several times a day), but may not be very critical. The job analyst can then multiply the frequency scores by the criticality scores to obtain an overall score for each task. So, if making coffee receives a frequency score of 4 (i.e., "every few hours to daily") and a criticality score of 0 (i.e., "not critical"), the overall score would be $4 \times 0 = 0$. Considering frequency scores alone would have given us the wrong impression that making coffee is a task that deserved a prominent role in the job description. Overall scores for all tasks can be ranked from highest to lowest to obtain a final list of tasks.

There are numerous job analysis questionnaires available on the Internet. These questionnaires, which can be administered online, using a paper survey, or in interview format, can be used for a variety of positions. For example, the state of Delaware uses a job analysis questionnaire available at http://www.delawarepersonnel.com/class/forms/jaq/jaq.htm. This questionnaire includes 18 multiple choice job content questions. Job content information is assessed through three factors: (1) knowledge and skills, (2) problem solving, and (3) accountability and end results. As a second example, the city of Alexandria Virginia, uses a job analysis questionnaire available at http://alexandriava.gov/class_comp/job_analysis.pdf. This instrument does not include multiple choice questions. Instead, employees answer more general questions about their jobs together with the allocation of the percentage of time employees spend performing each duty. In addition, respondents are encouraged to attach forms, work schedules, reports, memoranda, and other materials that may help explain the responses provided. Conducting a Google search for the phrase "job analysis question-naire" leads to several other instruments. Be aware that some of these instruments may have been created for specific types of jobs and industries (e.g., service jobs, nonsuper-visory jobs). Make sure you check the suitability of the instrument before using it in a different organizational context. Combining items and formats from various instru-ments already available may be the most effective way to proceed.

Writing a job description may seem like a daunting task. However, it does not have to be. Generic job descriptions can be obtained from the Occupational Informational Network (O*NET, http://online.onetcenter.org/gen_search_page). O*NET is a compre-hensive database of worker attributes and job characteristics that provides a common language for defining and describing occupations. The descriptions available via O*NET can serve as a foundation for a job description. O*NET descriptions can be easily adapted and changed to accommodate specific local characteristics. For example, see O*NET's generic description for truck drivers in the box "Summary Report for Tractor-Trailer Truck Drivers (from O*NET)." First, the summary description can be checked for accuracy and relevance by supervisors. Then, the list of KSAs provided by O*NET can be readily rated by incumbents (and additional KSAs may be added if needed).

O*NET can also be a very useful resource for small businesses because, for most of them, conducting a job analysis may not be feasible simply because there are not sufficient numbers of people from whom to collect data. In addition, O*NET can be used when organizations expand and new positions are created. One thing needs to be clear, however: jobs change. Thus, job descriptions must be checked for accuracy and updated as needed.

BOX 2.2

Summary Report for Tractor-Trailer Truck Drivers (from O*NET)

DESCRIPTION

Drive a tractor-trailer combination or a truck with a capacity of at least 26,000 gross vehicle weight (GVW) to transport and deliver goods, livestock, or materials in liq-uid, loose, or packaged form. May be required to unload truck. May require use of automated routing equipment. Requires commercial driver's license.

TASKS

- Drives tractor-trailer combination, apply-ing knowledge of commercial driving regulations, to transport and deliver products, livestock, or materials, usually over long distance.

- Maneuvers truck into loading or unloading position, following signals from loading crew as needed.

- Drives truck to weigh station before and after loading, and along route to document weight and conform to state regulations.

- Maintains driver log according to Interstate Commerce Commission (ICC) regulations.

- Inspects truck before and after trips and submits report indicating truck condition.

- Reads bill of lading to determine assignment.

- Fastens chain or binders to secure load on trailer during transit.

- Loads or unloads, or assists in loading and unloading truck.

(Continued)

(Continued)

- Works as member of two-person team driving tractor with sleeper bunk behind cab.
- Services truck with oil, fuel, and radiator fluid to maintain tractor-trailer truck.

KNOWLEDGE

- Transportation—Knowledge of principles and methods for moving people or goods by air, rail, sea, or road, including the relative costs and benefits.
- Geography—Knowledge of principles and methods for describing the features of land, sea, and air masses, including their physical characteristics, locations, interrelationships, and distribution of plant, animal, and human life.
- Mechanical—Knowledge of machines and tools, including their designs, uses, repair, and maintenance.
- Law and Government—Knowledge of laws, legal codes, court procedures, precedents, government regulations, executive orders, agency rules, and the democratic political process.
- Public Safety and Security—Knowledge of relevant equipment, policies, procedures, and strategies to promote effective local, state, or national security operations for the protection of people, data, property, and institutions.

SKILLS

- Operation and Control—Controlling operations of equipment or systems.
- Equipment Maintenance—Performing routine maintenance on equipment and determining when and what kind of maintenance is needed.
- Reading Comprehension—Understanding written sentences and paragraphs in work-related documents.
- Mathematics—Using mathematics to solve problems.
- Writing—Communicating effectively in writing as appropriate for the needs of the audience.

ABILITIES

- Far Vision—The ability to see details at a distance.
- Reaction Time—The ability to quickly respond (with the hand, finger, or foot) to a signal (sound, light, picture) when it appears.
- Response Orientation—The ability to choose quickly between two or more movements in response to two or more different signals (lights, sounds, pictures). It includes the speed with which the correct response is started with the hand, foot, or other body part.
- Static Strength—The ability to exert maximum muscle force to lift, push, pull, or carry objects.
- Near Vision—The ability to see details at close range (within a few feet of the observer).
- Spatial Orientation—The ability to know your location in relation to the environment or to know where other objects are in relation to you.
- Multilimb Coordination—The ability to coordinate two or more limbs (for example, two arms, two legs, or one leg and one arm) while sitting, standing, or lying down. It does not involve performing the activities while the whole body is in motion.
- Depth Perception—The ability to judge which of several objects is closer or farther away from you, or to judge the distance between you and an object.
- Manual Dexterity—The ability to quickly move your hand, your hand together with your arm, or your two hands to grasp, manipulate, or assemble objects.
- Rate Control—The ability to time your movements or the movement of a piece of equipment in anticipation of changes in the speed and direction of a moving object or scene.

Job descriptions are a key prerequisite for any performance management system because they provide the criteria (i.e., yardsticks) that will be used in measuring performance. Such criteria may concern behaviors (i.e., how to perform) or results (i.e., what outcomes should result from performance). In our truck driver example, a behavioral criterion could involve the skill "equipment maintenance." For example, a supervisor may rate the extent to which the employee "performs routine maintenance on equipment and determines when and what kind of maintenance is needed." Regarding results, these criteria usually fall into one of the following categories: (1) quality, (2) quantity, (3) cost-effectiveness, and (4) timeliness.[5] In the truck driver example, results-oriented criteria can include number of accidents (i.e., quality) and amount of load transported over a specific period of time (i.e., quantity).

Some organizations are becoming aware of the importance of considering prerequisites before implementing a performance management system. Take the case of Deaconess Hospital in Oklahoma City, Oklahoma, which includes a workforce of 750 physicians and a total of 1,600 employees (http://www.deaconessokc.org/). Deaconess Hospital has been able to effectively integrate employees' job descriptions within their performance management system. The need for this integration was reinforced by results from an employee survey revealing that employees did not know what they were being evaluated on. Therefore, with the input of employees, the hospital updated each of the 260 job descriptions. At present, each employee's job description is part of the performance review form. The new forms incorporate task performance standards as well as behaviors specific to individual jobs. For example, a nurse may be evaluated on "how well he or she safely, timely, and respectfully administers patient medication and on his or her planning and organization skills." In addition, Deaconess Hospital has been able to link each employee's performance to the strategy and goals of the organization. Specifically, all employees are rated on the following core behaviors considered to be of top strategic importance for this particular organization: (1) adaptability, (2) building customer loyalty, (3) building trust, and (4) contributing to team success.[6]

In summary, there are two important prerequisites that must exist before the implementation of a successful performance management system. First, there is a need to have good knowledge of the organization's mission and strategic goals. This knowledge, combined with knowledge regarding the mission and strategic goals of their unit, allows employees to make contributions that will have a positive impact on the unit and on the organization as a whole. Second, there is a need to have good knowledge of the job in question: what tasks need to be done, how they should be done, and what KSAs are needed. Such knowledge is obtained through a job analysis. If we have good information regarding a job, then it is easier to establish criteria for job success.

2.2　PERFORMANCE PLANNING

Employees should have a thorough knowledge of the performance management system. In fact, at the beginning of each performance cycle, the supervisor and the employee meet to discuss, and agree upon, what needs to be done and how it should be done. This performance planning discussion includes a consideration of both results and behaviors, as well as a developmental plan.

2.2.1 Results

Results refer to what needs to be done or the outcomes an employee must produce. A consideration of results needs to include the *key accountabilities,* or broad areas of a job for which the employee is responsible for producing results. This information is typically obtained from the job description. A discussion of results also includes specific *objectives* that the employee will achieve as part of each accountability. Objectives are statements of important and measurable outcomes. Finally, discussing results also means discussing *performance standards.* A performance standard is a yardstick used to evaluate how well employees have achieved each objective. Performance standards provide information on acceptable and unacceptable performance, for example, regarding quality, quantity, cost, and time.

Consider the job of university professors. Two key accountabilities are (1) teaching (preparation and delivery of instructional materials to students) and (2) research (creation and dissemination of new knowledge). An objective for teaching could be "to obtain a student evaluation of teaching performance of 3 on a 4-point scale." An objective for research could be "to publish two articles in scholarly refereed journals per year." Performance standards could be "to obtain a student evaluation of teaching performance of at least 2 on a 4-point scale" and "to publish at least one article in scholarly referred journals per year." Thus, the objective is the desired level of performance, whereas the standard is usually a minimum acceptable level of performance.

2.2.2 Behaviors

Although it is important to measure results, an exclusive emphasis on results can give a skewed or incomplete picture of employee performance. For example, for some jobs it may be difficult to come up with precise objectives and standards. For other jobs, employees may have control over how they do their jobs but not over the results of their behaviors. For example, for a salesperson, resulting sales figures could be affected more strongly by the assigned sales territory than by the salesperson's ability and performance. So, behaviors, or how a job is done, are an important component of the planning phase. This is probably the reason that results from a recent survey indicated that, in addition to sales figures, salespeople would like to be appraised based on such behavioral criteria as communications skills and product knowledge.[7]

A consideration of behaviors includes discussing *competencies,* which are measurable clusters of KSAs that are critical in determining how results will be achieved. Examples of competencies are customer service, written or oral communication, creative thinking, and dependability. Returning to the example of the professor, assume that teaching is done online and numerous technology-related problems exist, such that the resulting teaching evaluations are deficient (i.e., lower than the standard of 2). This is an example of a situation in which behaviors should be given more importance than results. In this situation, the evaluation could include competencies such as online communication skills (e.g., in the chat room).

2.2.3 Development plan

An important step before the review cycle begins is for the supervisor and employee to agree on a development plan. At a minimum, this plan should include identifying areas that need improvement and setting goals to be achieved in each area. Development plans usually include both results and behaviors. The topic of development plans is addressed in detail in Chapter 8.

In summary, performance planning includes the consideration of results and behaviors and the developmental plan. A discussion of results needs to include key accountabilities (i.e., broad areas for which an employee is responsible), specific objectives for each key accountability (i.e., goals to be reached), and performance standards (i.e., what constitutes acceptable and unacceptable levels of performance). A discussion of behaviors needs to include competencies (i.e., clusters of KSAs). Finally, the developmental plan includes a description of areas that need improving and goals to be achieved in each area.

Once the prerequisites are met and the planning phase has been completed, we are ready to begin the implementation of the performance management system. This includes performance execution, assessment, review, and renewal and recontracting.

2.3 PERFORMANCE EXECUTION

Once the review cycle begins, the employee strives to produce the results and display the behaviors agreed upon earlier as well as to work on developmental needs. The employee has primary responsibility and ownership of this process. Employee participation does not begin at the performance execution stage, however. As noted earlier, employees need to have active input in the development of the job descriptions, performance standards, and the creation of the rating form. In addition, at later stages, employees are active participants in the evaluation process in that they provide a self-assessment and the performance review interview is a two-way communication process. But, at the performance execution stage, the following factors need to be present:[8]

1. *Commitment to goal achievement.*   The employee must be committed to the goals that were set. One way to enhance commitment is to allow the employee to be an active participant in the process of setting the goals.
2. *Ongoing performance feedback and coaching.*   The employee should not wait until the review cycle is over to solicit performance feedback. Also, the employee should not wait until a serious problem develops to ask for coaching. The employee needs to take a proactive role in soliciting performance feedback and coaching from her supervisor.[9]
3. *Communication with supervisor.*   Supervisors are busy with multiple obligations. The burden is on the employee to communicate openly and regularly with the supervisor.
4. *Collecting and sharing performance data.*   The employee should provide the supervisor with regular updates on progress toward goal achievement, in terms of both behaviors and results.
5. *Preparing for performance reviews.*   The employee should not wait until the end of the review cycle approaches to prepare for the review. On the contrary, the employee should engage in an ongoing and realistic self-appraisal, so immediate corrective action can be taken if necessary. The usefulness of the self-appraisal process can be enhanced by gathering informal performance information from peers and customers (both internal and external).

Although the employee has primary responsibilities for performance execution, the supervisor also needs to do his or her share of the work. In fact, monitoring the performance of colleagues has been identified as a key competency by the Management Standards Center (www.management-standards.com, Unit 26). Supervisors have primary responsibility over the following issues:[10]

1. *Observation and documentation.*   Supervisors must observe and document performance on a daily basis. It is important to keep track of examples of both good and poor performance.
2. *Updates.*   As the organization's goals may change, it is important to update and revise initial objectives, standards, and key accountabilities (in the case of results) and competency areas (in the case of behaviors).
3. *Feedback.*   Feedback on progression toward goals and coaching to improve performance should be provided on a regular basis, and certainly before the review cycle is over.
4. *Resources.*   Supervisors should provide employees with resources and opportunities to participate in developmental activities. Thus, they should encourage (and sponsor) participation in training, classes, and special assignments. Overall, supervisors have a responsibility to ensure that the employee has the necessary supplies and funding to perform the job properly.
5. *Reinforcement.*   Supervisors must let employees know that their outstanding performance is noticed by reinforcing effective behaviors and progress toward goals. Also, supervisors should also provide feedback regarding negative performance and how to remedy the observed problem. Observation and communication are not sufficient. Performance problems must be diagnosed early on and appropriate steps taken as soon as the problem is discovered.

The summary list included in Table 2.1 makes it clear that both the employee and the manager are responsible for performance execution. As an example of this shared responsibility in an actual organization, consider the case of Lockheed Martin Corporation. Lockheed Martin Corporation, an advanced technology company, was formed in March 1995 with the merger of two of the world's premier technology companies: Lockheed Corporation and Martin Marietta Corporation. Lockheed Martin has approximately 130,000 employees worldwide. They are engaged in the research, design, development, manufacture, and integration of advanced technology systems, products, and services (www.lockheedmartin.com). Lockheed Martin's performance management system includes the active participation of both employees and their

TABLE 2.1   Performance Execution Stage: Areas for Which Employees and Managers Have Primary Responsibility

Employees	*Managers*
Commitment to goal achievement	Observation and documentation
Ongoing performance feedback and coaching	Updates
Communication with supervisor	Feedback
Collecting and sharing performance data	Resources
Preparing for performance reviews	Reinforcement

supervisors. Specifically, employees write their own performance management objectives based on organization and unit objectives. Then, managers approve the objectives and are encouraged to give ongoing feedback about the progress toward meeting the objectives. The actual performance appraisal form is an electronic, one-page computer screen. The program was designed to "involve employees in setting their own goals, to make those goals clear and to provide regular feedback on their progress toward achieving those goals."[11]

2.4 PERFORMANCE ASSESSMENT

In the assessment phase, both the employee and the manager are responsible for evaluating the extent to which the desired behaviors have been displayed, and whether the desired results have been achieved. Although many sources can be used to collect performance information (e.g., peers, subordinates), in most cases the direct supervisor provides the information. This also includes an evaluation of the extent to which the goals stated in the development plan have been achieved.

It is important that both the employee and the manager take ownership of the assessment process. The manager fills out her appraisal form, and the employee should also fill out his form. The fact that both parties are involved in the assessment provides good information to be used in the review phase. When both the employee and the supervisor are active participants in the evaluation process, there is a greater likelihood that the information will be used productively in the future. Specifically, the inclusion of self-ratings helps emphasize possible discrepancies between self-views and the views that important others (i.e., supervisors) have of our behavior. It is the discrepancy between these two views that is most likely to trigger development efforts, particularly when feedback from the supervisor is more negative than are employee self-evaluations.[12]

The inclusion of self-appraisals is also beneficial regarding important additional factors. Self-appraisals can reduce employees' defensiveness during an appraisal meeting and increase employee satisfaction with the performance management system, as well as enhance perceptions of accuracy and fairness and therefore acceptance of the system.[13] This point is addressed in more detail in later chapters.

In sum, both the employee and the supervisor must evaluate employee performance. Employee involvement in the process increases employee ownership and commitment to the system. In addition, it provides important information to be discussed during the performance review, which is discussed next.

2.5 PERFORMANCE REVIEW

The performance review stage involves the meeting between the employee and the manager to review their assessments. This meeting is usually called the *appraisal meeting* or *discussion*. The appraisal meeting is important because it provides for a formal setting in which the employee receives feedback on his of her performance. In spite of its importance in performance management, the appraisal meeting is often seen as the "Achilles' heel of the entire process."[14] This is because many managers are uncomfortable providing performance feedback, particularly when performance is deficient.[15] This high level of discomfort, which often translates into anxiety and the avoidance of the appraisal interview, can be mitigated through training those responsible for providing feedback, a topic that is discussed in detail in Chapters 6 and 9. At this point, however, let's emphasize that people are apprehensive about both receiving *and* giving performance information, and this apprehension reinforces the importance of a formal performance review as part of any performance management system.[16]

In most cases, the appraisal meeting is seen as a review of the past, that is, what was done (i.e., results) and how (i.e., behaviors). For example, a survey including over 150 organizations in Scotland showed that performance management systems in over 80% of organizations emphasize the past.[17] However, this meeting should also include a discussion of the employee's developmental progress as well as plans for the future. The conversation should include a discussion of goals and development plans that the employee will be expected to achieve over the period before the next review session. In addition, a good appraisal meeting includes information on what new compensation, if any, the employee may be receiving as a result of his performance. In short, the appraisal discussion focuses on the past (what has been done and how), the present (what compensation is received or denied as a result), and the future (goals to be attained before the upcoming review session).

As noted earlier, the discussion about past performance can be challenging, particularly when performance levels have not reached acceptable levels. Following is a script reflecting what the first few seconds of the appraisal meeting can be like.[18]

Sit down, Sally. I've been looking forward to this chance to talk with you about your work last year. I think this discussion can be helpful to both of us. I'd like to go through the process slowly and carefully. I've put aside 45 minutes for us to talk together. This is one of the most important things you and I will do together all year. I want to start by having you tell me how you see your own performance over the past year—what you feel you did particularly well and where you think you might have achieved more. Then I'd like to talk about the appraisal I wrote. I think the most effective way to start is by discussing those areas where you and I generally agree. Then we'll talk about those in which our views seem to differ. I'll give you my reasons, and I want to get your point of view. The most important part of the process is reviewing the specific goals and objectives of your job. I'd like to start there and spend most of our time together talking about the results you achieved this year. Then I'd like to look at the section that deals with job skills and competencies and any other key elements of the appraisal. When we've completed that, I'd like to talk about my overall rating and how I arrived at it. Why don't you start by telling me how you feel this past year has gone?

We discuss performance reviews in more detail in Chapter 9. For now, however, consider the centrality of the performance review stage in the performance management process by reading the box "Six Recommended Steps for Conducting Productive Performance Reviews"[19]

BOX 2.3

Six Recommended Steps for Conducting Productive Performance Reviews

1. Identify what the employee has done well and poorly by citing specific positive and negative behaviors.

2. Solicit feedback from your employee about these behaviors. Listen for reactions and explanations.

3. Discuss the implications of changing, or not changing, the behaviors. Positive feedback is best, but an employee must be made aware of what will happen if any poor performance continues.

4. Explain to the employee how skills used in past achievements can help him overcome any current performance problems.

5. Agree on an action plan. Encourage the employee to invest in improving his performance by asking questions such as "What ideas do you have for _____?" and "What suggestions do you have for _____?"

6. Set up a meeting to follow up and agree on the behaviors, actions, and attitudes to be be evaluated.

2.6 PERFORMANCE RENEWAL AND RECONTRACTING

The final stage in the performance process is renewal and recontracting. Essentially, this is identical to the performance planning component. The main difference is that the renewal and recontracting stage uses the insights and information from the other phases. For example, some of the goals may have been set unrealistically high given an unexpected economic downturn. This would lead to setting less ambitious goals for the upcoming review period.

The performance management process includes a cycle starting with prerequisites and ending with performance renewal and recontracting. But, the cycle is not over after the renewal and recontracting stage. In fact, the process starts all over again: there needs to be a discussion of prerequisites, including the organization's mission and strategic goals and the job's KSAs. Because markets change, customers' preferences and needs change, and products change, there is a need to continuously monitor the prerequisites so that performance planning, and all the subsequent stages, are consistent with the organization's strategic objectives. Recall that, in the end, one of the main goals of any performance management system is to promote the achievement of organization-wide goals. Obviously, if managers and employees are not aware of these strategic goals, it is unlikely the performance management system will be instrumental in accomplishing the strategic goals.

SUMMARY POINTS

- Performance management is an ongoing process. It never ends. Once established in an organization, it becomes part of an organization's culture. The performance management process includes six closely related components: (1) prerequisites, (2) performance planning, (3) performance execution, (4) performance assessment, (5) performance review, and (6) performance renewal and recontracting.

- Job analysis can be conducted using interviews, observation, or off-the-shelf questionnaires. Once a list of tasks has been compiled, all incumbents should have an opportunity to review the information and rate each task in terms of its frequency and criticality.

- Each of the six components of the performance management process plays an important role. If any of these components is implemented poorly, then the entire performance management system suffers. For example, lack of knowledge of the organization's mission and strategic goals and the job in question (i.e., prerequisites) will not allow performance planning (i.e., performance road map) to be aligned with organizational goals, which in turn will lead to poor performance execution. In short, a performance management system is only as good as its weakest component.

- The links between the various components need to be clearly established. For example, performance planning needs to be closely related to performance execution. Performance planning is a futile exercise if execution does not follow from it. The same applies to all the arrows linking the various components, as shown in Figure 2.1.

- The first component of the performance management process involves two prerequisites. First, there is a need to have good knowledge of the organization's mission and strategic goals. This knowledge, combined with knowledge regarding the mission and strategic goals of one's unit, allows employees to make contributions that will have a positive impact on their units and on the organization as a whole. Second, there is a need to have good knowledge of the job in question. A job analysis allows for the determination of the key components of a particular job: what tasks need to be done, how they should be done, and what

KSAs are needed. If we have good information regarding a job, then it is easier to establish criteria for job success.

- The second component of the performance management process involves performance planning. Performance planning includes the consideration of results and behavior, as well as a developmental plan. A discussion of results needs to include key accountabilities (i.e., broad areas for which an employee is responsible), specific objectives for each key accountability (i.e., goals to be reached), and performance standards (i.e., what are acceptable and unacceptable levels of performance). A discussion of behaviors needs to include competencies (i.e., clusters of KSAs). Finally, the developmental plan includes a description of areas that need improving and goals to be achieved in each area.

- The third component involves performance execution. Both the employee and the manager are responsible for performance execution. For example, the employee needs to be committed to goal achievement and should take a proactive role in seeking feedback from his or her supervisor. The burden is on the employee to communicate openly and regularly with the supervisor. Also, the employee has a responsibility to be prepared for the performance review by conducting regular and realistic self-appraisals. On the other hand, the supervisor also has important responsibilities. These include observing and documenting performance, updating the employee on any changes in the goals of the organization, and providing resources and reinforcement so the employee can succeed and continue to be motivated.

- The fourth component involves performance assessment. Both the employee and the supervisor must evaluate employee performance. Involvement of the employee in the process increases his or her ownership and commitment to the system. In addition, it provides important information to be discussed during the performance review. In the absence of self-appraisals, it is often not clear to supervisors if employees have a real understanding of what is expected of them.

- The fifth component involves performance review. This is when the employee and manager meet to discuss employee performance, and this meeting is usually called the appraisal meeting. This meeting usually emphasizes the past: what the employee has done and how. However, an effective appraisal meeting also focuses on the present and the future. The present involves the changes in compensation that may result from the results obtained. The future involves a discussion of goals and development plans that the employee will be expected to achieve during the period before the next review session.

- The final component involves performance renewal and recontracting. Essentially, this component is identical to the performance planning stage. However, performance renewal and recontracting uses information gathered during the review period to make adjustments as needed. For example, some new key accountabilities and competencies may be included. Conversely, some goals may have to be adjusted either upward or downward.

Case Study 2.1   Job Analysis Exercise

Please conduct a job analysis for the position "graduate student enrolled in a master's program in the general field of business." This job analysis can include interviewing incumbents (i.e., other students) as well as supervisors (i.e., faculty). In addition, of course, you can rely on your own knowledge of the "job."

As a result of your job analysis, follow the O*NET format and create a summary description for the position as well as a list of tasks, knowledge, skills, and abilities needed for successful performance. Use the box "Summary Report for Tractor-Trailer Truck Drivers (from O*NET)" as a template. ■

Case Study 2.2   Disrupted Links in the Performance Management Process at "Omega, Inc."[1]

Omega, Inc., is a small manufacturing company whose sales success or failure rests in the hands of sales representatives employed by franchised dealers operating independently. Omega faces a challenging situation because it does not have control over the people working for the independent dealerships. It is the performance of these individuals that dictates Omega's sales success. To make things more complicated, until recently there was no clear understanding of the role of the sales representatives and there were no formal sales processes in place. Sales representatives varied greatly in terms of their level of skill and knowledge, most put out little effort beyond taking orders, and they did not feel motivated to make additional sales. Finally, franchises varied greatly regarding their management strategies and follow-up with Omega.

Recently, understanding the need to improve the performance of sales representatives, Omega agreed to partially fund and

support a training program for them. The network of franchise owners in turn agreed to work together to implement a performance management system. As a first step in creating the performance management system, the franchise owners conducted a job analysis of the role of the sale representatives, wrote a job description, and distributed it to all sales representatives. The franchise owners also adopted a franchisewide mission statement primarily based on the need to provide high-quality customer service. This mission statement was posted in all franchise offices, and each franchise owner spoke with his employees about the contribution that individual sales had on achieving their mission. As a second step, the managers set performance goals (i.e., sales quotas) for each employee. Then, all sales representatives attended extensive training sessions. The employees received feedback based on their performance in the training course and then were reminded once again of their sales quotas.

---

[1]This case study is loosely based on J. Swinney and B. Couch, Sales Performance Improvement Getting Results Through a Franchise sales organization. International Society for Performance Improvement case studies (2003). Retrieved August 15, 2005 from ISPI Online at http://www.ispi.org/services/gotResults/2003/GotResults_Swinney.pdf

Back on the job, managers gave feedback to their employees regarding their standing in relation to their sales quotas. However, the employees had no way of monitoring their own progress toward their quotas, and performance feedback consisted of little more than reiterating monthly sales goals. There was not a performance appraisal form in place, so discussions were not documented. This lack of feedback continued and, while sales quotas were being reached for the first few months, franchise owners received complaints from customers about the low quality of customer service they were receiving. Subsequently, sales began to decline. Furthermore, many orders were often incorrect, forcing customers to return items to Omega.

While the new performance management process was an improvement over no performance management (at least initially), the franchise owners were still far from having a system that included a smooth transition between each of the

components of the performance management process. Based on Omega's situation, please answer the following questions.

1. Consider each of the links of the performance management process as shown in Figure 2.1:
   a. prerequisites → performance planning
   b. performance planning → performance execution
   c. performance execution → performance assessment
   d. performance assessment → performance review
   e. performance review → performance renewal and recontracting
   f. performance renewal and recontracting → prerequisites

   Discuss whether each of the links is present, and in what form, in the performance management system described.

2. Given your answers to question 1, what can be done to fix each of the disrupted links in the process? ◼

Case Study 2.3   Performance Management at the University of Ghana[2]

The University of Ghana in Legon, Ghana began in 1948 as an affiliate college of the University of London called University College of the Gold Coast. In 1961, the university was reorganized by an act of Parliament into what is today: the independent, degree-granting University of Ghana (http://www.ug.edu.gh/).

The Balme Library is the main library in the University of Ghana library system. Situated on the main Legon campus, it

coordinates a large number of libraries attached to the university's various schools, institutes, faculties, departments, and halls of residence, most of which are autonomous. The library started as the College Library in 1948 and was then situated in Achimota College, about 8 kilometers from the present Legon campus. In 1959, the College Library moved into its brand-new buildings at the Legon campus and was named after the University College

[2]This case study is loosely based on A. K. Martey, "Appraising the Performance of Library Staff in a Ghanaian Academic Library," *Library Management 23* (2002): 403–416.

of the Gold Coast's first principal, David Mowbrary Balme.

As in the case of many other modern university libraries worldwide that face resources challenges and the need to serve an increasingly diverse customer base, the Balme Library has implemented numerous initiatives. One such initiative is a performance management system. However, several of the components of the performance management process at the Balme Library are in need of improvement. First, there is no evidence that a systematic job analysis was conducted for any of the jobs at the library. Second, the forms that the employees are rated on contain vague items such as "general behavior." The forms include no specific definition of what "general behavior" is or examples explaining to employees (or managers) what would lead to a high or a low rating in this category. In addition, all library employees are rated on the same form, regardless of their job responsibilities. Third, there is no evidence that managers have worked with employees in setting mutually agreed-upon goals. Fourth, there is no formal or informal discussion of results and needed follow-up steps after the subordinates and managers complete their form. Not surprisingly, an employee survey revealed that more than 60% of the employees have never discussed their performance with their managers. Finally, employees are often rated by different people. For example, it is sometimes the case that the head of the library rates an employee, even though he may not be in direct contact with that employee.

Based on the above description, please answer the following questions.

1. Please identify one component in the performance management process at the Balme Library that has not been implemented effectively (there are several; choose only one).
2. Describe how the poor implementation of the specific component you have chosen has a negative impact on the flow of the performance management process as a whole.
3. Discuss what should be done to improve the implementation of the component you have chosen in question 1. ■

END NOTES

1. The general framework and labels for these components are based on D. Grote, *The Complete Guide to Performance Appraisal.* (New York: American Management Association, 1996), chap. 2.
2. Teo, S. (2000). Evidence of strategic HRM linkages in eleven Australian corporatized public sector organizations. *Public Personnel Management, 29,* 557–574.
3. Clifford, J. P. (1994). Job analysis: Why do it, and how should it be done? *Public Personnel Management, 23,* 321–340.
4. Rodriguez, D., Patel, R., Bright, A., Gregory, D., & Gowing, M. K. (2002). Developing competency models to promote integrated human-resource practices. *Human Resource Management, 41,* 309–324.
5. Banner, D. K., & Graber, J. M. (1985). Critical issues in performance appraisal. *Journal of Management Development, 4,* 27–35.
6. Erickson, P. B. (2002, March 24). Performance feedback boosts employee morale, experts in Oklahoma City say. *The Daily Oklahoman,* OK-Worker-Reviews section.
7. Pettijohn, L. S., Parker, R. S., Pettijohn, C. E., & Kent, J. L. (2001). Performance appraisals: Usage, criteria and observations. *Journal of Management Development, 20,* 754–781.
8. Grote, D. (1996). *The complete guide to performance appraisal* (pp. 22–24). New York: American Management Association.
9. VandeWalle, D., Ganesan, S., Challagalla, G. N., & Brown, S. P. (2000). An integrated model of feedback-seeking behavior: Disposition, context, and cognition. *Journal of Applied Psychology, 85,* 996–1003.

10. Grote, D. (1996). *The complete guide to performance appraisal* (pp. 27–32). New York: American Management Association.

11. The best appraisals of workers can be simple; objectivity, feedback are important features. (2003, December 14). *The Baltimore Sun,* p. D6.

12. Brutus, S., London, M., & Martineau, J. (1999). The impact of 360-degree feedback on planning for career development. *Journal of Management Development, 18,* 676–693.

13. Shore, T. H., Adams, J. S., & Tashchian, A. (1998). Effects of self-appraisal information, appraisal purpose, and feedback target on performance appraisal ratings. *Journal of Business and Psychology, 12,* 283–298.

14. Kikoski, J. F. (1999). Effective communication in the performance appraisal interview: Face-to-face communication for public managers in the culturally diverse workplace. *Public Personnel Management, 28,* 301–322.

15. Ghorpade, J., & Chen, M. M. (1995). Creating quality-driven performance appraisal systems. *Academy of Management Executive, 9,* 32–39.

16. London, M. (2003). *Job feedback: Giving, seeking, and using feedback for performance improvement* (2nd ed.). Mahwah, NJ: Lawrence Erlbaum.

17. Soltani, E. (2003). Towards a TQM-driven HR performance evaluation: An empirical study. *Employee Relations, 25,* 347–370.

18. Grote, D. (1998). Painless performance appraisals focus on results, behaviors. *HR Magazine, 43*(11), 52–56.

19. Grossman, J. H., & Parkinson, J. R. (2002). *Becoming a successful manager: How to make a smooth transition from managing yourself to managing others* (pp. 142–145). Chicago: McGraw-Hill Professional.

Performance Management and Strategic Planning

Strategy is a style of thinking, a conscious and deliberate process, an intensive implementation system, the science of insuring future success.

—PETE JOHNSON

Learning Objectives

By the end of this chapter, you will be able to do the following:

■ Define strategic planning and its overall goal.

■ Describe the various specific purposes of a strategic plan.

■ Explain why the usefulness of a performance management system relies to a large degree on its relationship with the organization and unit's strategic plans.

■ Understand how to create an organization's strategic plan, including an environmental analysis resulting in a mission statement, vision statement, goals, and strategies.

■ Conduct an environmental analysis that includes a consideration of both internal (strengths and weaknesses) and external (opportunities and threats) trends.

■ Understand how a gap analysis resulting from a consideration of internal and external trends dictates an organization's mission.

■ Define the concept of a mission statement and describe the necessary components of a good mission statement.

■ Define the concept of a vision statement and understand its relationship to the mission statement.

■ Describe the basic components of a good vision statement.

■ Create organizational- and unit-level mission and vision statements.

■ Understand the relationship between mission and vision statements, goals, and strategies.

■ Understand the relationship between an organization's vision, mission, goals, and strategies and the vision, mission, goals, and strategies of each of its divisions or units.

■ Understand the relationship between a unit's vision, mission, goals, and strategies and individual job descriptions.

■ Explain why job descriptions must be linked to the organization and unit's strategic plans.

■ Understand how a strategic plan determines various choices regarding performance management system design.

■ Explain why a consideration of strategic issues is a building block for creating support for a performance management system.

In Chapters 1 and 2 we discussed the fact that good performance management systems encourage employees to make tangible and important contributions toward the organization's strategic objectives. When these contributions to the top organizational and unit priorities are made clear, performance management systems are likely to receive crucial top management support. Without this support, it is unlikely that a performance management system will be successful. How, then, are these strategic organizational objectives identified? How does an organization know what the "target" should be, what it is trying to accomplish, and how to do it? These questions are answered by considering an organization's strategic plan.

3.1 DEFINITION AND PURPOSES OF STRATEGIC PLANNING

Strategic planning is a process that involves describing the organization's destination, assessing barriers that stand in the way of that destination, and selecting approaches for moving forward. The main goal of strategic planning is to allocate resources in a way that provides organizations with a competitive advantage.[1] Overall, a strategic plan serves as a blueprint that defines how the organization will allocate its resources in pursuit of its goals.

Strategic planning serves the following purposes: First and foremost, strategic planning allows organizations to define their identity. In other words, it provides organizations with a clearer sense of who they are and what their purpose is. Second, strategic planning helps organizations prepare for the future because it clarifies the desired destination. Knowing where the organization wants to go is a key first step in planning how to get there. Third, strategic planning allows organizations to analyze their environment, and doing so enhances their ability to adapt to environmental changes and even anticipate future changes. Although knowledge of the environment does not guarantee that an organization will be more likely to change and adapt, knowledge is the first step toward possible adaptation. Fourth, strategic planning provides organizations with focus and allows them to allocate resources to what matters most. In turn, the improved allocation of resources is likely to stimulate growth and improve profitability. Fifth, strategic planning can produce a culture of cooperation within the organization given

TABLE 3.1   Strategic Plan: Purposes
Helps define the organization's identity
Helps organizations prepare for the future
Enhances ability to adapt to environmental changes
Provides focus and allows for better allocation of resources
Produces an organizational culture of cooperation
Allows for the consideration of new options and opportunities
Provides employees with information to direct daily activities

that a common set of goals is created. Such a culture of cooperation can gain organizations a key competitive advantage. Sixth, strategic planning can be a good corporate eye-opener because it generates new options and opportunities to be considered. New opportunities to be considered may include expanding to new markets or offering new products. Finally, strategic planning can be a powerful tool to guide employees' daily activities because it identifies the behaviors and results that really matter. A strategic plan provides critical information to be used in the performance management system. To summarize, Table 3.1 lists key purposes of a strategic plan.

3.2 PROCESS OF LINKING PERFORMANCE MANAGEMENT TO THE STRATEGIC PLAN

The mere presence of a strategic plan does not guarantee that this information will be used effectively as part of the performance management system. In fact, countless organizations spend thousands of hours creating strategic plans that lead to no tangible actions. Many organizations spend too much time and effort crafting their mission and vision statements without any concrete follow-up actions. The process then ends up being a huge waste of time and a source of frustration and long-lasting cynicism. Thus, to ensure that strategy cascades down the organization and leads to concrete actions, there a needs to be a conscious effort to link the strategic plan with individual performance.

Figure 3.1 provides a useful framework for understanding the relationship among an organization's strategic plan, a unit's strategic plan, job descriptions, and individual and team performance. The organization's strategic plan includes a mission statement, vision statement, as well as goals and strategies that will allow for the fulfillment of the mission and vision. The strategies are created with the participation of managers at all levels. The higher the level of involvement, the more likely it is that managers will see the resulting strategies favorably.[2] Once organizational strategies are defined, senior management proceeds to meet with department or unit managers, who in turn solicit input from all people within their units to create unit-level mission and vision statements, goals, and strategies. A critical issue is to ensure that each unit or department's mission and vision statements, goals, and strategies are consistent with those at the organizational level. Then job descriptions are revised to make sure they are consistent with unit and organizational priorities. Finally, the performance management system includes results, behaviors, and developmental plans consistent with the organizational- and department-level priorities as well as the individual job descriptions.

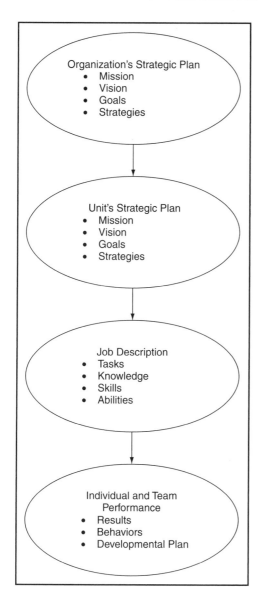

FIGURE 3.1 **Link Among Organization and Unit Strategic Plans, Job Descriptions, and Individual and Team Performance**

Does the process of aligning organizational, unit, and individual priorities actually work in practice? Is this doable? The answer to these questions is Yes. And, the benefits of doing so are widely documented. For example, consider the case of Key Bank USA, a financial services company with assets of $84 billion that provides investment management, retail and commercial banking, consumer finance, and investment banking products and services. Key Bank of Utah successfully developed a performance management system that is aligned with the strategic plan of the organization.[3] To do this, the bank first involved managers at all hierarchical levels to develop an organization mission statement. Next, they developed goals and strategies that would help achieve Key Bank's mission. The mission statement, goals, and strategies at the organizational level served as the foundation for developing the strategies for individual departments and units. To develop these, senior managers met with each department manager to discuss the organization's goals and strategies and to explain the importance of having similar items in place in each department. Subsequently, each of the departmental managers met with their employees to develop a department mission statement and goals. One important premise in this exercise was that each department's mission statement and objectives had to be aligned with the corporate mission statement, goals, and strategies. Once organizational and departmental goals and strategies were aligned, managers and employees reviewed individual job descriptions. Each job description was tailored so that individual job responsibilities were clear and they contributed to meeting the department and organization's objectives. Involving employees in this process helped them to gain a clear understanding of how their performance affected the department and, in turn, the organization.

Finally, based on the key responsibilities identified, the performance management system included behaviors, results, and developmental plans. For example, each employee record included information on various responsibilities, standards expected, goals to be reached, and actions to be taken to improve performance in the future. A summary of the entire process implemented at Key Bank of Utah is shown in Figure 3.2.

What happened after Key Bank of Utah implemented this system? In general terms, Key Bank was able to enjoy several positive consequences of aligning corporate, departmental, and individual goals. After the implementation of its new performance management system, Key Bank found several meaningful benefits, including the following:

- Managers knew that employees were focused on meeting important goals.
- Employees had more decision-making power.
- Lower-level managers had a better understanding of higher-level managers' decisions.
- Communication increased and improved (among managers, between managers and employees, etc.).

In sum to be most useful, organizations' performance management systems must rely on their strategic plans. The behaviors, results, and developmental plans of all employees must be aligned with the vision, mission, goals, and strategies of the organization and unit. Organizations can expect greater returns from implementing a performance management system when such alignment is in place.

3.2.1 Strategic Planning

The development of an organization's strategic plan requires a careful analysis of the organization's competitive situation, the organization's current position and destination, the development of the organization's strategic goals, the design of a plan of action and implementation, and the allocation of resources (human, organizational, physical) that will increase the likelihood of achieving the stated goals.[4]

There are several steps that must be considered in the creation of a successful strategic plan. These include (1) the conduct of an environmental analysis (i.e., the

FIGURE 3.2 Summary of Alignment of Performance Management and Strategic Plan at Key Bank of Utah

- *Mission statement*: The mission of the corporation is to operate as a high-performing financial institution providing a wide range of profitable, competitive, and superior financial services in our market.
- *Goals*: To attract and retain an outstanding staff who are highly motivated and productive and who vigorously pursue revenue-generating and cost-reduction strategies.
- *Strategy*: ...Critically review our existing branches and departments to ensure that all branches are consistent in their goals, strategies, and profit objectives.

- *Mission (Department Level)*: Increase the knowledge, management skills, and decision-making abilities of our branch managers so that we will minimize losses and other operating expenses while maximizing the profitability of our branching systems.

- *Position Description for HR Manager:* Administers a comprehensive human resources program in the division to ensure the expertise, effectiveness, motivation, and depth (including providing appropriate management succession) to the division's staff members.

- *Individual Performance*: Information on various responsibilities, standards expected, goals to be reached, and actions to be taken to improve performance in the future.

identification of the internal and external parameters of the environment in which the organization operates); (2) the creation of an organizational mission (i.e., statement of what the organization is all about); (3) the creation of an organizational vision (i.e., statement of where the organization intends to be in the long term, say, about 10 years); (4) setting goals (i.e., what the organization intends to do in the short term, say, one to three years); and (5) the creation of strategies that will allow the organization to fulfill its mission and vision and achieve its goals (i.e., descriptions of game plans or how-to procedures to reach the stated objectives). Once each of these issues has been defined, organizational strategies are created so that the mission and vision are fulfilled and the stated goals are met.

The strategic planning process is not linear, however. For example, there may first be a rough draft of the organization's mission and vision and *then* the conduct of an environmental analysis may follow to help define the mission and vision more clearly. In other words, the mission and vision may be drafted first and the environmental analysis may follow second. The important point is that there is a constant interplay among these issues: the vision and mission affect the type of environmental analysis to be conducted, and the results of an environmental analysis are used to revise the mission and vision. By necessity, we need to discuss them one by one. However, keep in mind that they affect and inform each other on an ongoing basis. Let's begin with a discussion of environmental analysis.

3.2.1.1 Environmental Analysis

The first step in conducting a strategic plan is to step back to take in the "big picture." This is accomplished through what is called an environmental analysis. An environmental analysis identifies external and internal parameters with the purpose of understanding broad issues related to the industry where the organization operates so that decisions can be made against the backdrop of a broader context.[5]

An examination of the *external environment* includes a consideration of opportunities and threats. Opportunities are characteristics of the environment that can help the organization succeed. Examples of such opportunities might be markets not currently being served, untapped labor pools, and new technological advances. On the other hand, threats are characteristics of the external environment that can prevent the organization from being successful. Examples of such threats range from economic recession to the innovative products of competitors. For example, consider the case of Frontier, which is currently the second largest jet carrier at Denver International Airport with an average of 200 daily departures and arrivals. Frontier is an affordable fare airline that provides service to 41 cities, 37 in the United States and 4 in Mexico. Frontier commenced operations in July 1994 given two key opportunities in the external environment. First, a major competing airline engaged in a dramatic downsizing of its Denver operations, leading to service gaps in various major markets that Frontier filled. Second, the city of Denver replaced the heavily congested Stapleton Airport with the much larger Denver International Airport.[6] In February 2004, United Airlines, the largest carrier operating out of Denver International Airport, made changes in the environment that may have a direct impact on Frontier's strategic plan: United Airlines launched its own low-fare affiliate. The new affiliate, Ted, is going toe-to-toe with Frontier. Peter McDonald, vice president for operations for United Airlines, reported that

Ted's cost per available seat mile is in the ballpark of Frontier's 8.3 cents.[7] So, what had been an opportunity for Frontier may no longer remain one, given the launching of Ted.

The following is a nonexhaustive list of external factors that should be considered in any environmental analysis:

- *Economic.* For example, is there an economic recession on the horizon? Or, is the current economic recession likely to end in the near future? How would these economic trends affect our business?
- *Political/legal.* For example, how will political changes domestically or in the international markets we are planning on entering affect our entry strategy?
- *Social.* For example, what is the impact of an aging workforce on our organization?
- *Technological.* For example, what technological changes are anticipated in our industry and how will these changes affect how we do business?
- *Competitors.* For example, how do the strategies and products of our competitors affect our own strategies and products? Can we anticipate our competitors' next move?
- *Customers.* For example, what do our customers want now, and what will they want in the next five years or so? Can we anticipate such needs?
- *Suppliers.* For example, what is the relationship with our suppliers now and is it likely to change, and in what way, in the near future?

An examination of external trends is important for all types of organizations. However, this issue is particularly important for multinational organizations because they are concerned with both domestic and international trends. In fact, monitoring the external environment is so important in the strategic planning of multinational organizations that a survey of U.S. multinational corporations showed that 89% of departments responsible for the assessment of the external environment report directly to a member of the board of directors.[8]

An examination of the *internal environment* includes a consideration of strengths and weaknesses. Strengths are internal characteristics that the organization can use to its advantage. For example, what are the organization's assets and the staff's key skills? At Frontier, several key executives from other airlines were recruited, an important strength that was considered before launching the airline in 1994. These executives created a senior management team with long-term experience in the Denver market.

Weaknesses are internal characteristics that are likely to hinder the success of the organization. These could include an obsolete organizational structure that does not allow for effective organization across units; the misalignment of organizational, unit, and individual level goals; and so forth.

The following is a nonexhaustive list of internal issues that should be considered in any environmental analysis:

- *Organizational structure.* For example, is the current structure conducive to fast and effective communication?
- *Organizational culture.* Organizational culture includes the unwritten norms and values espoused by the members of the organization. For example, is the

current organizational culture likely to encourage or hinder innovation and entrepreneurial behaviors on the part of middle-level managers?

- *Politics.* For example, are the various units competing for resources in such a way that any type of cross-unit collaboration is virtually impossible? Or, are units likely to be open and collaborative in cross-unit projects?
- *Processes.* For example, are the supply chains working properly? Can customers reach us when they need to and receive a satisfying response when they do?
- *Size.* For example, is the organization too small or too large? Are we growing too fast? Will we be able to manage growth (or downsizing) effectively?

Table 3.2 includes a summary list of internal and external trends to consider in conducting an environmental analysis. Think about your current employer (or latest employer, if you are not currently employed). Take a look at Table 3.2. Where does your organization stand regarding each of these important internal and external issues? Regarding the external issues, what are some of the opportunities and threats? Regarding the internal issues, what are some of the strengths and weaknesses?

Once external and internal issues have been considered, information is collected regarding opportunities, threats, strengths, and weaknesses. This information is used to conduct a *gap analysis*, which analyzes the external environment in relation to the internal environment. The pairing of external opportunities and threats with internal strengths and weaknesses leads to the following situations (ranked from most to least competitive):

1. Opportunity + Strength = *Leverage.* The best combination of external and internal factors occurs when there is an opportunity in the environment and a matching strength within the organization to take advantage of that opportunity. These are obvious directions that the organization should pursue. Consider the case of IBM, the world's largest information technology company, as well as the world's largest business and technology services provider (US$36 billion). In the past few years, IBM concluded that the PC-driven client-server computing model no longer applies and that network-based computing is taking over. This shifted the focus to servers, databases, and software for transaction management. Furthermore, IBM recognized the upsurge of network-connected devices including PDAs, cell phones, and video game systems. To take advantage of this

TABLE 3.2 Trends to Consider in Conducting an Environmental Analysis	
Internal	*External*
Organizational structure	Economic
Organizational culture	Political/legal
Politics	Social
Processes	Technological
Size	Competitors
	Customers
	Suppliers

external opportunity, IBM now focuses its resources on supporting network systems, developing software for the network-connected devices, and manufacturing specialized components. IBM has also improved its server technology and revamped its storage systems. IBM built up its software capabilities through internal development and outside acquisitions. In short, IBM has now found a leverage factor by identifing internal strengths that match external opportunities, which in turn leads to a successful business model.

2. Opportunity + Weakness = *Constraint.*   In a constraint situation, the external opportunity is present. However, the internal situation is not conducive to taking advantage of the external opportunity. At IBM, this situation could have taken place if IBM did not have the internal capabilities to develop software for the network-connected devices and specialized components. The external opportunity would still be there, but the absent internal capabilities would not turn the external opportunity into an advantageous business scenario.

3. Threat + Strength = *Vulnerability.*   In this situation, there is an external threat, but this threat can be contained because of the presence of internal strengths. If this had been the case at IBM, the company would not have been able to take advantage of a new situation, but nevertheless existing strengths would have allowed IBM to continue to operate in other areas.

4. Threat + Weakness = *Problem.*   In the worst scenario, there is an external threat and an accompanying internal weakness. For example, in the 1980s, IBM refused to adapt to the demands of the emerging microcomputer market (i.e., today's PCs). IBM did not have the internal capability to address customers' needs for PCs and instead continued to focus on its internal strength: the mainframe computer. IBM's poor performance in the early 1990s was a direct consequence of this problem situation: the external threat (market demand for PCs) was met with an internal weakness (lack of ability to shift internal focus from the mainframe to the PC).

Consider the organization you are currently working for, or the organization for which you have worked most recently. Try to identify one leverage and one problem based on an analysis of opportunities, threats, strengths, and weaknesses. What was the situation like? What were the results?

In sum, the process of creating a strategic plan begins with an environmental analysis, which considers internal as well as external trends. Internal trends can be classified as either strengths or weaknesses, and external trends can be classified as either opportunities or threats. A gap analysis consists of pairing strengths and weaknesses with opportunities and threats and determining whether the situation is advantageous (i.e., leverage), disadvantageous (i.e., problem), or somewhere in between (i.e., constraint and vulnerability).

3.2.1.2 Mission

Once the environmental analysis is completed and the gap analysis reveals an organization's leverage, constraints, vulnerabilities, and problems, the members of the organization determine who they are and what they do. This information will then be incorporated into the organization's mission statement. The mission statement summarizes the organization's most important reason for its existence. Mission statements provide information on the purpose of the organization and its scope. Good mission statements provide answers to the following questions:

- Why does the organization exist?
- What is the scope of the organization's activities?
- Who are the customers served?
- What are the products or services offered?

Consider the mission statement for the Coca-Cola Company:[9]

> The Coca-Cola Company exists to benefit and refresh everyone it touches. The basic proposition of our company is simple, solid and timeless. When we bring refreshment, value, joy and fun to our stakeholders, then we successfully nurture and protect our brands, particularly Coca-Cola. That is key to fulfilling our ultimate obligation to provide consistently attractive returns to the owners of our business.

Presumably, this mission statement was preceded by an environmental analysis examining internal and external trends. However, we do not have information on this. What we do know is that this mission statement provides some information regarding the four questions noted earlier. Based on this mission statement, we have information on why the company exists (i.e., "to benefit and refresh everyone it touches") and the scope of the organization's activities (i.e., "bringing refreshment, value, joy and fun"). There is also information on the organization's ultimate goal (i.e., "to provide consistently attractive returns"). However, the mission statement does not include information on who are the customers served and what are the products and services offered. Although the Coca-Cola brand is mentioned, there is no information on other products (e.g., Sprite, Minute Maid, Powerade, Dasani, and so forth).

More specific and detailed information is needed if Coca-Cola's mission statement is to be used by its various units to create their own mission statements. More detailed information is also needed if both the organization and unit mission statements will be used as input for individual job descriptions and for managing individual and team performance. In general, thorough mission statements include the following components:

- Basic product or service to be offered (does what?)
- Primary markets or customer groups to be served (to whom?)
- Unique benefits and advantages of products or services (with what benefits?)
- Technology to be used in production or delivery
- Fundamental concern for survival through growth and profitability

Mission statements also typically include information on the organization's values and beliefs, including:

- Managerial philosophy of the organization
- Public image sought by the organization
- Self-concept of business adopted by employees and stockholders

In sum, a mission statement defines why the organization exists, the scope of its activities, the customers served, and the products and services offered. Mission statements also include specific information, such as the technology used in production or delivery, and the unique benefits or advantages of the organization's products and services. Finally, a mission statement can include a statement of values and beliefs, such as the organization's managerial philosophy.

3.2.1.3 Vision

An organization's vision is a statement of future aspirations. In other words, the vision statement includes a description of what the organization would like to become in the future (about 10 years in the future). Vision statements are typically written after the mission statement is completed because the organization needs to know who they are and what their purpose is before they can figure out who they will be in the future. Note, however, that mission and vision statements are often combined and, therefore, in many cases it is difficult to differentiate one from the other.[10] In such cases, the vision statement usually includes two components: a core ideology, which is what is referred to as the mission, and an envisioned future, which is what is referred to as the vision per se. The core ideology contains the core purpose and core values of an organization and the envisioned future specifies long-term objectives and a picture of what the organization aspires to.

Rayovac Corporation provides an example of combining mission and vision into one statement. Rayovac is a global consumer products company including such brands as Remington (shaving accessories and hair care products) and VARTA (consumer batteries). It was founded in 1906 as the French Battery Company in Madison, Wisconsin, and was renamed the Rayovac Company in the mid-1930s. Currently, it is a publicly held company employing 3,300 individuals worldwide. Rayovac's combined mission and vision statement is the following:

> Seek long term growth in both sales and profits by providing innovative, high quality products that create significant value for our customers. Establish long term partnerships with customers, suppliers and employees by creating an environment where empowerment, participation, and openness are encouraged and rewarded. Maintain a leadership position in all targeted markets by providing world class customer service.[11]

This statement includes components of a mission statement (e.g., Rayovac provides innovative products that create significant value for its customers) as well as components of a vision statement (e.g., maintain a leadership position in all targeted markets). This produces a statement combining the present (i.e., who the company is, what it does) with the future (i.e., aspirations).

Other organizations make a more explicit differentiation between the mission and vision statements. Consider the vision statement for Greif, a global company headquartered in Delaware, Ohio, with approximately 9,800 employees providing industrial packaging products and services in over 40 countries in Africa, Asia, Australia, Europe, North America, and South America.[12] Greif reported US$1.6 billion in net sales for the fiscal year that ended October 31, 2002. Greif's five-year vision statement is the following:

- We will achieve superior return on assets while consistently increasing revenue.
- We will strive to be one of the most desirable companies to work for in our industries, focusing on establishing a work atmosphere in which our employees can excel.

- We will continually add value to our customer relationships, with an emphasis on providing packaging solutions on a global scale.
- We will capitalize on our leadership position and pursue profitable growth in the Industrial Packaging & Services business.
- We will pursue internal growth in addition to strategic acquisitions to profitably expand the Paper, Packaging & Services business.
- We will grow our Timber business both in terms of land holdings and revenue generation.

Greif's vision statement is clearly future oriented. It provides direction and focus. In addition, it includes several features that are required of useful vision statements. First, it focuses attention on what is most important and thus eliminates unproductive activities. Second, it provides a context from which to evaluate new external opportunities and threats. For example, the vision statement indicates that new opportunities for profitable growth in the industrial packaging and services business should be pursued. In addition, good vision statements have the following characteristics, not all of which are present in Greif's vision statement:

- *Brief.*   A vision statement should be brief so that employees can remember it.
- *Verifiable.*   A good vision statement should be able to stand the reality test. For example, how can we verify if Greif indeed becomes "one of the most desirable companies to work for in our industries, focusing on establishing a work atmosphere in which our employees can excel"?
- *Bound by a timeline.*   A good vision statement specifies a timeline for the fulfillment of various aspirations.
- *Current.*   Outdated vision statements are not useful. Vision statements should be updated on an ongoing basis, ideally as soon as the old vision is fulfilled.
- *Focused.*   A good vision statement is not a laundry list of aspirations, but rather focuses on just a few (perhaps not more than three or four) aspects of an organization's performance that are important to future success.
- *Understandable.*   Vision statements need to be written in a clear and straightforward manner so that they are understood by all employees.
- *Inspiring.*   Good vision statements make employees feel good about their organization's direction and motivate them to help achieve the vision.
- *A stretch.*   Consider Microsoft's vision statement of "putting a computer on every desk and in every home," which was the vision when CEO Bill Gates started the MS-DOS operating system in the 1980s. This vision statement was such a stretch that it was considered ludicrous at a time when the mainframe computer still reigned supreme and the first minicomputer models (now PCs) were being made and sold. But that vision is now a reality. Microsoft has come up with a new vision: "putting a computer in every car and every pocket."[13]

In sum, a vision statement includes a description of future aspirations. Whereas the mission statement emphasizes the present, the vision statement emphasizes the future. Table 3.3 includes a list of the features that should be present in a good vision statement. Think about your current employer (or latest employer, if you are not currently employed). Take a look at Table 3.3. How many of these features are reflected in your organization's vision statement?

TABLE 3.3   Characteristics of Good Vision Statements
Brief
Verifiable
Bound by a timeline
Current
Focused
Understandable
Inspiring
A stretch

3.2.1.4 Goals

Once an organization has analyzed its external opportunities and threats as well as internal strengths and weaknesses and defined its mission and vision, it can realistically establish goals that will further its mission. The purpose of setting such goals is to formalize statements about what the organization hopes to achieve in the medium- to long-range period (i.e., within the next three years or so). Goals provide more specific information regarding how the mission will be implemented. Goals can also be a source of motivation and provide employees a more tangible target to strive for. Goals also provide a good basis for decisions by keeping desired outcomes in mind. And, finally, goals provide the basis for performance measurement because they allow for a comparison of what needs to be achieved versus what each unit, group, and individual is achieving.

Consider the case of Harley-Davidson, Inc., the motorcycle manufacturer. In January 2004, Jeffrey L. Bleustein, chairman and chief executive officer, set the following goals:

> As we begin our 101st year, we expect to grow the business further with our proven ability to deliver a continuous stream of exciting new motorcycles, related products and services. We have set a new goal for the Company to be able to satisfy a yearly demand of 400,000 Harley-Davidson motorcycles in 2007. By offering innovative products and services, and by driving productivity gains in all facets of our business, we are confident that we can deliver an earnings growth rate in the mid-teens for the foreseeable future.[14]

In the case of Harley-Davidson, these goals provide a clear direction for the organization. In fact, they provide useful information to guide unit-level goals as well as individual and team performance. The entire organization now has a clear sense of focus because all members know that there is a goal to deliver 400,000 motorcycles in 2007.

3.2.1.5 Strategies

At this point, we know what the organization is all about (mission), what it wants to be in the future (vision), and some intermediate steps to follow to get there (goals). What remains is a discussion of how to fulfill the mission and vision and how to achieve the stated goals. This is done by creating strategies, which are descriptions of game plans or how-to procedures to reach the stated objectives. The strategies could address issues of growth, survival, turnaround, stability, innovation, and leadership, among others.

The human resources (HR) function plays a critical role in creating and implementing the strategies that will allow the organization to realize its mission and vision. Specifically, the HR function can make the following contributions:

- *Communicate knowledge of strategic plan.* The HR function can be a good conduit to communicate the various components of the strategic plan (e.g., mission, vision, and goals) to all the employees.
- *Outline knowledge, skills, and abilities (KSAs) needed for strategy implementation.* The HR function, through job analyses and the resulting job descriptions, serves as a repository of knowledge regarding what KSAs are needed for a successful implementation of the strategic plan. Thus, the HR function is in a unique situation to provide information about whether the current workforce has the KSAs needed to support the strategic plan and, if not, to offer suggestions about what types of employees should be hired and what types of plans should be put in place to develop the needed KSAs internally.
- *Propose reward systems.* The HR function can provide useful information on what type of reward system should be implemented to motivate employees to support the strategic plan.

3.2.2 Developing Strategic Plans at the Unit Level

As shown in Figure 3.1, the organization's strategic plan has a direct impact on the units' strategic plans. The case of Key Bank of Utah described earlier illustrates how the branch administration division had a mission statement that was aligned with the overall organizational mission statement. Similarly, the vision statement, goals, and strategies of the various units need to be congruent with the overall organizational vision, goals, and strategies. Consider the case of Microsoft Corporation's mission statement:

> To enable people and businesses throughout the world to realize their full potential. Delivering on this mission requires a clearly defined set of values and tenets. Our company values are not new, but have recently been articulated to reinforce our new mission. Achieving our mission requires great people who are bright, creative, and energetic, and who possess the following values:
>
> - Integrity and honesty
> - Passion for customers, partners, and technology
> - Open and respectful with others and dedicated to making them better
> - Willingness to take on big challenges and see them through
> - Self critical, questioning and committed to personal excellence and self improvement
> - Accountable for commitments, results, and quality to customers, shareholders, partners and employees.[15]

Now, consider the mission statement of one of Microsoft's units: Training and Education:

> With the charter to enable Microsoft engineering workgroups to realize their full potential for innovation and performance through world-class

learning strategies, Microsoft Training and Education (MSTE) provides performance support strategies to support the overall corporation's software engineering efforts. Our efforts include the design, development, and delivery of learning programs, online information, and resources for Microsoft employees. MSTE's integrated suite of technical offerings supports our goal of having a significant impact on Microsoft's business. We promote best practices, cross-group communication, Microsoft expertise and Industry expertise.

As you can see, the mission of the training and education unit is consistent with the overall mission in that the *realization of full potential* plays a central role. Of course, MSTE's mission is more focused on issues specifically relevant to the training and education function. Nevertheless, the link between the two mission statements is readily apparent.

The congruence between the mission of the organization and its various units is important regardless of the type of industry and size of the organization. High-performing organizations have a clear alignment in the mission and vision of the overall and unit-level mission and vision statements. Consider the case of Norfolk State University (NSU, http://www.nsu.edu/), located in Norfolk, Virginia. NSU has a current enrollment of about 8,000 students, it is the fifth-largest historically African American university in the United States, and serves many students who are the first in their families to attend college. It offers over 50 academic programs, including 37 undergraduate, 14 master's, and two doctoral degree programs. NSU has five main schools: School of Business, School of Education, School of Liberal Arts, School of Social Work, and School of Science and Technology. The university's mission statement is the following:

> To provide an affordable, high-quality education for an ethnically and culturally diverse student population, equipping them with the capability to become productive citizens who continuously contribute to a global and rapidly changing society.[16]

Now, consider the mission statement for the School of Business:

> The mission of the School of Business at Norfolk State University is to provide a high quality, management education to a diverse student population. This is accomplished primarily through teaching and the development of instructional and other processes which ensure that students are equipped to be productive citizens in a global society.[17]

Note that both mission statements are clearly aligned and refer to similar issues including the (1) delivery of a high-quality education to a (2) diverse student body, with the goal of (3) educating productive citizens who will contribute to a (4) global society.

In sum, the organization's strategic plan including the mission, vision, goals, and strategies cascades down to all organizational levels. Thus, each division or unit also creates its own strategic plan, which should be consistent with the organization's overall plan.

3.2.3 Job Descriptions

Continuing with the sequence of components shown in Figure 3.1, job descriptions also need to be congruent with the organization and unit mission, vision, goals, and strategies.

We discussed the job analysis process leading to the creation of job descriptions in Chapter 2. Once the strategic plan is completed, some rewriting of the existing job descriptions may be in order. Recall the job description for Trailer Truck Driver as used by the Civilian Personnel Management Service (U.S. Department of Defense) (see the accompanying box).

This description provides information on the various tasks performed together with a description of some of the KSAs required for the position. But what is the link with the organization and unit strategic plans? How do the specific tasks make a contribution to the strategic priorities of the transportation division and the organization as a whole? This description includes only cursory and indirect information regarding these issues. For example, one can assume that the proficient handling of bills of lading, expense accounts, and other papers pertinent to the shipment contributes toward a smooth shipping operation, and therefore makes a contribution to the transportation division. However, this link is not sufficiently clear.

On the other hand, consider a job announcement describing the position of Performance Solutions Group Manager in Microsoft's training and education unit (see the accompanying box).

This job description makes the link between the individual position and MSTE quite clear. First, the description includes MSTE's mission statement so that individuals become aware of how their specific role fits within the overall mission of the department. Second, the job description includes language to the effect that the work must lead to an "industry leading" product, which is consistent not only with MSTE's mission but with Microsoft's overall mission as well. Third, in the needed qualifications section, there is a clear overlap between those needed for this specific position and those mentioned in MSTE's as well as Microsoft's overall mission. In short, the person

---

BOX 3.1

Job Description for Trailer Truck Driver:
Civilian Personnel Management Service, U.S. Department of Defense

Operates gasoline or diesel powered truck or truck tractor equipped with two or more driving wheels and with four or more forward speed transmissions, which may include two or more gear ranges. These vehicles are coupled to a trailer or semi-trailer by use of a turntable (fifth wheel) or pintle (pivot) hook. Drives over public roads to transport materials, merchandise, or equipment. Performs difficult driving tasks such as backing truck to loading platform, turning narrow corners, negotiating narrow passageways, and keeping truck and trailer under control, particularly on wet or icy highways. May assist in loading and unloading truck. May also handle manifest, bills of lading, expense accounts, and other papers pertinent to the shipment.

BOX 3.2

Job Description for Performance Solutions Group Manager at Microsoft

As the Performance Solutions Group Manager, you will be accountable for developing and delivering on a portal strategy that touches over 20,000 employees worldwide and involves a complex data delivery system. Additionally, the person is responsible for defining the cutting edge tool suite used by the team to develop and maintain the portal, the content housed by the group, and all e-learning solutions. Key initiatives include redesigning the Engineering Excellence Guide within the next 6 months and evolving it over the next 18 months to 3 years to become the industry leading performance support site. Key challenges include maintaining and managing the cutting edge tool suite used by the team and driving a clear vision for an industry leading portal and content delivery plan.

Qualifications for this position are a minimum of five years of senior management experience, preferably in knowledge management, e-learning, or web-based product development roles; ability to think strategically and exercise sound business judgment on behalf of MS; excellent leadership, communication, interpersonal, and organizational skills; firsthand experience delivering/shipping web-based learning and content management solutions; proven record of successful team management; and ability to work well independently and under pressure, while being flexible and adaptable to rapid change. Knowledge of performance support and training procedures, standards, and processes is preferred.

With the charter to enable Microsoft engineering workgroups to realize their full potential for innovation and performance through world-class learning strategies, Microsoft Training and Education (MSTE) provides performance support strategies to support the overall corporation's software engineering efforts. Our efforts include the design, development, and delivery of learning programs, online information, and resources for Microsoft employees. MSTE's integrated suite of technical offerings supports our goal of having a significant impact on Microsoft's business. We promote best practices, cross-group communication, Microsoft expertise and Industry expertise.

---

working as Performance Solutions Group Manager has a clear sense not only of her position, but also of how behaviors and expected results are consistent with expectations about MSTE and Microsoft in general.

In sum, the tasks and KSAs included in individual job descriptions must be congruent with the organization and unit's strategic plans. In other words, job descriptions should include activities that, if executed well, will help execute the mission and vision. Job descriptions that are detached from strategic priorities will lead to performance evaluations focused on behaviors and results that are not central to an organization's success.

3.2.4 Individual and Team Performance

Finally, the performance management system needs to motivate employees to display the behaviors and produce the results required to support the organization and the unit's mission, vision, and goals. Developmental plans need to be aligned with unit and organizational priorities as well. Well-designed performance management systems define a clear path from organizational mission, vision, and goals to individual and team performance. This is critical because organizational success is a direct function of the alignment between collective and individual objectives.

In addition to serving as a necessary guide for individual and team performance, knowledge of organization- and unit-level mission and vision provides information on how to design the performance management system. Specifically, there are many choices in how the system is designed. For example, the system might place more emphasis on behaviors (i.e., processes) as opposed to results (i.e., outcomes), or the system might emphasize more short-term criteria (i.e., quarterly goals) as opposed to long-term criteria (triennial). Some of these choices are presented in Table 3.4.

Knowledge of the organization and unit vision and mission allows the HR function to make informed decisions about design choices. More detailed information on each of the factors guiding each of these design choices is provided in subsequent chapters. For now, as one illustration, assume an organization is producing a mature product in a fairly stable industry. In this situation, an emphasis on behaviors rather than results may be preferred because the relationship between processes and outcomes is well known and the top priority is that employees display reliable and consistent behaviors in making the product. Regardless of the type of criteria used, be it behaviors or results, these must be observable (i.e., the person rating the criteria needs to have the ability to observe what is rated) and verifiable (i.e., there needs to be evidence to confirm the criteria rated). As a second example, consider the actual case of Dell computers. Dell is one of the top players in the personal computer industry through its mode of online direct selling. Dell's main strategic business strategy is to be a low-cost leader in an industry that deals with a product that is increasingly seen as a commodity. However, in addition to a low-cost strategy, Dell also has a customer relationship business strategy of maintaining customer service at a high level, while reducing costs. So, Dell's performance management system provides a strong link between individual goals and organizational performance by including a results component (i.e., cost) and a behavioral component (i.e., customer service).[18] At Dell, both low cost and high levels of customer service (for both internal and external customers) are important dimensions of the performance management system. Also, the system is not only strongly linked to the strategic objectives (i.e., low cost and high levels of customer service), but it is also linked to the organization's "winning culture" (i.e., achievement of personal and business objectives through its focus on interaction between managers and team members).

In summary, the criteria measured in the performance management system are behaviors or results (or both) that must be relevant to the unit and the organization.

TABLE 3.4 Some Choices in Performance Management System Design

Criteria: Behavioral criteria vs. results criteria

Participation: Low employee participation vs. high employee participation

Temporal dimension: Short-term criteria vs. long-term criteria

Level of criteria: Individual criteria vs. team/group criteria

System orientation: Developmental orientation vs. administrative orientation

Rewards: Pay for performance (i.e., merit-based) vs. pay for tenure/position

Performance criteria need to make a contribution to the strategic priorities. It is unlikely that a performance management system will make an important contribution to the organization's bottom line if (1) there is no clear sense of direction about where the organization and unit are going, or (2) there is a clear sense of direction but this information is not reflected in the job descriptions and the actual behaviors and results measured.

3.3 BUILDING SUPPORT

Given the many competing projects and usual scarcity of resources, some organizations may be reluctant to implement a performance management system. Primarily, the reason is a lack of any perceived value added to a system that requires many resources (particularly time from supervisors) and that seems to produce little tangible payoffs. The need to align organization and unit priorities with the performance management system is one of the key factors contributing to obtaining the much needed top management support for the system.

Top management is likely to ask, "Why is performance management important?" One answer to this question is that performance management is the primary tool that will allow top management to carry out their vision. The performance management system, when aligned with organization and unit priorities, is a critical tool to (1) allow all employees to understand where the organization stands and where it needs to go, and (2) provide tools to employees (i.e., motivation, developmental resources) so that their behaviors and results will help the organization get there. Fundamentally, the implementation of any performance management system requires that the "What's in it for me?" question be answered convincingly. In the case of top management, the answer to the "What's in it for me?" question is that performance management can serve as a primary tool to realize their vision.

Building support for the system does not stop with top management, however. All participants in the system need to understand the role they play and also receive a clear answer to the "What's in it for me?" question. Communication about the system is key. This includes a clear description of the system's mechanics (e.g., when the performance planning meetings will take place, how to handle disagreements between supervisor and employees) and the system's consequences (e.g., relationship between performance evaluation and rewards). As discussed in Chapter 1, not involving people in the process of system design and implementation can create resistance and the performance management system may result in more harm than good.

Consider the role that good communication played in the launching of a revamped performance management system at Bankers Life and Casualty (http://www.bankerslife.com), an insurance company specializing in insurance for seniors headquartered in Chicago. In November 2000, Edward M. Berube was appointed as its new president and CEO. Berube understood that Bankers Life and Casualty was facing important challenges, including new customer demands, the impact of the Internet, outsourcing, and increased competition. So, Bankers Life and Casualty engaged in a very aggressive marketing campaign, which included retaining actor Dick Van Dyke as its company spokesperson. In spite of these efforts, however, internal focus groups revealed that while employees understood the organization's strategic plan, they did not understand what role each person was supposed to play in helping the organization execute its strategy. In other words, employees did not have a clear understanding of how each person could help achieve the organization's strategic goals, including focusing on the following three key areas: (1) distribution scope, scale, and productivity; (2) home office productivity and unit costs; and (3) product revenue and profitability.

Bankers Life and Casualty realized that a better link between strategy and individual and team performance could be established by improving its performance management process. Therefore, the HR department proceeded to overhaul the performance management system so that the three areas of strategic importance just outlined would be part of everyone's performance evaluation and improvement efforts. The design and implementation of the new system was a *joint venture* between the HR and the communications departments. First, the HR and communications team spoke candidly with the CEO about his expectations. The CEO responded with overwhelming support, stating that the performance management system would be implemented to every employee on preestablished dates, and that he would hold his team accountable for making this happen. Then, to implement the performance management system, each unit met with its VP. During these meetings, each VP discussed how his or her unit's goals were linked to the corporate goals. Next, HR and communications led discussions surrounding goal setting, giving feedback, and writing developmental plans. Then, managers were given the opportunity to share any feedback, concerns, or questions that they had about the program. During this forum, managers exchanged success stories and offered advice to one another. These success stories were then shared with the CEO. The CEO then shared these stories with those who reported directly to him to strengthen the visibility of his support for the program.

In short, the performance management system at Bankers Life and Casualty helped all employees understand their contributions to the organization's strategic plan. This was a key issue that motivated the CEO to give unqualified support to the system. This support gave a clear message to the rest of the organization that the performance management system was an important initiative. The support of the CEO and other top executives, combined with a high degree of participation from all employees and their ability to voice concerns and provide feedback regarding the system, were critical factors in the success of the performance management system at Bankers Life and Casualty.

SUMMARY POINTS

- Strategic planning involves defining the organization's present and future identity. The overall purpose of a strategic plan is to serve as a blueprint that allows organizations to allocate resources in a way that provides the organization with a competitive advantage.
- Strategic planning serves several purposes, including defining an organization's identity, preparing for the future, analyzing the environment, providing focus, creating a culture of cooperation, generating new options, and serving as a guide for the daily activities of all organizational members.
- Performance management systems must rely on the strategic plan to be useful. The behaviors, results, and

developmental plans of all employees must be aligned with the vision, mission, goals, and strategies of the organization and unit.

- The process of creating a strategic plan begins with an environmental analysis, which considers internal (e.g., organizational structure, processes, etc.) as well as external (e.g., economic, technological, etc.) trends. Internal trends can be classified as either strengths or weaknesses, and external trends can be classified as either opportunities or threats. A gap analysis consists of pairing strengths and weaknesses with opportunities and threats and determining whether the situation is advantageous (i.e., leverage), disadvantageous (i.e., problem), or somewhere in between (i.e., constraint and vulnerability).

- The second step in creating a strategic plan is to write a mission statement based on the results of the gap analysis. A mission statement defines why the organization exists, the scope of its activities, the customers served, and the products and services offered. Mission statements also include information about what technology is used in production or delivery, and the unique benefits or advantages of the organization's products and services. Finally, a mission statement can include a statement of values and beliefs, such as the organization's managerial philosophy.

- The third component of a strategic plan is the vision statement, which includes a description of future aspirations. Whereas the mission statement emphasizes the present, the vision statement emphasizes the future. However, in many cases the mission and vision statements are combined into one. For vision statements to be most useful they must be brief, verifiable, bound by a timeline, current, focused, understandable, inspiring, and a stretch.

- Once the mission and vision statements are created, the next step in the strategic planning process is to generate specific goals that will help fulfill the mission and vision. Goals provide more specific information regarding how the mission and vision will be implemented. Typically, goals span a five-year period.

- The final step in the strategic planning process is to identify strategies that will help achieve the stated goals. These strategies are game plans and usually address issues surrounding growth, survival, turnaround, stability, innovation, and leadership. The HR department plays an important role in identifying strategies because its members have knowledge of the organization's mission and vision as well as the organization's internal capabilities, or what is called an organization's human capital.

- The organization's strategic plan, including the mission, vision, goals, and strategies, cascades down to all organizational levels. Thus, each division or unit also creates its own strategic plan, which should be consistent with the organization's overall plan.

- The tasks and KSAs included in individual job descriptions must be congruent with the organization's and unit's strategic plans. In other words, job descriptions should include activities that, if executed well, will in turn help execute the mission and vision. Job descriptions that are detached from strategic priorities will lead to performance evaluations focused on behaviors and results that are not central to an organization's success.

- The various choices in designing the performance management system are directly affected by an organization's strategic plan. Different missions and visions lead to different types of systems, for example, emphasizing behaviors (i.e., processes) as opposed to results (i.e., outcomes).

- Top management must be aware that the performance management system is a primary tool to execute an organization's strategic plan. This awareness will lead to top management's support for the system. In addition, all organizational members need to be able to answer the "What's in it for me?" question regarding the system. Implementing the performance management system will require considerable effort on the part of all those involved. Those doing the evaluation and those being evaluated should know how the system will benefit them directly.

Case Study 3.1 Evaluating Vision and Mission Statements at Harley-Davidson

Consider the mission and vision statements for Harley-Davidson (http://www.harley-davidson.com):[1]

Harley-Davidson's Mission Statement: We fulfill dreams through the experience of motorcycling, by providing to motorcyclists and to the general public an expanding line of motorcycles and branded products and services in selected market segments.

Harley-Davidson's Vision Statement: Harley-Davidson, Inc. is an action-oriented, international company, a leader in its commitment to continuously improve our mutually beneficial relationships with stakeholders (customers, suppliers, employees, shareholders, governments and society). Harley-Davidson believes the key to success is to balance stakeholders' interests through the empowerment of all employees to focus on value-added activities.

The table here summarizes the key characteristics of ideal mission and vision statements as discussed in Chapter 3. Please use this table to evaluate the mission and vision statements of Harley-Davidson. Use the Y/N column in the table to indicate whether each of the features is present or not in Harley-Davidson's mission and vision statements. Then prepare a brief report addressing the following questions:

1. How many of the eight characteristics of an ideal mission statement are present in Harley-Davidson's mission statement?
2. How many of the eight characteristics of an ideal vision statement are present in Harley-Davidson's vision statement?
3. Given the purposes that a mission statement and a vision statement are ideally serving, please compare the mission and vision statement of Harley-Davidson based on whether these statements are achieving their respective objectives. Do they both serve their respective purposes? Collectively, are they useful tools to link organizational priorities with individual and team performance? ■

	Y/N	Characteristics
Mission statement—summarizes the organization's most important reason for its existence.		Basic product/service to be offered (does what)
		Primary markets or customer groups to be served (to whom)
		Unique benefits, features, and advantages of products/services (with what benefits)
		Technology to be used in production or delivery
		Fundamental concern for survival through growth and profitability
		Managerial philosophy of the firm
		Public image sought by organizations

---

[1]Harley-Davidson Motor Company. Available online at http://www.ideafinder.com/features/century/h-d.htm. Retrieval date: August 15, 2005.

	Y/N	Characteristics
		Self-concept of business adopted by employees and stockholders
Vision—Statement of future aspirations.		Brief—So that employees can remember it Verifiable—Able to stand the reality test Bound by a timeline—specifies a timeline for fulfillment of the various aspirations Current—updated on an ongoing basis Focused—lists a few (3–4) aspects of organization's performance that are important to future success Understandable—written in a clear and straightforward manner so that they are understood by all employees Inspiring—makes employees feel good about their organization's direction and motivates them to help achieve the vision Stretch—goal not easily attained

Case Study 3.2   Dilbert's Mission Statement Generator

Please visit Dilbert's Web page and play the "mission statement generator" game (http://www.dilbert.com/comics/dilbert/games/career/bin/ms.cgi). Generate two different mission statements and provide a critique of the resulting statements based on whether they comply with the characteristics of an ideal statement. Because generated statements will vary, please also provide a critique of the following statement: "We strive to continually adminis-trate timely opportunities and enthusiasti-cally utilize enterprise-wide technology while promoting personal employee growth." In addition, answer the following questions:

1. What are the dangers of having a flawed mission statement?
2. How does a flawed statement affect the development of a unit's mission state-ment and subsequent individual job descriptions and goals? ■

Case Study 3.3   Linking Individual with Unit and Organizational Priorities

Obtain a copy of the job description for your current or most recent job. If this is not feasible, obtain a copy of a job description of someone you know. Then, obtain a copy of the mission statements for the organization and unit in question.

Revise the job description so that it is aligned with the unit and organizational strategic priorities. Revisions may include adding tasks and KSAs important in the mission statement that are not already included in the job description. ■

END NOTES

1. Addams, H. L., & Embley, K. (1988). Performance management systems: From strategic planning to employee productivity. *Personnel, 65,* 55–60.

2. Collier, N., Fishwick, F., & Floyd, S. W. (2004). Managerial involvement and perceptions of strategy process. *Long Range Planning, 37,* 67–83.

3. Adapted from Addams and Embley (1988), op. cit.

4. Adapted from C. D. Fisher, L. F. Schoenfeldt, and J. B. Shaw. *Human Resource Management,* 5th ed. (Boston: Houghton Mifflin, 2003).

5. The discussion regarding environmental analysis is adapted from W. Drohan, "Principles of Strategic Planning," *Association Management* 49(1997): 85–87.

6. Company profile. Available online at http://www.frontierairlines.com/about/profile.asp

7. Low-cost Ted may help United fly out of bankruptcy. (2004, February 13) *USA Today.* Available online at http://www.usatoday.com/travel/news/2004-02-13-ted-wrap_x.htm. Retrieval date: August 15, 2005.

8. Kennedy, C. R., Jr. (1984). The external environment-strategic planning interface: U.S. multinational corporate practices in the 1980s. *Journal of International Business Studies, 15,* 99–108.

9. The Coca-Cola promise. Available online at http://www2.coca-cola.com/ourcompany/ourpromise.html. Retrieval date: August 15, 2005.

10. Collins, J. C., & Porras, J. I. (1996, September–October). Building your company's vision. *Harvard Business Review,* 74(5), 65–77.

11. Mission and vision statements. Available online at http://www.rayovac.com/about/info/mis_and.shtml. Retrieval date: January 5, 2005.

12. Company profile. Available online at http://www.greif.com/about/vision.php. Retrieval date: January 5, 2005.

13. Bill Gates. Available online at http://www.microsoft.com/billgates/speeches/industry&tech/iayf2005.asp. Retrieval date: August 19, 2005.

14. Harley-Davidson reports record fourth quarter and 18th consecutive record year. Available online at http://www.harley-davidson.com/CO/NEW/en/PressRelease_Date.asp?locale=en_US&bmLocale=en_US&id_in=552&dspmm=1&dspyy=2004. Retrieval date: August 15, 2005.

15. Microsoft Corporation. Mission and values. Available on-line at http://www.microsoft.com/mscorp/mission/. Retrieval date: January 10, 2005.

16. Mission statement of NSU. Available online at http://www.nsu.edu/about/mission.html. Retrieval date: August 15, 2005.

17. The School of Business mission statement. Available online at http://www.nsu.edu/business/Administration/Mission.html. Retrieval date: August 15, 2005.

18. Building people capability. Available online at http://www1.ap.dell.com/content/topics/topic.aspx/global/hybrid/careers/content/8012aa1f-fa50-4634-ac65-fa149b26228f?c=au&l=en&s=corp. Retrieval date: August 15, 2005.

C H A P T E R

4

Defining Performance and Choosing a Measurement Approach

How you measure the performance of your managers directly affects the way they act.

—GUSTAVE FLAUBERT

Learning Objectives

By the end of this chapter, you will be able to do the following:

■ Define what performance is and it is not.

■ Understand the evaluative and multidimensional nature of performance.

■ Identify the various factors that determine performance, including declarative knowledge, procedural knowledge, and motivation.

■ Gather information about a performance problem and understand which of the three main determinants of performance need to be addressed to solve the problem.

■ Design a performance management system that includes both task and contextual performance dimensions.

■ Understand that performers should be placed within a context: a performer in a specific situation engaging in behaviors leading to specific results.

■ Adopt a trait approach to measuring performance, which basically focuses on the performer and ignores the situation, his or her behaviors, and the results produced.

■ Adopt a behavior approach to measuring performance, which basically focuses on how the job is done and ignores the performer's traits and results produced.

■ Adopt a results approach to measuring performance, which basically focuses on the outcomes of work and ignores the performer's traits as well as the manner in which the work is done.

■ Understand the situations under which a trait, behavior, or results approach to measuring performance may be most appropriate.

This chapter marks the beginning of Part II of this text, which describes how to implement
a performance management system. Whereas Part I addressed strategic and more macro-
organizational issues, Part II addresses more operational concerns, such as the determinants of
performance and how to measure performance. Let's begin by defining performance.

4.1 DEFINING PERFORMANCE

Performance management systems usually include measures of both behaviors (what
an employee does) and results (the outcomes of an employee's behavior). However,
the definition of performance does not include the results of an employee's behaviors,
but only the behaviors themselves. Performance is about behavior or what employees
do, and not about what employees produce or the outcomes of their work.

Also, there are two additional characteristics of the behaviors we label performance.[1] First, they are *evaluative*. This means that such behaviors can be judged as
negative, neutral, or positive for individual and organizational effectiveness. In other
words, the value of these behaviors can vary based on whether they make a contribution toward the accomplishment of individual, unit, and organizational goals. Second,
performance is *multidimensional*.[2] This means that there are many different kinds of
behaviors that have the capacity to advance (or hinder) organizational goals.

As an example, consider a set of behaviors that can be grouped under the general
label "contribution to effectiveness of others in the work unit." This set of behaviors
can be defined as follows:

> Works with others within and outside the unit in a manner that improves
> their effectiveness; shares information and resources; develops effective
> working relationships; builds consensus; constructively manages conflict.

Contribution to effectiveness of others in the work unit could be assessed using a
scale including anchors demonstrating various levels of competence. For example,
anchors could be words and phrases such as "outstanding," "significantly exceeds standards," "fully meets standards," "does not fully meet standards," and "unacceptable."
This illustrates the evaluative nature of performance because this set of behaviors is
judged as positive, neutral, or negative. In addition, this example illustrates the multidimensional nature of performance because there are several behaviors that, combined,
affect the overall perceived contribution that an employee makes to the effectiveness
of others in the work unit. In other words, we would be missing important information
if we only considered, for example, "shares information and resources" and did not
consider the additional behaviors listed earlier.

Because not all behaviors are observable, performance management systems
often include measures of results or consequences that we infer are the direct result of
employees' behaviors. Take the case of a salesperson whose job consists of visiting
clients to offer them new products or services. The salesperson's supervisor is back in
the home office and does not have an opportunity to observe the salesperson's behaviors firsthand. In this case sales volume may be used as a proxy for a behavioral

measure. In other words, the supervisor makes the assumption that if the salesperson is able to produce high sales figures, then she is probably engaging in the right behaviors.

4.2 DETERMINANTS OF PERFORMANCE

What factors cause an employee to perform at a certain level? Why do certain individuals perform better than others? A combination of three factors allows some people to perform at higher levels than others: (1) *declarative knowledge*, (2) *procedural knowledge*, and (3) *motivation*.[3] Declarative knowledge is information about facts and things, including information regarding a given task's requirements, labels, principles, and goals. Procedural knowledge is a combination of knowing what to do and how to do it and includes cognitive, physical, perceptual, motor, and interpersonal skills. Finally, motivation involves three types of choice behaviors:

1. Choice to expend effort (e.g., "I will go to work today")
2. Choice of level of effort (e.g., "I will put in my best effort at work" versus "I will not try very hard")
3. Choice to persist in the expenditure of that level of effort (e.g., "I will give up after a little while" versus "I will persist no matter what")

Table 4.1 summarizes the components of declarative knowledge, procedural knowledge, and motivation. All three determinants of performance must be present for performance to reach high levels. In other words, the three determinants have a multiplicative relationship, such that

$$\text{Performance} = \text{Declarative Knowledge} \times \text{Procedural Knowledge} \times \text{Motivation}$$

If any of the determinants has a value of 0, then performance also has a value of 0. For example, consider the case of Jane, a sales clerk who works in a national clothing retail chain. Jane has excellent declarative knowledge regarding the merchandise. Specifically, she knows all of the brands, prices, sizing charts, and sales promotions. We would consider her declarative knowledge to be very high. Jane is also intelligent and physically able to conduct all of the necessary tasks. We would consider Jane's procedural knowledge also to be very high. However, Jane does not show motivation to perform. When customers enter the store, she does not approach them; instead, she sits behind the cash register and talks on the phone. When her manager is in the store, she shows a high level of effort, but her coworkers complain that as soon as the manager leaves, Jane stops working. Therefore, her overall performance is likely to be poor because although she has the declarative and procedural knowledge necessary to do the job, she is not motivated to apply them to her job when her supervisor is not watching her.

TABLE 4.1 Factors Determining Performance		
Declarative Knowledge	*Procedural Knowledge*	*Motivation*
Facts	Cognitive skill	Choice to perform
Principles	Psychomotor skill	Level of effort
Goals	Physical skill	Persistence of effort
	Interpersonal skill	

4.2.1 Implications for Addressing Performance Problems

The fact that performance is affected by the combined effect of three different factors has implications for addressing performance problems. In order to properly address performance problems, managers must find information that will allow them to understand if the source of the problem is declarative knowledge, procedural knowledge, motivation, or any combination of these three factors. If an employee lacks motivation but the manager believes the source of the problem is declarative knowledge, the manager may send the employee to a company-sponsored training program so he can acquire the knowledge that is presumably lacking. This would obviously be a waste of time and resources for the individual, manager, and organization in Jane's case because it is lack of motivation, and not lack of declarative knowledge, that is causing her poor performance. This is why performance management systems need not only to measure performance but also to provide information on the source of any performance deficiencies.

4.2.2 Factors Influencing Determinants of Performance

The factors that determine performance are affected by both the employee (i.e., abilities and previous experience) and human resources (HR) practices and the work environment. For example, some companies offer more opportunities for training than do others. At the top of the list in terms of annual training investment are IBM ($1 billion), Accenture ($717 million), and Ford Motor ($500 million).[4] In these companies, declarative knowledge is not likely to be a big problem because when lack of knowledge is identified, employees have multiple opportunities to fill in the gap. However, performance problems may be related more to procedural knowledge and motivation. In terms of procedural knowledge, employees may actually have the knowledge to perform certain tasks but may not have the skill to do them because of lack of opportunity for practice. In terms of motivation, downsizing interventions may have caused a "survivor syndrome," which includes retained employees' feeling frustration, resentment, and even anger. These feelings are likely to have strong negative effects on motivation, and employees may expend minimal energy on their jobs.

Thus, there are three individual characteristics that determine performance: procedural knowledge, declarative knowledge, and motivation. In addition, HR practices and the work environment can also affect performance. When addressing performance problems, managers first need to identify which of these factors is hampering performance. Then managers can help the employee improve his or her performance.

4.3 PERFORMANCE DIMENSIONS

As noted earlier, performance is multidimensional, meaning that we need to consider many different types of behaviors to understand performance. Although we can identify many specific behaviors, two types of behaviors or performance facets stand out: task performance and contextual performance.[5] Some authors also use the labels *prosocial behaviors* and *organizational citizenship behaviors* in referring to contextual performance.[6]

Contextual and task performance must be considered separately because they do not necessarily occur in tandem. An employee can be highly proficient at her task, but be an underperformer regarding contextual performance.[7] Task performance is defined as

- activities that transform raw materials into the goods and services that are produced by the organization
- activities that help with the transformation process by replenishing the supply of raw materials, distributing its finished products, or providing important planning, coordination, supervising, or staff functions that enable it to function effectively and efficiently[8]

Contextual performance is defined as those behaviors that contribute to the organization's effectiveness by providing a good environment in which task performance can occur. Contextual performance includes behaviors such as the following:

- persisting with enthusiasm and exerting extra effort as necessary to complete one's own task activities successfully (e.g., being punctual and rarely absent, expending extra effort on the job)
- volunteering to carry out task activities that are not formally part of the job (e.g., suggesting organizational improvements, making constructive suggestions)
- helping and cooperating with others (e.g., assisting and helping coworkers and customers)
- following organizational rules and procedures (e.g., following orders and regulations, showing respect for authority, complying with organizational values and policies)
- endorsing, supporting, and defending organizational objectives (e.g., organizational loyalty, representing the organization favorably to outsiders)

Both task and contextual performance are important dimensions to take into account in performance management systems. Imagine what would happen to an organization in which all employees are outstanding regarding task performance but do not perform well regarding contextual performance. What if a colleague whose cubicle is next to yours needs to take a bathroom break and asks you to answer the phone if it rings because an important client will call at any moment? What if we said, "That is not MY job"? Many organizations now realize that there is a need to focus on both task and contextual performance because organizations cannot function properly without a minimum dose of contextual behaviors on the part of all employees.

Consider the case of TRW, Inc., a global company operating four business segments: automotive, aeronautical systems, space and electronics, and information systems (http://www.trw.com). TRW had more than $16 billion in annual revenues in 2001 and employed close to 100,000 people. With increasing market pressures and sluggish growth, TRW wanted to become more performance driven, experiment in new markets, and offer greater value to its shareholders. To do so, the senior management team developed what they labeled the "TRW behaviors." These behaviors are communicated throughout the company and have a prominent role in the performance management process. The majority of the TRW behaviors actually focus on *contextual performance*. Specifically, the TRW behaviors emphasize many of the elements of contextual performance, including teamwork and trust.

TABLE 4.2	Main Differences between Task and Contextual Performance
Task Performance	*Contextual Performance*
Varies across jobs	Fairly similar across jobs
Likely to be role prescribed	Not likely to be role prescribed
Antecedents: abilities and skills	Antecedents: personality

Table 4.2 summarizes the main differences between task and contextual performance. First, task performance varies across jobs. For example, the tasks performed by an HR manager are different from those performed by a line manager. The tasks performed by a senior HR manager (i.e., more strategic in nature) differ from those performed by an entry-level HR analyst (i.e., more operational in nature). On the other hand, contextual performance is fairly similar across functional and hierarchical levels. All employees, regardless of job title, function, and responsibilities, are equally responsible for, for example, volunteering to carry out task activities that are not formally part of the job. Second, task performance is likely to be role prescribed, meaning that task performance is usually included in one's job description. On the other hand, contextual performance behaviors are usually not role prescribed and, instead, are typically expected without making them explicit. Finally, task performance is mainly influenced by abilities and skills (e.g., cognitive, physical), whereas contextual performance is mainly influenced by personality (e.g., conscientiousness).[9]

There are numerous pressing reasons why both task and contextual performance dimensions should be included in a performance management system. First, global competition is raising the levels of effort required of employees. Thus, whereas it may have sufficed in the past to have a workforce that was competent regarding task performance, today's globalized world and accompanying competitive forces make it imperative that the workforce also engage in contextual performance. It is difficult to compete if an organization employs a workforce that does not engage in contextual behaviors. Second, related to the issue of global competition is the need to offer outstanding customer service. Contextual performance behaviors can make a profound impact on customer satisfaction. Imagine what a big difference it makes, from a customer perspective, when an employee puts in extra effort to satisfy a customer's needs. Third, many organizations are forming employees into teams. Although some teams may not be permanent because they are created to complete specific short-term tasks, the reality of today's world of work is that teams are here to stay. Interpersonal cooperation is a key determinant of team effectiveness. Thus, contextual performance becomes particularly relevant for teamwork. Finally, when supervisors evaluate performance, it is difficult for them to ignore the contextual performance dimension, even though the evaluation form they are using may not include any specific questions about contextual performance.[10] Consequently, since contextual performance has an impact on performance ratings even when only task performance is measured, it makes sense to include contextual performance more explicitly. Measuring contextual performance explicitly is also important because, unless carefully defined, it is often more subjective and subject to bias compared to measuring task performance.

In short, performance includes both a task and a contextual dimension. Both should be considered because both dimensions contribute to organizational success. In the case of both task and contextual performance, each behavior should be defined clearly so that employees understand what is expected of them. Organizations that include both task and contextual dimensions are likely to be more successful, as in the case of O2 Ireland, Ireland's second largest mobile phone operator. Headquartered in Dublin, O2 Ireland employs over 1,450 people. In 2000, O2 Ireland implemented a performance management system in its 320-seat customer care center in Limerick. O2's performance management system includes task-related facets centered in hard metrics regarding productivity as well as contextual-related facets such as involvement in staff socialization and contribution to team development. The targets set for each employee are also aligned with company objectives. O2 concluded that this focus on both task and contextual performance has led to higher levels of customer service and employee satisfaction.

4.4 APPROACHES TO MEASURING PERFORMANCE

Before we discuss how to measure performance, we must remember that employees do not perform in a vacuum. Figure 4.1 shows that employees work in an organizational context, engaging in certain behaviors that produce certain results. The same employee may behave differently (and produce different results) if placed in a different situation (e.g., working with a different supervisor or using better or worse equipment).

Given the model shown in Figure 4.1, there are three approaches that can be used to measure performance. These are the *trait, behavior,* and *results* approaches.[11]

4.4.1 Trait Approach

The trait approach emphasizes the individual performer and ignores the specific situation, behaviors, and results. If one adopts the trait approach, raters evaluate relatively stable traits. These can include abilities such as cognitive abilities (which are not easily trainable) or personality (which is not likely to change over time). For example, performance measurement may consist of assessing an employee's intelligence and conscientiousness at the end of each review period. This approach is justified based on the positive relationship found between abilities (such as intelligence) and personality traits (such as conscientiousness) and desirable work-related behaviors.[12,13] Several vendors provide tools to assess relatively stable traits such as these, sometimes with the capability of administering them online. Vendors who describe their products online include ddi.com, appliedpsych.com, epredix.com, kenexa.com, personneldecisions.com, and earsonreidlondonhouse.com/assessments/psi.htm.

FIGURE 4.1   Job Performance in Context[16]

| A performer (individual or team with certain **traits**) | In a given work situation | Engages in certain behaviors | That produce various results |

What are some of the challenges of implementing a system that emphasizes the measurement of traits only? First, traits are not under the control of individuals. In most cases, they are fairly stable over one's life span. They are not likely to change even if an individual is willing to exert substantial effort to do so. Consequently, employees may feel that a system based on traits is not fair because the development of these traits is usually beyond their control.[14] Second, the fact that an individual possesses a certain trait (e.g., intelligence) does not mean that this trait will necessarily lead to desired results and behaviors. As noted in Figure 4.1, individuals are embedded in specific situations. If the equipment is faulty and coworkers are uncooperative, even a very intelligent and conscientious employee is not likely to engage in behaviors conducive to supporting the organization's goals.

In spite of these challenges, there are situations in which a trait-oriented approach can be fruitful. For example, as part of its business strategy, an organization may anticipate drastic structural changes that will result in the reorganization of most functions and the resulting reallocation of employees. In such a circumstance, it may be useful to assess the traits possessed by the various individuals so that fair and appropriate decisions are made regarding the allocation of HR resources across the newly created organizational units. However, this is a fairly unique circumstance. In most organizations, performance is not measured using the trait approach. Two more popular approaches to measuring performance are based on behaviors and results, discussed next.

4.4.2 Behavior Approach

The behavior approach emphasizes what employees do on the job and does not consider employees' traits or the outcomes resulting from their behaviors. This is basically a process-oriented approach that emphasizes *how* an employee does the job.

The behavior approach is most appropriate under the following circumstances:

- *The link between behaviors and results is not obvious.* Sometimes the relationship between behaviors and the desired outcomes is not clear. In some cases, the desired result may not be achieved in spite of the fact that the right behaviors are in place. For example, a salesperson may not be able to close a deal because of a downturn in the economy. In other cases, results may be achieved in spite of the absence of the correct behaviors. For example, a pilot may not check all the items in the preflight checklist but the flight may nevertheless be successful (i.e., take off and land safely and on time). When the link between behaviors and results is not always obvious, it is beneficial to focus on behaviors as opposed to outcomes.
- *Outcomes occur in the distant future.* When the desired results will not be seen for months, or even years, the measurement of behaviors is beneficial. Take the case of NASA's Mars Exploration Rover Mission program. NASA launched the exploration rover Spirit on June 10, 2003, which landed on Mars on January 3, 2004, after traveling 487 million kilometers (302.6 million miles). Its twin, the exploration rover Opportunity, was launched on July 7, 2003, and landed on the opposite side of Mars on January 24, 2004. From launching to landing, this mission took about six months to complete. In this circumstance, it is certainly appropriate to assess the performance of the

engineers involved in the mission by measuring their behaviors in short intervals during this six-month period rather than waiting until the final result
(i.e., successful or unsuccessful landing) is observed.

- *Poor results are due to causes beyond the performer's control.*   When the
  results of an employee's performance are beyond the employee's control,
  then it makes sense to emphasize the measurement of behaviors. For example, consider a situation involving two assembly-line workers, one of them
  working the day shift and the other the night shift. When the assembly line
  gets stuck because of technical problems, the employee working during the
  day receives immediate technical assistance, so the assembly line is back in
  motion in less than five minutes. In contrast, the employee working the night
  shift has very little technical support and, therefore, when the assembly line
  breaks down, it takes about 45 minutes for it to be up and running again. If
  we measured results, we would conclude that the performance of the day-
  shift employee is far superior to that of the night-shift employee, but this
  would be an incorrect conclusion. Both employees may be equally competent
  and do the job equally well. The results produced by these employees are
  uneven because they depend on the amount and quality of technical assistance they receive when the assembly line is stuck.

We discuss the specific steps involved in measuring behaviors in Chapter 5. Next,
let's discuss the results approach to measuring performance.

4.4.3 Results Approach

The results approach emphasizes the outcomes and results produced by the employees. It does not consider the traits that employees may possess or how employees do
the job. This is basically a bottom-line approach that is not concerned about employee
behaviors and processes and, instead, focuses on what is produced (e.g., sales, number
of accounts acquired, time spent with clients on the telephone, number of errors).
Defining and measuring results usually takes less time than defining and measuring
behaviors needed to achieve these results. Also, the results approach is usually seen as
more cost-effective because results can be less expensive to track than behaviors.
Overall, data resulting from a results approach seem to be objective and are intuitively
very appealing.

The results approach is most appropriate under the following circumstances:

- *Workers are skilled in the needed behaviors.*   An emphasis on results is
  appropriate when workers have the necessary knowledge and skills to do
  the work. In such situations, workers know what specific behaviors are
  needed to achieve the desired results and they are also sufficiently skilled
  to know what to do to correct any process-related problems when the
  desired results are not obtained. Consider the example of a professional
  basketball player. A free throw is an unhindered shot made from the foul
  line that is given to one team to penalize the other team for committing a
  foul. Free throw shooting often makes the difference between winning and
  losing in many close basketball games. Professional players know that there
  is really no secret to becoming a great free throw shooter: just hours and
  hours of dedicated practice besides actual basketball play. So, in assessing

the performance of professional basketball players, free throw shooting percentage is a key results-oriented performance indicator because most players have the skills to do it well. It's just a matter of assessing whether they do it or not.

- *Behaviors and results are obviously related.* In some situations certain results can be obtained only if a worker engages in certain specific behaviors. This is the case of jobs involving repetitive tasks such as assembly-line work or newspaper delivery. Take the case of a person delivering newspapers. Performance can be measured adopting a results approach: whether the newspaper is delivered to all intended customers within a particular time frame. For the employee to obtain this result, she needs to pick up the papers at a specific time and use the most effective delivery route. If these behaviors are not present, the paper is not delivered on time.
- *Results show consistent improvement over time.* When results improve consistently over time, it is an indication that workers are aware of the behaviors needed to complete the job successfully. In these situations, it is appropriate to adopt a results approach to assessing performance.
- *There are many ways to do the job right.* When there are different ways in which one can do the tasks required for a job, a results approach is appropriate. An emphasis on results can be beneficial because it could encourage employees to achieve the desired outcomes in creative and innovative ways.

Table 4.3 summarizes conditions under which a behavior or a results approach may be best suited for assessing performance. However, these approaches are not mutually exclusive. In fact, measuring *both* behavior and results is the approach adopted by many organizations. Consider the case of The Limited, Inc., a retailer headquartered in Columbus, Ohio.[15] The Limited, Inc., operates 14 retail stores and five strategic business units, including Victoria's Secret, Express, Limited, Bath & Body Works, and Abercrombie and Fitch. The Limited aims to foster an entrepreneurial culture for its managers. Therefore, managers who thrive in the company have a history of delivering impressive business results. The Limited decided to design a new performance management system that is now used uniformly by all The Limited companies. With the involvement of outside consultants and employees, The Limited developed a performance management system wherein

TABLE 4.3 Behavior Approach versus Results Approach

Adopting a behavior approach to measuring performance is most appropriate when . . .
- The link between behaviors and results is not obvious
- Outcomes occur in the distant future
- Poor results are due to causes beyond the performer's control

Adopting a results approach to measuring performance is most appropriate when . . .
- Workers are skilled in the needed behaviors
- Behaviors and results are obviously related
- Results show consistent improvement over time
- There are many ways to do the job right

managers are measured on business results including total sales, market share, and expense/sale growth ratio, as well as leadership competencies that are tailored to The Limited. A few of these competencies include developing fashion sense, financial acumen, and entrepreneurial drive. Overall, The Limited has been pleased with the new system because it helps align individual goals with business strategy and results. Raters like the new system as well because behavioral anchors help define the competencies, which make ratings more straightforward. Finally, employees comment that they appreciate the new focus on *how* results are achieved, as opposed to focusing only on *what* is achieved (i.e., sales).

SUMMARY POINTS

- Performance is about behavior or what employees do, and not about what employees produce or the outcomes of their work. However, performance management systems typically include the measurement of both behaviors (how the work is done) and results (the outcomes of one's work). Performance is evaluative (i.e., we judge it based on whether it helps advance or hinder organizational goals) and multidimensional (i.e., many behaviors are needed to describe an employee's performance).

- Performance is determined by a combination of declarative knowledge (i.e., information), procedural knowledge (i.e., know how), and motivation (willingness to perform). Thus, Performance = Declarative Knowledge × Procedural Knowledge × Motivation. If any of the three determinants of performance has a very small value (e.g., very little procedural knowledge), then performance will have a low level also. All three determinants of performance must be present for performance to reach satisfactory (and better) levels.

- There are two important facets of performance: task and contextual. Task performance refers to the specific activities required by one's job. Contextual performance refers to the activities required to be a good "organizational citizen" (e.g., helping coworkers, supporting company initiatives). Both task and contextual performance are needed for organizational success and both should be included in a performance management system.

- Employees do not perform in a vacuum. Employees work in a specific situation, engaging in specific behaviors that produce certain results. An emphasis on the employee leads to a trait-based approach to assessing performance. An emphasis on behaviors leads to a behavior-based approach to assessing performance. An emphasis on results leads to a results-based approach to assessing performance. The relative emphasis given to each of these approaches to measuring performance should be influenced by the organization's business strategy. For example, an organization emphasizing research and development as its main strategy would be concerned about results that are not easily observable in the short term. Thus, an emphasis on behaviors would be consistent with such a business strategy.

- A traits approach emphasizes individual traits that remain fairly stable throughout an individual's life span (e.g., cognitive abilities or personality). This approach may be most appropriate when an organization anticipates drastic structural changes. A major disadvantage of this approach is that traits are not under the control of individuals and, even when individuals possess a specific positive trait (e.g., high intelligence), this does not necessarily mean that the employee will engage in productive behaviors that lead to desired results.

- A behavior approach emphasizes what employees do (i.e., how work is done). This approach is most appropriate when (1) the link between behaviors and results is not obvious, (2) outcomes occur in the distant future, and (3) poor results are due to causes beyond the employee's control. A behavior approach may not be the best choice if most of these conditions are not present. In most situations, however, the inclusion of at least some behavior-based measures is beneficial.

- A results approach emphasizes the outcomes and results produced by employees. This is basically a bottom-line approach that is not concerned with how the work is done as long as certain specific results are obtained. This approach is most appropriate when (1) workers are skilled in the needed behaviors, (2) behaviors and results are obviously related, (3) results show consistent improvement over time, and (4) there are many ways to do the job right. An emphasis on results can be beneficial because it could encourage employees to achieve the desired outcomes in creative and innovative ways. On the other hand, measuring only results is typically not welcomed by employees even in types of jobs for which the expected result is very clear (e.g., as in the case of sales jobs).

Case Study 4.1   Diagnosing the Causes of Poor Performance

Heather works in the training department of a large information technology (IT) organization. She is in charge of designing and delivering interpersonal skills training, including communication skills, networking, and new manager training classes. Heather has excellent knowledge of how to design a training class. She incorporates behavioral modeling and practice into all of her classes. She has also conducted research on what good communication consists of, how to network, and what new managers need to know to be successful. However, individuals who attend Heather's training classes often give her low ratings, stating that she has a hard time answering specific questions in classes and that she does not seem approachable after the classes when individuals want to ask questions.

1. You are Heather's manager. In your opinion, what is causing Heather's poor performance? Is it due to a deficiency in declarative knowledge or procedural knowledge?

2. What can be done to remedy the performance problem? ∎

Case Study 4.2   Differentiating Task from Contextual Performance

Consider the following adaptation of a job description for the position of a district business manager for a sales organization in Bristol-Myers Squibb (BMS) (www.bms.com). BMS produces in pharmaceuticals, infant formulas and nutritional products, ostomy and advanced wound care products, cardiovascular imaging, and over-the-counter products. Some of their brands include Enfamil, Cardiolite, and Plavix. Their stated mission is to "extend and enhance human life by providing the highest-quality pharmaceutical and related health care products." In addition, all employees live by the BMS pledge: "We pledge—to our patients and customers, to our employees and partners, to our shareholders and neighbors, and to the world we serve—to act on our belief that the priceless ingredient of every product is the honor and integrity of its maker."

DBM Job Responsibilities: The following are the core performance objectives for the district business manager (DBM) position. Create the environment to build an innovative culture, create and articulate a vision, drive innovation by embracing diversity and change, set the example and thereby shape the culture. Develop and communicate the business plan, understand and explain BMS strategies, translate national plan to business plans for districts and territories, set goals and expectations of performance, set priorities and allocate resources. Execute the business plan, execute and implement the plan, maximize rank order lists (ROL) medical education professional relationships, achieve optimum coverage frequency of highest potential physicians, take accountability, and achieve results. Building relationships focused on customer retention, develop relationships (i.e., networks), influence others (i.e., internal and external), develop self and others. Strong skills in the following areas required: written and oral communication, negotiation, strategic analysis, leadership, team building, and coaching.

1. Based on the DBM job description, extract a list of task and contextual performance behaviors. Refer to Table 4.2 for a review of the differences between task and contextual performance. ■

Case Study 4.3 Choosing a Performance Measurement Approach at Paychex, Inc.

The following job description is for an account executive at Paychex, Inc. (www. paychex.com). Paychex, Inc., is a leading national provider of payroll, human resources, and benefits outsourcing solutions for small- to medium-sized businesses. Paychex is headquartered in Rochester, New York, but the company has more than 100 offices and serves hundreds of thousands of clients nationwide. Account executives often make sales calls individually, so their managers do not always directly observe their performance. Furthermore, managers are also responsible for sales in their markets and for staying up-to-date on payroll laws. However, account executives are responsible for training new account executives and networking in the industries in which they sell products. For example, if an account manager is responsible for retail companies, then that account executive is expected to attend retail trade shows and professional meetings to identify potential clients and to stay current with the issues facing the retail industry.

Account Executive Job Responsibilities:

- Performing client needs analysis to ensure that the major market services product can meet a client's requirements and expectations.

- Establishing clients on the host processing system.
- Acting as primary contact for the client during the conversion process.
- Supporting clients during the first few payrolls.
- Completing the required documentation to turn the client over to customer service for ongoing support.
- Scheduling and making client calls, and when necessary supporting sales representatives in presales efforts.
- Keeping abreast of the major market services system and software changes, major changes and trends in the PC industry, and changes in wage and tax law.

1. Based on the above description, assess whether Paychex should use a behavior approach, results approach, or a combination of both to measure performance.
2. Using the accompanying table as a guide, place checkmarks next to the descriptions that apply to the job of account executive. Then explain why you chose the approach you did. ■

Behavior approach to measuring performance is most appropriate when
the link between behaviors and results is not obvious outcomes occur in the distant future poor results are due to causes beyond the performer's control
Results approach to measuring performance is most appropriate when
workers are skilled in the necessary behaviors behaviors and results are obviously related results show consistent improvement over time there are many ways to do the job right

End Notes

1. Motowidlo, S. J., Borman, W. C., & Schmit, M. J. (1997). A theory of individual differences in task and contextual performance. *Human Performance, 10*, 71–83.

2. Murphy, K. R., & Shiarella, A. H. (1997). Implications of the multidimensional nature of job performance for the validity of selection tests: Multivariate frameworks for studying test validity. *Personnel Psychology, 50*, 823–854.

3. McCloy, R. A., Campbell, J. P., & Cudeck, R. (1994). A confirmatory test of a model of performance determinants. *Journal of Applied Psychology, 79*, 493–505.

4. Edward Jones, A.G. Edwards lauded for training efforts (2002, February 20). *St. Louis Business Journal*, available online at http://stlouis.bizjournals.com/stlouis/stories/2002/02/18/daily31.html. Retrieval date: August 15, 2005.

5. Borman, W. C., Penner, L.A., Allen, T. D., & Motowidlo, S. (2001). Personality predictors of citizenship performance. *International Journal of Selection and Assessment, 9*, 52–69.

6. Borman, W. C. (2004). The concept of organizational citizenship. *Current Directions in Psychological Science, 13*, 238–241.

7. Borman, W. C., Hanson, M., & Hedge, J. (1997). Personnel selection. *Annual Review of Psychology, 48*, 299–337.

8. Cascio, W. F., & Aguinis, H. (2001). The Federal Uniform Guidelines on Employee Selection Procedures (1978): An update on selected issues. *Review of Public Personnel Administration, 21*, 200–218.

9. Arvey, R. D., & Murphy, K. R. (1998). Performance evaluation in work settings. *Annual Review of Psychology, 49*, 141–168.

10. Van Scotter, J. R., Motowidlo, S. J., & Cross, T. C. (2000). Effects of task performance and contextual performance on systemic rewards. *Journal of Applied Psychology, 85*, 526–535.

11. The discussion of each of these approaches is based on D. Grote. *The Complete Guide to Performance Appraisal* (New York: American Management Association, 1996), chap. 3.

12. Viswesvaran, C., & Ones, D. S. (2000). Perspectives on models of job performance. *International Journal of Selection and Assessment, 8*, 216–226.

13. Schmidt, F. L. (2002). The role of general cognitive ability and job performance: Why there cannot be a debate. *Human Performance, 15*, 187–210.

14. Smither, J. W., & Walker, A. G. (2004). Are the characteristics of narrative comments related to improvement in multirater feedback ratings over time? *Journal of Applied Psychology, 89*, 575–581.

15. Heneman, R. L., & Thomas, A. L. (1997). The Limited, Inc.: Using strategic performance management to drive brand leadership. *Compensation and Benefits Review, 29*, 33–40.

16. Grote, D. (1996). Adapted from *The complete guide to performance appraisal* (Fig. 3-1, p. 37). New York: American Management Association.

Measuring Results and Behaviors

The reason most people never reach their goals is that they don't define them, or ever seriously consider them as believable or achievable. Winners can tell you where they are going, what they plan to do along the way, and who will be sharing the adventure with them.

—DENIS WATLEY

Learning Objectives

By the end of this chapter, you will be able to do the following:

- Adopt a results approach to measuring performance, including the development of accountabilities, objectives, and standards.

- Determine accountabilities and their relative importance.

- Identify objectives that are specific and clear, challenging, agreed upon, significant, prioritized, bound by time, achievable, fully communicated, flexible, and limited in number.

- Identify performance standards that are related to the position, concrete, specific, measurable, practical to measure, meaningful, realistic and achievable, and reviewed regularly.

- Adopt a behavior approach to measuring performance, including the identification and assessment of competencies.

- Develop competencies that are defined clearly, provide a description of specific behavioral indicators that can be observed when someone demonstrates a competency effectively, provide a description of specific behaviors that are likely to occur when someone doesn't demonstrate a competency effectively (what a competency is not), and include suggestions for developing them further.

- Develop comparative performance measurement systems such as simple rank order, alternation rank order, paired comparisons, and forced distribution (being aware of the relative advantages and disadvantages of each).

- Develop absolute performance measurement systems such as essays, behavior checklists, critical incidents, and graphic rating scales, and understand their advantages and disadvantages.

Chapter 4 provided a definition of performance and described the trait, results, and behavior approaches to measuring performance. In this chapter, we provide a more detailed description of how to measure performance, adopting the two most common approaches: results and behavior.

5.1 MEASURING RESULTS

Chapter 2 included some information about how to assess performance when a results approach is adopted. If one adopts a results approach, one needs to ask the following key questions:

- What are the different areas in which this individual is expected to focus efforts (key accountabilities)?
- Within each area, what are the expected objectives?
- How do we know how well the results have been achieved (performance standards)?[1]

As a reminder, key accountabilities are broad areas of a job for which the employee is responsible for producing results. A discussion of results also includes specific objectives that the employee will achieve as part of each accountability. Objectives are statements of important and measurable outcomes. Finally, discussing results also means discussing performance standards. A performance standard is a yardstick used to evaluate how well employees have achieved each objective. Performance standards provide information on acceptable and unacceptable performance, for example, regarding quality, quantity, cost, and time. Organizations that implement a management by objectives (MBO) philosophy are likely to implement performance management systems, including objectives and standards. An emphasis on objectives and standards is likely to allow employees to translate organizational goals into individual goals, which is a key goal of MBO philosophies.[2]

5.1.1 Determining Accountabilities

The first step in determining accountabilities is to collect information about the job. The primary source is, of course, the job description that resulted from the job analysis and a consideration of unit- and organization-level strategic priorities. The job description provides information on the tasks performed. Tasks included in the job description can be grouped into clusters of tasks based on their degree of relatedness. Each of these clusters or accountabilities is a broad area of the job for which the employee is responsible for producing results.

Once the accountabilities are identified, we need to determine their relative degree of importance. To understand this issue, we need to ask the following questions:

- What percentage of the employee's time is spent performing each accountability?
- If the accountability were performed inadequately, would there be a significant impact on the work unit's mission?
- Is there a significant consequence of error? Could inadequate performance of the accountability contribute to the injury or death of the employee or others, serious property damage, and loss of time and money?

Although determining accountabilities may at first seem like a daunting task, it is not that difficult. Let's discuss an example based on a real job in a real organization to illustrate how it is done. Consider the position of Training Specialist/Consultant—Leadership & Team Development for Target Corporation, a growth company focused exclusively on general merchandise retailing (www.target.com). The job description is the following:

Identifies the training and development needs of Target Corporation's work force (in collaboration with partners), with primary emphasis on exempt team members. Designs and delivers training and development workshops and programs and maintains on ongoing evaluation of the effectiveness of those programs. Assumes leadership and strategic responsibility for assigned processes. May supervise the non-exempt staff.

Based on the job description, and additional information found on Target's Web page regarding the company's strategic priorities, a list of the accountabilities, consequences of performing them inadequately, consequences of making errors, and percentage of time spent in each follows:

- *Process leadership.*   Leads the strategy and direction of assigned processes. Coordinates related projects and directs or manages resources. This is extremely important to the functioning of Target leadership and the ability of executives to meet strategic business goals. If this position is managed improperly, then it will lead to a loss of time and money in training costs and leadership ineffectiveness. (40% of time)
- *Supervision of nonexempt staff.*   Supervises nonexempt staff working in the unit. This is relatively important to the functioning of the work unit. If nonexempt staff are supervised improperly, then the development of the employees and the ability to meet business targets will be compromised. (10% of time)
- *Coaching.*   Conducts one-on-one executive coaching with managers and executives. This is extremely important to the development of internal leaders. If managers and executives are not coached to improve their performance, there is a loss of time and money associated with their poor performance as well as the cost of replacing them if necessary. (20% of time)
- *Team building consultation.*   Assists company leaders in designing and delivering their own team building sessions and other interventions. This is relatively important to the successfulness of teams at Target. Mismanagement of this function will result in teams not meeting their full potential and wasting time and resources on conducting the team sessions. (10% of time)
- *Assessment instrument feedback.*   Delivers feedback based on scores obtained on assessment instruments of skills, ability, personality, and other individual characteristics. This is relatively important to the development of leaders. If assessment is incorrect, it could derail leader development. (10% of time)
- *Product improvement.*   Continuously seeks and implements opportunities to use technology to increase the effectiveness of leadership and team development programs. This is important to the effectiveness of training delivery, and could result in significant gains in efficiencies of the systems if carried out effectively. (10% of time)

5.1.2 Determining Objectives

Once the accountabilities have been identified, the next step in measuring results is to determine specific objectives. Objectives are statements of an important and measurable outcome that, when accomplished, will help ensure success for the accountability. The purpose of establishing objectives is to identify a limited number of highly important results that, when achieved, will have a dramatic impact on the overall success of the organization. After objectives are set, employees should receive feedback on their progress toward attaining the objective. Rewards should be allocated to those employees who have reached their objectives.

Objectives are clearly important because they help employees guide their efforts. But to serve a useful function, objectives must have the following characteristics:[3]

1. *Specific and clear.*   Objectives must be easy to understand. In addition, they must be verifiable and measurable, for example; a directive: "Cut travel cost by 20%."
2. *Challenging.*   Objectives need to be challenging (but not impossible to achieve). They must be a stretch, but employees should feel that the objective is reachable.
3. *Agreed upon.*   To be most effective, objectives need to result from an agreement between the manager and the employee. Employees need an opportunity to participate in setting objectives. Participation in the process increases objective aspirations and acceptance, and it decreases objective resistance.
4. *Significant.*   Objectives must be important to the organization. Employees must believe that if the objective is achieved, it will make a critical impact on the overall success of the organization. In addition, achieving the objective should give the employee the feeling of congruence between the employee's performance and the goals of the organization. This, in turn, is likely to enhance feelings of value to the organization.
5. *Prioritized.*   Not all objectives are created equal. Thus, objectives should be prioritized and tackled one by one.
6. *Bound by time.*   Good objectives have deadlines and mileposts. Objectives lacking a time dimension are likely to be neglected.
7. *Achievable.*   Good objectives are doable. That is, employees should have sufficient skills and training to achieve them. If they don't, then the organization should make resources available so that the necessary skills are learned and equipment is made available to achieve the goals.
8. *Fully communicated.*   In addition to the manager and employee in question, the other organizational members who may be affected by the objectives need to be aware of them.
9. *Flexible.*   Good objectives are not immutable. They can and likely will change based on changes in the work or business environments.
10. *Limited in number.*   Too many objectives may become impossible to achieve, but too few may not make a sufficient contribution to the organization. So, objectives must be limited in number. Between 5 and 10 objectives per review period is a manageable number, but this can change based on the position and organization in question.

TABLE 5.1 Characteristics of Good Objectives
Specific and clear
Challenging
Agreed upon
Significant
Prioritized
Bound by time
Achievable
Fully communicated
Flexible
Limited in number

Several organizations set goals following these guidelines. For example, Microsoft Corporation has a long history of using individual goals in its performance management system. The goals at Microsoft are described by the acronym SMART: specific, measurable, results-based, and time-specific.[4]

Table 5.1 summarizes the characteristics of good objectives. Using this list as our guide, let's return to the position Training Specialist/Consultant—Leadership & Team Development at Target Corporation.

Examples of objectives (one or two per accountability) are the following:

- *Process leadership.* Develop leadership development processes and training programs within budget and time commitments. Meet budget targets and improve executive leader's "leadership readiness" scores across organization by 20% in the coming fiscal year.
- *Supervision of nonexempt staff.* Receive acceptable managerial effectiveness rating scores from your nonexempt staff in the coming fiscal year.
- *Coaching.* Improve the managerial effectiveness scores of executive coaching clients in the coming fiscal year.
- *Team-building consultation.* Deliver necessary team-training sessions throughout the year within budget and with an acceptable satisfaction rating (as measured by the follow-up survey that is sent to every team) with team-training sessions in the coming fiscal year.
- *Assessment instrument feedback.* Deliver assessment feedback with an acceptable approval rating from your coaching clients in the coming fiscal year.
- *Product improvement.* Improve satisfaction with training delivery scores in the coming fiscal year while staying on budget.

Do these objectives comply with each of the 10 characteristics of good objectives listed in Table 5.1?

5.1.3 Determining Performance Standards

Once accountabilities and objectives have been determined, the next step is to define performance standards. These are yardsticks designed to help people understand to what extent the objective has been achieved. The standards provide raters with information on what to look for to determine the level of performance that has been achieved. Standards can refer to various aspects of a specific objective, including quality, quantity, and time. Each of these aspects can be considered criteria to be used in judging the extent to which an objective has been achieved.

- Quality: how well the objective has been achieved. This can include usefulness, responsiveness, effect obtained (e.g., problem resolution), acceptance rate, error rate, and feedback from users or customers (e.g., customer complaints, error rates, returns).
- Quantity: how much has been produced, how many, how often, and at what cost.
- Time: due dates, adherence to schedule, cycle times, deadlines (how quickly) (e.g., timetables, progress reports).

Standards must include an action, the desired result, a due date, and some type of quality or quantity indicator. For example, a standard might be the following: *Reduce overtime from 150 hours/month to 50 hours/month by December 1, 2007 at a cost not to exceed $12,000.* The action is *reduce*, the due date is *December 1, 2007*, and the indicators are the *reduction in hours from 150 to 50* and *at a cost not to exceed $12,000*.

Standards usually describe fully satisfactory performance. But once a standard has been created, one can create standards that describe minimum performance and outstanding performance. For example, the minimum standard could be the following: *Reduce overtime from 150 hours/month to 75 hours/month by December 1, 2007 at a cost not to exceed $12,000.* The standard suggesting outstanding performance could be the following: *Reduce overtime from 150 hours/month to 40 hours/month by October 1, 2007 at a cost not to exceed $12,000.*

In writing standards, consider the following characteristics that often determine whether one has a useful standard or not:

1. *Related to the position.*   Good standards are based on the job's key elements and tasks, and not on individual traits or person-to-person comparisons.
2. *Concrete, specific, and measurable.*   Good standards are observable and verifiable. They allow us to distinguish between different performance levels. A good standard allows supervisors to measure the employee's actual performance to determine if it is below expectations, fully satisfactory, or above expectations. Standards are specific and concrete so that there should be no dispute over whether and how well they were met.
3. *Practical to measure.*   Good standards provide necessary information about performance in the most efficient way possible. Good standards are created by taking into account the cost, accuracy, and availability of the needed data.
4. *Meaningful.*   Good standards are about what is important and relevant to the purpose of the job, to the achievement of the organization's mission and objectives, and to the user or recipient of the product or service.
5. *Realistic and achievable.*   Standards are possible to accomplish, but they require a stretch. There should be no apparent barriers to achieving the standard. Employees should be able to reach the standards within the specified time frame.
6. *Reviewed regularly.*   Information should be available on a regular basis to learn if the employee has reached the standard and, if not, remedial action should be taken.[5]

TABLE 5.2   Characteristics of Good Performance Standards
Related to the position
Concrete, specific, and measurable
Practical to measure
Meaningful
Realistic and achievable
Reviewed regularly

Table 5.2 lists the characteristics described here that are typical of good standards. Using this list as a guide, let's once again return to the position of Training Specialist/Consultant—Leadership & Team Development at Target Corporation.

Examples of standards (one per objective for each accountability) are the following:

- *Process leadership.*   Increased the executive leader's "leadership readiness" scores across organization by 20% by December 31, 2007 at a cost not to exceed $70,000.
- *Supervision of nonexempt staff.*   Received managerial effectiveness rating scores of 80% approval from your nonexempt staff in December 2007.
- *Coaching.*   Improve the managerial effectiveness scores of executive coaching clients by 5% in December 2007.
- *Team-building consultation.*   Designed and delivered 95% of scheduled team-building sessions with a cost not to exceed $30,000 for an 85% satisfaction rating with team-training sessions by December 2007.
- *Assessment instrument feedback.*   Delivered assessment feedback with an 85% approval rating from your coaching clients in December 2007.
- *Product improvement.*   Improve satisfaction with training delivery scores by 5% by December 31, 2007 at a cost not to exceed $30,000.

5.2 MEASURING BEHAVIORS

Chapter 2 provided an introduction to the topic of measuring behaviors. A behavior approach to measuring performance includes the assessment of competencies. Competencies are measurable clusters of knowledge, skills, and abilities (KSAs) that are critical in determining how results will be achieved. Examples of competencies are customer service, written or oral communication, creative thinking, and dependability. We can consider two types of competencies: first, differentiating competencies, which are those that allow us to distinguish between average and superior performers; and, second, threshold competencies, which are those that everyone needs to display to do the job to a minimally adequate standard. For example, for the position Information Technology (IT) Project Manager, a differentiating competency is process management. Process management is defined as the "ability to manage projective activities." For the same position, a threshold competency is change management.[6] The change management competency includes knowledge of behavioral sciences, operational and relational skills, and sensitivity to motivators. Therefore, in order for an information technology project manager to be truly effective, she has to possess process management and change management competencies.

As noted earlier, competencies should be defined in behavioral terms. Take the case of a professor teaching an online course. An important competency could be "communication." This competency is defined as the set of behaviors that enables a professor to convey information so that students are able to receive it and understand it. For example, one such behavior might be whether the professor is conveying information during preassigned times and dates. That is, if the professor is not present at the chat room at the prespecified dates and times, no communication is possible.

To understand the extent to which an employee possesses a competency, we measure indicators. Each indicator is an observable behavior that gives us information regarding the competency in question. In other words, we don't measure the competency directly, but we measure indicators that tell us whether the competency is present or not.

Figure 5.1 shows the relationship between a competency and its indicators. A competency can have several indicators. Figure 5.1 shows a competency with five indicators. An indicator is a behavior that, if displayed, suggests that the competency is present. In the example of the competency communication for a professor teaching an online course, one indicator is whether the professor shows up at the chat room at the preestablished dates and times. Another behavioral indicator of the competency communication could be whether the responses provided by the professor address the questions asked by the students or whether the answers are only tangential to the questions asked. As another example, consider the two competencies that define good leadership: consideration and initiation structure.[7] Consideration is the degree to which the leader looks after the well-being of his followers. Initiating structure is the degree to which the leader lays out task responsibilities. Five indicators whose presence would indicate the existence of the consideration competency are the following:

- Supports subordinates' projects.
- Asks about the well-being of employees' lives outside of work.
- Encourages subordinates to reach their established goals.
- Gets to know employees personally.
- Shows respect for employees' work and home lives.

In describing a competency, the following components must be present:

1. Definition of competency.
2. Description of specific behavioral indicators that can be observed when someone demonstrates a competency effectively.

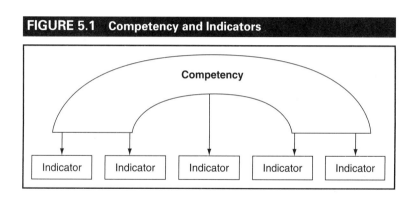

FIGURE 5.1 Competency and Indicators

3. Description of specific behaviors that are likely to occur when someone doesn't demonstrate a competency effectively (what a competency is not).

4. List of suggestions for developing the competency in question.[8]

Using the competency consideration, let's discuss the four essential elements in describing a competency. We defined consideration: it is the degree to which a leader shows concern and respect for followers, looks out for their welfare, and expresses appreciation and support. Next, we listed five indicators or behaviors that can be observed when a leader is exhibiting consideration leadership. Leaders who do not show consideration may speak with subordinates only regarding task assignments, repeatedly keep employees late with no consideration of home lives and take no interest in an employee's career goals, and assign tasks based only on current expertise. Finally, how do leaders develop the consideration competency? One suggestion would be to ask employees, on a regular basis, how their lives outside of work are going. This may lead to knowledge about an employee's family and interests outside of work.

In contrast to the measurement of results, the measurement of competencies is intrinsically judgmental. Competencies are measured using data provided by individuals who make a judgment regarding the presence of the competency. In other words, the behaviors displayed by the employees are observed and judged by raters (typically, the direct supervisor, but raters might also include peers, customers, subordinates, and the employee himself).

There are two types of systems used to evaluate competencies: *comparative systems* and *absolute systems*. Comparative systems base the measurement on comparing employees with one other. Absolute systems base the measurement on comparing employees with a prespecified performance standard.

Table 5.3 includes a list of the various types of comparative and absolute systems that could be used. Let's discuss how to implement each of these types of systems and some advantages and disadvantages of each.[9]

5.2.1 Comparative Systems

Comparative systems of measuring behaviors imply that employees are compared to one other. If a *simple rank order* system is used, employees are simply ranked from best performer to worst performer. Alternatively, in an *alternation rank order* procedure, the supervisor initially lists all employees. Then, the supervisor selects the best performer (#1), then the worst performer (#n), then the second best (#2), then the second worst (#n − 1), and so forth, alternating from the top to the bottom of the list until all employees have been ranked.

TABLE 5.3 **Comparative and Absolute Behavioral Measurement Systems**

Comparative	*Absolute*
Simple rank order	Essays
Alternation rank order	Behavior checklists
Paired comparisons	Critical incidents
Forced distribution	Graphic rating scales

Paired comparisons is another comparative system. In contrast to the simple and alternation rank order procedures, explicit comparisons are made between all pairs of employees to be evaluated.[10] In other words, supervisors systematically compare the performance of each employee against the performance of all other employees. The number of pairs of employees to be compared is computed by the following equation:

$$\frac{n(n-1)}{2}$$

where *n* is the number of employees to be evaluated. If a supervisor needs to evaluate the performance of 8 employees, she would have to make $[8(8-1)]/2 = 28$ comparisons. The supervisor's job is to choose the better of each pair, and each individual's rank is determined by counting the number of times he or she was rated as better.

A fourth comparison method is called *forced distribution.* In this type of system, employees are apportioned according to an approximately normal distribution. So, for example, 20% of employees must be classified as exceeding expectations, 70% must be classified as meeting expectations, and 10% must be classified as not meeting expectations. General Electric is one such organization that adopted a forced distribution system. Former GE CEO Jack Welch labeled GE's forced distribution system the "vitality curve." In his view, forced ranking enables managers to better manage low-achieving performers. GE's success in implementing a forced ranking system is cited as the model by many of the 20% of U.S. companies that have adopted it in recent years. At GE, each year 10% of managers are assigned the "C" grade and if they don't improve they are asked to leave the company.[11]

What are some of the advantages of using comparative measurement methods? First, these types of measurement procedures are usually easy to explain. Second, decisions resulting from these types of systems are fairly straightforward: it is easy to see which employees are where in the distributions. Third, they tend to control several biases and errors made by those rating performance better than do those in absolute systems. Such errors include leniency (i.e., giving high scores to most employees), severity (i.e., giving low scores to most employees), and central tendency (i.e., not giving any above-expectations or below-expectations ratings).

On the other hand, there are also disadvantages associated with the use of comparative systems. First, employees usually are compared only in terms of a single overall category. Employees are not compared based on individual behaviors, or even individual competencies, but instead are compared based on an overall assessment of performance. As a consequence, the resulting rankings are not sufficiently specific so that employees can receive useful feedback, and also these rankings may be subject to legal challenge. Second, because the resulting data are based on rankings and not actual scores, we don't have information on the relative distance between employees. All we know is that employee A received a higher score than employee B, but we don't know if this difference is, for example, similar to that between employee B and employee C.

Finally, there are specific issues that should be considered in the implementation of a forced distribution method. This method assumes that performance scores are normally distributed, with some employees performing very highly, some poorly, and the majority in between. However, this assumption may not hold true for all units within an organization. Some units may have a high performing culture and systems in place so that the majority of members perform at a very high level. Conversely, other units may have a majority of members who perform at a below-expectations level. Another disadvantage of implementing a forced distribution system is that such a system may discourage employees from engaging in contextual performance behaviors. After all, some employees may think, "The better my colleague does, the smaller the chance that I will be rated at the top of the distribution, so why should I help her do her job?" Obviously, this can undermine teamwork and the goals of the organization; it is important to consider what the culture of the organization is before implementing this type of system. If there is a culture with an unhealthy level of competitiveness, then a forced distribution may produce an effect opposite to what is intended and create performance problems. Finally, a forced distribution system is very difficult to implement in an organization that is not experiencing any growth. This is especially true for an organization that is experiencing cutbacks. If it is the same group or, even worse, a smaller group being evaluated one year later, people who had been in the middle position are by default moved to the bottom, even if their performance has not changed. This is because the employees who were rated at the bottom previously are no longer with the organization. It is not easy for employees to understand why, given the same level of performance, they are now placed in the C instead of the B category. University of Southern California professor Ed Lawler gives a great example of a forced distribution system using a salamander as a comparison: the salamander's tail grows back once you chop it off, but this doesn't happen in companies. In companies, if a forced distribution system is used and a prespecified percentage of employees is let go every year because someone has to be placed in the C category, at some point you will be cutting into the "bone" of the organization. Computer simulations have confirmed that the benefits of implementing a forced distribution system in terms of performance improvement are most noticeable in the first several years of program implementation.[12]

5.2.2 Absolute Systems

In absolute systems, supervisors provide evaluations of an employee's performance without making direct reference to other employees. The simplest absolute system consists of a supervisor writing an *essay* describing each employee's strengths and weaknesses, and making suggestions for improvement. One advantage of the essay system is that supervisors have the potential to provide detailed feedback to employees regarding their performance. On the other hand, essays are almost totally unstructured, so some supervisors may choose to be more detailed than others. Some supervisors may be better at writing essays than others. Because of this variability, comparisons across individuals, groups, or units are virtually impossible because essays written by different supervisors, and even by the same supervisor regarding different employees, may address different aspects of an employee's performance. Finally, essays do not provide any quantitative information, making it difficult to use them in some personnel decisions (e.g., allocation of rewards).

A second type of absolute system involves a *behavior checklist*, which consists of a form listing behavioral statements that are indicators of the various competencies to be measured. The supervisor's task is to indicate ("check") statements that describe the employee being rated. When this type of measurement system is in place, supervisors are not so much evaluators as they are "reporters" of employee behavior. Because it is likely that all behaviors rated are present to some extent, behavior checklists usually include a description of the behavior in question (e.g., "the employee arrives at work on time")

FIGURE 5.2   Example of Behavior Checklist Item

The employee arrives at work on time.

1	2	3	4	5
Never	Sometimes	Often	Fairly Often	Always

followed by several response categories, such as "always," "very often," "fairly often," "occasionally," and "never." The rater simply checks the response category she feels best describes the employee. Each response category is weighted—for example, from 5 ("always") to 1 ("never") if the statement describes desirable behavior such as arriving at work on time. Then, an overall score for each employee is computed by adding the weights of the responses that were checked for each item. Figure 5.2 includes an example of an item from a form adopting a behavior checklist measurement approach.

How do we select response categories for behavior checklist scales? Often, this is a quite arbitrary decision and equal intervals between scale points are simply assumed. For example, in Figure 5.2, we would assume that the distance between "never" and "sometimes" is the same as the distance between "fairly often" and "always" (i.e., 1 point in each case). Great care must be taken in how the anchors are selected. Table 5.4 includes anchors that can be used for scales involving frequency and amount.[13]

TABLE 5.4   Anchors for Checklists of Frequency and Amount

Anchors for Checklists of Frequency

Seven-Point Scale	*Five-Point Scale*
Always	Always
Constantly	Very often
Often	Fairly often
Fairly often	Occasionally
Sometimes	Never
Once in a while	
Never	

Anchors for Checklists of Amount

Seven-Point Scale	*Five-Point Scale*
All	All
An extraordinary amount of	An extreme amount of
A great amount of	Quite a bit of
Quite a bit of	Some
A moderate amount of	None
Somewhat	
None	

Table 5.4 includes anchors to be used in both 7-point and 5-point scales. However, for most systems the use of a 5-point scale should be sufficient to capture an employee's performance on the behavior being rated. One advantage of using 5-point scales is that they are less complex than are 7-point scales. Also, 5-point scales are superior to 3-point scales because they are more likely to motivate performance improvement because employees believe it is more doable to move up one level on a 5-point scale than it is on a 3-point scale.[14]

Table 5.5 includes anchors that can be used in scales involving agreement and evaluation.[15] This table includes 13 anchors that can be chosen if one uses a scale of evaluation and 13 anchors that can be used if a scale of agreement is used.

TABLE 5.5   Anchors to Be Used in Checklists of Evaluation and Agreement

Anchors for Checklists of Evaluation

Terrible	1.6
Bad	3.3
Inferior	3.6
Poor	3.8
Unsatisfactory	3.9
Mediocre	5.3
Passable	5.5
Decent	6.0
Fair	6.1
Average	6.4
Satisfactory	6.9
Good	7.5
Excellent	9.6

Anchors for Checklists of Agreement

Slightly	2.5
A little	2.7
Mildly	4.1
Somewhat	4.4
In part	4.7
Halfway	4.8
Tend to	5.3
Inclined to	5.4
Moderately	5.4
Generally	6.8
Pretty much	7.0
On the whole	7.4
Very much	9.1

Table 5.5 also includes ratings that can be used to choose anchors for a scale of evaluation or agreement. In creating scales, we must choose anchors that are approximately equally spaced based on the ratings included in Table 5.5. So, if we were to create a 5-point scale of evaluation using the information provided in this table, one possible set of anchors might be the following:

1. Terrible
2. Unsatisfactory
3. Decent
4. Good
5. Excellent

In this set of anchors, the distance between all pairs of adjacent anchors ranges between 1.5 and 2.3 points. Note, however, that the use of the anchor "terrible" has a very negative connotation, so we may want to use a less negative anchor, such as "bad" or "inferior." In this case, we would be choosing an anchor that is closer to the next one ("unsatisfactory") than we may wish, but using the new anchor may lead to less defensive and overall negative reactions on the part of employees who receive this rating.

In summary, behavior checklists are easy to use and to understand.[16] On the other hand, detailed and useful feedback is difficult to extract from the numerical rating provided. Overall, however, the practical advantages of checklists probably account for their current widespread popularity.

Every job includes some critical behaviors that make a crucial difference between doing a job effectively and doing it ineffectively. The *critical incidents* measurement approach involves gathering reports of situations in which employees performed behaviors that were especially effective or ineffective in accomplishing their jobs.[17] The recorded critical incidents provide a starting point for assessing performance. For example, consider the following incident as recorded by a high school principal regarding the performance of Tom Jones, the head of the disability services office:

> A sophomore with learning disabilities was experiencing difficulty in writing. Her parents wanted a laptop computer for her. Tom Jones ordered a computer and it was delivered to the student's teacher. No training was provided to the child, her teacher, or her parents. The laptop was never used.

This recorded incident is actually the synthesis of a series of incidents:

1. A problem was detected (a student with a special need was identified).
2. Corrective action was taken (the computer was ordered).
3. Corrective action was initially positive (the computer was delivered).
4. Corrective action was subsequently deficient (the computer was not used because of the lack of training).

When critical incidents are collected, this measurement method allows supervisors to focus on actual job behavior rather than on vaguely defined traits. On the other hand, collecting critical incidents is very time-consuming. As is the case with essays, it is difficult to attach a score quantifying the impact of the incident (either positive or negative). A revised version of the critical incidents technique involves summarizing critical incidents and giving them to supervisors in the form of scales (e.g., behavior checklist). One example following up on the critical incident involving Tom Jones might be the following:

Addresses learning needs of special needs students efficiently

| Strongly Agree | Agree | Undecided | Disagree | Strongly Disagree |

   A second variation of the critical incidents technique is the approach adopted in the performance management system implemented by the city of Irving, Texas.[18] First, the city identified core competencies and classified them as core values, skill group competencies, or performance essentials. Then, the team in charge of implementing the system wrote dozens of examples of different levels of performance on each competency from ineffective to highly effective. In other words, this team was in charge of compiling critical incidents illustrating various performance levels for each competency. Then, managers used this list by simply circling the behavior that best described each of the employees in the work unit.

   As an example, consider the competency Adaptability/Flexibility. For this competency, critical incidents were used to illustrate various performance levels:

Completely Ineffective	Somewhat Ineffective	Effective	Highly Effective	Exceptional
Able to focus on only one task at a time	Easily distracted from work assignments/ activities	Handles a variety of work assignments/ activities with few difficulties	Handles a variety of work assignments/ activities concurrently	Easily juggles a large number of assignments and activities
Avoids or attempts to undermine changes	Complains about necessary changes	Accepts reasons for change	Understands and responds to reasons for change	Encourages and instructs others about the benefits of change
Refuses to adopt changes policies	Makes only those changes with which they agree	Adapts to changing circumstances and attitudes of others	Adapts to changes and develops job aids to assist others	Welcomes change and looks for new opportunities it provides
Considers only own opinion when seeking solution	Occasionally listens to others but supports own solutions	Listens to others and seeks solutions acceptable to all	Ensures that everyone's thoughts and opinions are considered in reaching a solution	Actively seeks input in addition to recognized sources and facilitates implementation of solution

   A third variation of the critical incidents technique is the use of behaviorally anchored rating scales (BARS), which are described next as one of several types of graphic rating scales. The *graphic rating scale* is the most popular tool to measure performance. The aim of graphic rating scales is to ensure that the response categories (ratings of behavior) are clearly defined, that interpretation of the rating by an outside party is clear, and that the supervisor and the employee understand the rating. An example of a graphic rating scale used to rate the performance of a project manager is the following:

Project management awareness is the knowledge of project management planning, updating status, working within budget, and delivering project on time and within budget. Rate _____'s project management awareness using the following scale:

1	2	3	4	5
Unaware or not interested	Needs additional training	Aware of responsibilities	Excellent knowledge and performance of skills	Superior performance of skill; ability to train others

BARS include the use of graphic rating scales that use critical incidents as anchors.[19] BARS improve on the graphic rating scales by first having a group of employees identify all of the important dimensions of a job. Then, another group of employees generates critical incidents illustrating low, average, and high skills of performance for each dimension. A third group of employees and supervisors takes each dimension and the accompanying definitions and a randomized list of critical incidents. They must match the critical incidents with the correct dimensions. Finally, a group of judges assigns a scale value to each incident. Consider the following BARS for measuring job knowledge:

Job Knowledge: The amount of job-related knowledge and skills that an employee possesses.

5	*Exceptional*: Employee consistently displays high level of job knowledge in all areas of his or her job. Other employees go to this person for training.
4	*Advanced*: Shows high levels of job knowledge in most areas of his or her job. Consistently completes all normal tasks. Employee continues searching for more job knowledge, and may seek guidance in some areas.
3	*Competent*: Employee shows an average level of job knowledge in all areas of the job. May need assistance completing difficult tasks.
2	*Improvement Needed*: Does not consistently meet deadlines or complete tasks required for this job. Does not attempt to acquire new skills or knowledge to improve performance.
1	*Major Improvement Needed*: Typically performs tasks incorrectly or not at all. Employee has no appreciation for improving his or her performance.

Consider the following BARS that assesses one of 10 performance dimensions identified as important for auditors:[20]

Knowledge of Accounting and Auditing Standards/Theory: Technical foundation, application of knowledge on the job, ability to identify problem areas and weigh theory vs. practice.

3	*High Point Performance*: Displays very strong technical foundation, able to proficiently apply knowledge on the job, willingly researches areas, able to identify problems, can weigh theory vs. practice considerations.
2	*Midpoint Performance*: Can resolve normal accounting issues, has adequate technical foundation and skills, application requires some refinement, has some problems in weighing theory vs. practice, can identify major problem areas.
1	*Low Point Performance*: Displays weak accounting knowledge and/or technical ability to apply knowledge to situations/issues on an engagement, has difficulty in identifying problems and/or weighing factors of theory vs. practice.

For graphic rating scales to be most useful and accurate, they must include the following features:

- The meaning of each response category is clear.
- The individual who is interpreting the ratings (e.g., an HR manager) can tell clearly what response was intended.
- The performance dimension being rated is defined clearly for the rater.

Compare the two examples of BARS shown earlier. Which is better regarding each of these three features? How can these BARS be revised and improved?

In summary, several types of methods are available for assessing performance. These methods differ in terms of practicality (i.e., some take more time and effort to be developed than others), usefulness for administrative purposes (i.e., some are less useful than others because they don't provide a clear quantification of performance), and usefulness for users (i.e., some are less useful than others in terms of the feedback they produce that allows employees to improve performance in the future). Practicality and usefulness are key considerations in choosing one type of measurement procedure over another.

SUMMARY POINTS

- The first step in measuring performance by adopting a results approach is to identify accountabilities. Accountabilities are the various areas in which an individual is expected to focus.
- Once all key accountabilities are identified, the second step in the results approach is to set objectives for each. Objectives should be (1) specific and clear, (2) challenging, (3) agreed upon, (4) significant, (5) prioritized, (6) bound by time, (7) achievable, (8) fully communicated, (9) flexible, and (10) limited in number.
- Finally, the third step in the results approach involves determining performance standards. These are yardsticks designed to help people understand to

what extent the objective has been achieved. In creating standards, we must consider the dimensions of quality, quantity, and time. Good standards are (1) related to the position; (2) concrete, specific, and measurable; (3) practical to measure; (4) meaningful; (5) realistic and achievable; and (6) reviewed regularly.

- The first step in measuring performance adopting a behavior approach involves identifying competencies. Competencies are measurable clusters of KSAs that are critical in determining how results will be achieved. Examples of competencies are customer service, written or oral communication, creative thinking, and dependability.

- The second step in the behavior approach involves identifying indicators that will allow us to understand the extent to which each individual possesses the competency in question. These indicators are behavioral manifestations of the underlying (unobservable) competency.

- In describing a competency, one must first clearly define it, then describe behavioral indicators showing the presence of the competency, describe behavioral indicators showing the absence of the competency, and list suggestions for developing the competency.

- Once the indicators are identified, the third step in the behavior approach includes choosing an appropriate measurement system, either comparative or absolute.

- Comparative systems base the measurement on comparing employees with one other and include simple rank order, alternation rank order, paired comparisons, and forced distribution. Comparative systems are easy to explain and the resulting data are easy to interpret, which facilitates administrative decisions. On the other hand, employees are usually compared to one other in terms of one overall single category instead of in terms of specific behaviors or competencies. This produces less useful feedback that employees can use for their future improvement.

- Absolute systems include evaluations of employees' performance without making direct reference to other employees. Such systems include essays, behavior checklists, critical incidents, and graphic rating scales. Essays are difficult to quantify but produce useful and often detailed feedback. Behavior checklists are easy to use and understand but the scale points used are often arbitrary and we cannot assume that a 1-point difference has the same meaning along the entire scale (i.e., the difference between an employee who scores 5 and an employee who scores 4 may not have the same meaning as the difference between an employee who scores 3 and one who scores a 2). Critical incidents allow supervisors to focus on actual job behavior rather than on vaguely defined traits, but gathering critical incident data may be quite time-consuming. Graphic rating scales are arguably the most frequently used measurement method to assess performance. For this type of measurement to be most useful, the meaning of each response category should be clear, the individual interpreting the ratings (e.g., HR manager) should be able to tell clearly what response was intended, and the performance dimension being rated should be defined clearly for the rater.

Case Study 5.1 Accountabilities, Objectives, and Standards

Below is an actual job description for a sourcing and procurement internship position for Disney Consumer Products/Studios. Based on the information in the job description, create accountabilities, objectives, and standards for this position.

Title

Graduate Associate, Sourcing & Procurement (Disney Consumer Products/Studios) http://jobsearch.disneycareers.newjobs.com/

The Position

- Provide analytical support for sourcing projects impacting business units, specifically targeting Disney Consumer Products & Studios.
- Benchmark current pricing models and develop new approaches to pricing/buying various products and services that yield creative and business advantage.
- Support the continuing efforts to increase the percentage of spend influenced, specifically as it relates to Business Units where we have had only a minor impact.
- Assist in the development of: spend profiles, key stakeholder lists, savings opportunities where existing contracts are leveraged, savings opportunities in commodity areas that have not been sourced.
- Assist in developing overall Sourcing & Procurement strategy for partnering with business units, specifically targeting Disney Consumer Products & Studios.

The Company

The Walt Disney Company is a diversified, international family entertainment and media company with 2003 annual revenues of $27.1 billion. Its operations include theme parks and resorts, filmed entertainment, including motion pictures and television shows, home video and DVD products, records, broadcast and cable networks, Internet and direct marketing, consumer products, radio and television stations, theatrical productions, publishing activities, and professional sports enterprises.

The Ideal Candidate

- Ability to conceptualize issues and problems and develop hypotheses around appropriate responses.
- Intellectual curiosity and professional commitment to excellence.
- Superior analytical skills defined by an ability to identify and rearticulate critical aspects of a business situation from a large data pool (both qualitative and quantitative).
- Superior Microsoft Excel modeling skills.
- Strong written and verbal communication skills with the ability to build relationships.
- Ability to work independently.
- Demonstrated ability to manage multiple tasks, meanwhile retaining focus on project deliverables and strategic priorities.

The Opportunity

This will be an opportunity for an MBA intern to utilize project management skills he or she has learned in the classroom. The intern will be faced with difficult and/or skeptical clients and will learn how to work with them. They will have an opportunity to execute portions of the Sourcing methodology and work on teams. This will also be an opportunity for those individuals who have not experienced working in Corporate America, and for those that have had some experience, to further their learnings. The intern will gain experience from working in the Media and Entertainment industry. Through these various experiences, we hope the intern will find value in the internship we are offering. ∎

Case Study 5.2 Evaluating Objectives and Standards

Using the results from Case Study 5.1, use the accompanying checklist to evaluate each objective and standard you produced. For each objective and standard, use the first column in the checklist and place a check mark next to each of the ideal characteristics if the characteristic is present. Then, use the Comments column to provide a description of why or why not each objective and standard meets the ideal. Finally, review your tables and provide an overall assessment of the quality of the objectives and standards you created. ∎

Objectives must have the following characteristics:	Comments
Specific and clear	
Challenging	
Agreed upon	
Significant	
Prioritized	
Bound by time	
Achievable	
Fully communicated	
Flexible	
Limited in number	
Performance standards must have the following characteristics:	Comments
Related to the position	
Concrete, specific, and measurable	
Practical to measure	
Meaningful	
Realistic and achievable	
Reviewed regularly	

Case Study 5.3 Measuring Competencies at the Department of Transportation[1]

The Department of Transportation (DOT) of a large midwestern state uses core competencies to measure performance in its organization. Two of its core competencies on which all employees are measured are "organizational knowledge" and "learning and strategic systems thinking." Organizational knowledge is defined as follows: "Understands the DOT's culture. Accurately explains the DOT's organizational structure, major products/services, and how various parts of the organization contribute to one other. Gets work done through formal channels and informal networks. Understands and can explain the origin and reasoning behind key policies, practices, and procedures. Understands, accepts, and communicates political realities and implications." Learning and strategic systems think-

ing is defined as follows: "Accepts responsibility for continued improvement/learning. Appreciates and can explain the mission of each individual work unit and the importance of the time between them to make the entire operation whole. Acquires new skills and competencies and can explain how they benefit the DOT. Regularly takes all transportation forms (i.e., bicycle, light rail, highway, etc.) into accounting planning and problem solving. Seeks information and ideas from multiple sources. Freely and intentionally shares ideas with others."

Using the accompanying table as a guide, evaluate each of these two competencies and place a check mark next to each of the components of a good competency description if the component is present.

In describing a competency, the following components must be present:	
	Definition
	Description of specific behavioral indicators that can be observed when someone demonstrates a competency effectively
	Description of specific behaviors that are likely to occur when someone doesn't demonstrate a competency effectively (what a competency is not)
	List of suggestions for developing the competency in question

Next, using the organizational knowledge and learning and strategic systems thinking competencies create a 5-point graphic rating scale for each indicator using anchors of frequency, amount, agreement, or evaluation. ■

---

[1]Adapted from D. Grote, "Public Sector Organizations: Today's Innovative Leaders in Performance Management," *Public Personnel Management, 29*(Spring 2000): 1–20.

Case Study 5.4   Creating BARS-Based Graphic Rating Scales for Evaluating Business Student Performance in Team Projects

In many universities, students are required to conduct team projects. A description of these "job" duties is the following:

Work with team members to deliver project outcomes on time and according to specifications. Complete all individual assignments to the highest quality, completing necessary background research, making any mathematical analysis, and preparing final documents. Foster a good working environment.

Please do the following:
1. Generate a list of competencies for the position described.
2. Identify a list of critical behavioral indicators for each competency.
3. Generate critical incidents (high, average, and poor performance) for each behavioral indicator.
4. Create graphic rating scales using BARS to measure each competency. ∎

END NOTES

1. The following discussion of accountabilities, objectives, and standards is based on D. Grote. *The Complete Guide to Performance Appraisal* (New York: AMACOM, 1996), chap. 4.
2. Daley, D. M. (1991). Great expectations, or a tale of two systems: employee attitudes toward graphic rating scales and mbo-based performance appraisal. *Public Administration Quarterly, 15*, 188–209.
3. Adapted from D. Grote, *The Complete Guide to Performance Appraisal* (New York: AMACOM, 1996) 91–94.
4. Shaw, K. N. (2004). Changing the goal-setting process at Microsoft. *Academy of Management Executive, 18*, 139–142.
5. Adapted from D. L. Kirkpatrick, *How to Improve Performance Through Appraisal and Coaching* (New York: AMACOM, 1982) 35–36.
6. Kendra, K. A., & Taplin, L. J. (2004). Change agent competencies for information technology project managers. *Consulting Psychology Journal: Practice & Research, 56*, 20–34.
7. Judge, T. A., Piccolo, R. F., & Illies, R. I. (2004). The forgotten ones? The validity of consideration and initiating structure in leadership research. *Journal of Applied Psychology, 89*, 36–51.
8. Grote, D. (1996). *The complete guide to performance appraisal* (p. 118). New York: AMACOM.
9. The material that follows on comparative and absolute systems is based primarily on W. F., Cascio and H. Aguinis, *Applied Psychology in Human Resources Management*, 6th ed. (Upper Saddle River, NJ: Prentice Hall, 2005).
10. Siegel, L. (1982). Paired comparison evaluations of managerial effectiveness by peers and supervisors. *Personnel Psychology, 37*, 703–710.
11. Davis, P., & Rogers, B. (2003). Managing the "C" performer: An alternative to forced ranking of appraisals. Available online at http://www.workinfo.com/free/Downloads/150.htm. Retrival date: August 15, 2005.
12. Scullen, S. E., Bergey, P. K., & Aiman-Smith, L. (2005). Forced distribution rating systems and

the improvement of workforce potential: A baseline simulation. *Personnel Psychology, 58,* 1–32.

13. This table is based on B. M. Bass, W. F. Cascio, and E. J. O'Connor, "Magnitude Estimations of Expressions of Frequency and Amount," *Journal of Applied Psychology, 59*(1974): 313–320.

14. Bartol, K. M., Durham, C. C., & Poon, J. M. L. (2001). Influence of performance evaluation rating segmentation on motivation and fairness perceptions. *Journal of Applied Psychology, 86,* 1106–1119.

15. This table is based on P. Spector, "Choosing Response Categories for Summated Rating Scales," *Journal of Applied Psychology, 61* (1976): 374–375.

16. Hennessy, J., Mabey, B., & Warr, P. (1998). Assessment centre observation procedures: An experimental comparison of traditional, checklist and coding methods. *International Journal of Selection and Assessment, 6,* 222–231.

17. Pulakos, E. D., Arad, S., Donovan, M. A., & Plamondon, K. E. (2000). Adaptability in the workplace: Development of a taxonomy of adaptive performance. *Journal of Applied Psychology, 85,* 612–624.

18. Grote, D. (2000, Spring). Public sector organizations: Today's innovative leaders in performance management. *Public Personnel Management, 29,* 1–20.

19. Cocanougher, A. B., & Ivancevich, J. M. (1978). "BARS" performance rating for sales force personnel. *Journal of Marketing, 42,* 87–95.

20. Harrell, A., & Wright, A. (1990). Empirical evidence on the validity and reliability of Behaviorally Anchored Rating Scales for auditors. *Auditing, 9,* 134–149.

CHAPTER

Gathering Performance Information

Unless a reviewer has the courage to give you unqualified praise, I say ignore the bastard.

—JOHN STEINBECK

Learning Objectives

By the end of this chapter, you will be able to do the following:

■ Understand why each of several basic components are included in the appraisal form.

■ Design effective appraisal forms.

■ Compute an overall employee performance score based on information found on the appraisal form.

■ Select an appropriate time period to document performance as part of a performance review.

■ Determine how many formal meetings are needed between the subordinate and the supervisor to discuss performance issues.

■ Understand advantages and disadvantages of using supervisors, peers, subordinates, self, and customers as sources of performance information.

■ Know how to deal with potential disagreements involved with different sources evaluating the performance of the same employee.

■ Understand the psychological mechanisms leading to the inflation and deflation of performance ratings.

■ Understand that the implementation of training programs can address intentional and unintentional rating distortion.

 As discussed in Chapter 2, the performance management process includes several stages: prerequisites, performance planning, performance execution, performance assessment, performance review, and performance renewal and recontracting. An important component of the performance assessment stage is the use of appraisal forms. These forms are instruments used to document and evaluate performance. Chapters 4 and 5 provided a description of the various approaches and techniques that can be used to measure performance, but this chapter provides a more exhaustive description of the use of appraisal forms and their content. In addition, this chapter describes other issues related to the administration of appraisal forms, such as how often the supervisor and subordinate should meet to discuss performance issues and how to choose the source(s) of performance data (e.g., supervisors, self, subordinates, peers, or customers). The chapter concludes with a discussion of reasons why raters are likely, either intentionally or unintentionally, to distort performance ratings and what can be done to improve the accuracy of ratings.

6.1 APPRAISAL FORMS

At the core of any performance management system is the assessment of performance. Information on performance is collected using forms, which can be filled out on paper or electronically. One advantage of filling out forms electronically is that the information is stored and it can easily be shared, for example, between the manager filling out the form and the human resources (HR) department. Also, having the data available in electronic form can help in subsequent analyses, for example, in making comparisons of the relative average performance levels of various units within the organization.

Regardless of whether they are electronic or paper, appraisal forms usually include a combination of the following components.[1]

- *Basic employee information.*   This section of the form includes basic employee information such as job title, division, department and other work group information, employee number, and pay grade or salary classification. In addition, forms usually include the dates of the evaluation period, the number of months and years the rater has supervised or worked with the employee, an employee's starting date with the company, and starting date in the current job, the reason for appraisal, current salary and position in range, and the date of the next scheduled evaluation.

- *Accountabilities, objectives, and standards.*   If performance measurement adopts a results approach, this section of the form would include the name and description of each accountability, objectives agreed upon by manager and employee, and the extent to which the objectives have been achieved. In many instances, the objectives are weighted in terms of importance, which facilitates the calculation of an overall performance score. Finally, this section can also include a subsection describing conditions under which performance was achieved, which may help explain why performance achieved the (high or low) level described. For example, a supervisor may have the opportunity to describe specific circumstances surrounding performance during the review period, including a tough economy, the introduction of a new line of products, and so forth.

- *Competencies and indicators.*   If performance measurement adopts a behavior approach, this section of the form includes a definition of the various competencies to be assessed, together with their behavioral indicators.

- *Major achievements and contributions.* Some forms include a section in which a rater is asked to list the two or three major accomplishments of the individual being rated during the review period. These could refer to results, behaviors, or both.
- *Developmental achievements.* This section of the form includes information on the extent to which the developmental goals set for the review period have been achieved. This can include a summary of activities, such as workshops attended and courses taken as well as results, such as new skills learned. Evidence of having learned new skills can be documented, for example, by obtaining a professional certification. Although some organizations include developmental achievements in the appraisal form, others choose to include them in a separate form. Sun Microsystems is an example of an organization that separates these forms. Some organizations do not include development content as part of the appraisal form because it is often difficult for employees to focus constructively on development if they have received a less-than-ideal performance review.
- *Developmental needs, plans, and goals.* This section of the form is future oriented and includes information on specific goals and timetables in terms of employee development. As noted before, some organizations choose to create a separate development form and do not include this information as part of the performance appraisal form.
- *Stakeholder input.* Some forms include sections to be filled out by other stakeholders, such as customers with whom the employee interacts. Overall, stakeholders are defined as people who have first-hand knowledge of and are affected by the employee's performance. In most cases, input from other stakeholders is collected from them by using forms separate from the main appraisal because not all sources of performance information are in the position to rate the same performance dimensions. For example, an employee may be rated on the competency "teamwork" by peers and on the competency "reliability" by a customer. A more detailed discussion of the use of various sources of performance information is offered later in this chapter.
- *Employee comments.* This section includes reactions and comments provided by the employee being rated. In addition to allowing formal employee input, which improves the perceived fairness of the system, the inclusion of this section helps with legal issues because it documents that the employee has had an opportunity to participate in the evaluation process.
- *Signatures.* The final section of most forms includes a section in which the employee being rated, the rater, and the rater's supervisor provide their signatures to show they have seen and discussed the content of the form. The HR department may also provide approval of the content of the form.

Table 6.1 summarizes the major components of appraisal forms. Let's consider some examples to see which of these components are present in each.

TABLE 6.1	Major Components of Appraisal Forms

Basic employee information

Accountabilities, objectives, and standards

Competencies and indicators

Major achievements and contributions

Developmental achievements [could be included in a separate form]

Developmental needs, plans, and goals [could be included in a separate form]

Stakeholder input

Employee comments

Signatures

First, consider the form included in Figure 6.1. This is a generic form that can be used for almost any position in a company. Let's evaluate this form in relation to the components listed in Table 6.1. First, the form asks for the employee's basic information. Second, while the form asks the manager to list the expected versus the actual accountabilities, it does not include objectives or standards. Third, the form includes five competencies, but does not include a definition of those competencies nor does it list the indicators to look for to determine whether the employee has mastered the relevant competencies. The form

FIGURE 6.1	Basic Performance Review Form

Performance Review Form

Employee Name: _____

Title: _____

Manager: _____

Date of Appraisal Meeting: _____

Employee Performance Reviews improve employee performance and development by encouraging communication, establishing performance expectations, identifying developmental needs, and setting goals to improve performance. Performance reviews also provide an ongoing record of employee performance, which is helpful for both the supervisor and employee.

Use the form below to list examples of outstanding performance or achievements, as well as areas of performance that need improvement. Please provide open comments on your employee's performance. Complete each section and list examples of performance where applicable.

1. Job description/key responsibilities/required tasks:

_____

_____

_____

_____

2. Note expected accomplishments vs. actual accomplishments:

_____

_____

_____

_____

FIGURE 6.1   Continued

3. List the areas where the employee developed in ways enabling him or her to take on additional responsibilities or be eligible for high-profile assignments:

_____
_____
_____
_____

4. Areas of development for upcoming quarter (i.e., communication skills, teamwork, project management skills, budgeting experience, etc.):

_____
_____
_____
_____

5. Goals for upcoming quarter (Please list S.M.A.R.T. goals):

_____
_____
_____
_____

Please circle the number below that best describes the employee's performance in the following areas:

Areas of concentration	Did not meet expectations	Achieved most expectations	Achieved expectations	Achieved expectations and exceeded on a few	Significantly exceeded expectations
Teamwork	1	2	3	4	5
Leadership	1	2	3	4	5
Business acumen	1	2	3	4	5
Customer service	1	2	3	4	5
Project management	1	2	3	4	5

Average Performance Score	

Employee Use Only:
Please provide comments and examples of behaviors to describe your performance in the past quarter.

_____
_____
_____

| Manager Signature | Date | Employee Signature | Date |

does include space to list the major achievements, development needs, and employee comments. However, the form does not solicit information from all relevant stakeholders. In short, the following table summarizes which of the components are present:

	Major Components of Appraisal Forms: Evaluation of Form in Figure 6.1
X	Basic employee information
	Accountabilities, objectives, and standards
	Competencies and indicators
X	Major achievements and contributions
X	Developmental achievements
X	Developmental needs, plans, and goals
	Stakeholder input
X	Employee comments
X	Signatures

As a second example, consider the form included in Figure 6.2. Similar to the form in Figure 6.1, this form has a section for basic employee information, developmental areas, goals, and employee comments. This form does not include

FIGURE 6.2 Employee Performance Appraisal Form

Employee Performance Appraisal

Employee Name: _____

Department: _____

Date of Hire: _____

Date of Performance Review: _____

Ratings: Please rate the employee on the following factors:

	Did not meet expectations	Achieved most expectations	Achieved expectations	Achieved expectations and exceeded on a few	Significantly exceeded expectations
Flexibility	1	2	3	4	5
Teamwork	1	2	3	4	5
Oral communication	1	2	3	4	5
Written communication	1	2	3	4	5
Initiative	1	2	3	4	5
Decision making	1	2	3	4	5
Job knowledge	1	2	3	4	5
Quality work	1	2	3	4	5
Productivity	1	2	3	4	5
				Total Points:	

FIGURE 6.2   Continued

Level of Performance	Description of Performance	Increase
Unsatisfactory (0–15 pts)	Did not meet the responsibilities associated with position. Place on personal improvement performance plan.	NA
Needs improvement (16–31 pts)	Met main responsibilities, but did not fulfill all responsibilities. Inconsistent level of performance across tasks.	1–2%
Fulfills responsibilities (32–37 pts)	Fulfilled all key responsibilities. Consistently performs to established work standards.	3–4%
Exceeds responsibilities (38–48 pts)	Fulfilled key responsibilities, and took on more and completed additional responsibilities. Consistently a high performer.	4–5%
Far exceedsresponsibilities (49–55 pts)	Far exceeded the job responsibilities in all areas and took charge of major projects. Consistent high performer and expert at position.	5–6%

Note: Percentage increases listed are to be used as a guideline.

Employee strengths/areas of expertise:

_____

_____

_____

_____

Developmental areas:

_____

_____

_____

_____

Goals for upcoming year in relation to job responsibilities and developmental areas:

_____

_____

_____

_____

Employee comments (optional):

_____

_____

_____

_____

Employee:_____   Date:_____

Reviewer:_____   Date:_____

a list of the employee's accountabilities, objectives, and standards. The competencies needed for the position are listed, but not the behavioral indicators to look for to evaluate the presence of the competency. Furthermore, unlike the form in Figure 6.1, the employee's developmental and major achievements are not acknowledged and stakeholders are not asked for their input. In short, the following components are present:

Major Components of Appraisal Forms: Evaluation of Form in Figure 6.2	
X	Basic employee information
	Accountabilities, objectives, and standards
	Competencies and indicators
	Major achievements and contributions
	Developmental achievements
X	Developmental needs, plans, and goals
	Stakeholder input
X	Employee comments
X	Signatures

This analysis shows that although the forms included in Figures 6.1 and 6.2 seem to be quite complete and thorough, they are not. Thus, before implementing appraisal forms, check that all their necessary components are present.

6.2 CHARACTERISTICS OF APPRAISAL FORMS

We should be aware that there is no such thing as a universally correct appraisal form. In some cases, a form may emphasize competencies and ignore results. This would be the case if the system adopts a behavior as opposed to results approach to measuring performance. In others, the form may emphasize developmental issues and minimize, or even completely ignore, both behaviors and results. In such cases, the form would be used for developmental purposes only and not for administrative purposes. One size does not fit all and different components are appropriate based on the purposes of the appraisal.

In spite of the large variability in terms of format and components, there are certain desirable features that make appraisal forms particularly effective:

- *Simplicity.* Forms must be easy to understand, easy to administer, quick to complete, clear, and concise. If forms are too long, convoluted, and complicated, it is likely that the performance assessment process will not be effective.
- *Relevancy.* Good forms include information related directly to the tasks and responsibilities of the job. Otherwise, they will be seen as an administrative burden and not a tool for performance improvement.

- *Descriptiveness.*   Good forms require that the raters provide evidence of performance regardless of the performance level. The form should be sufficiently descriptive that an outside party (e.g., supervisor's supervisor or HR department) has a clear understanding of the performance information conveyed.
- *Adaptability.*   Good forms allow managers in different functions and departments to adapt them to their particular needs and situations. This feature encourages widespread use of the form.
- *Comprehensiveness.*   Good forms include all the major areas of performance for a particular position for the entire review period.
- *Definitional clarity.*   Desirable competencies and results are clearly defined for all raters so that everyone evaluates the same attributes. This feature enhances consistency of ratings across raters and levels of the organization.
- *Communication.*   The meaning of each of the components of the form must be successfully communicated to all people participating in the evaluation process. This enhances acceptance of the system and motivation to participate in it both as rater and ratee.
- *Time Orientation.*   Good forms help clarify expectations about performance. They address not only the past but also the future.[2]

Table 6.2 includes a summary of features that are desirable in all forms regardless of specific content and format. Let's consider the two illustrative forms discussed earlier to see how they fare in relation to these desirable features. First, consider the form shown in Figure 6.1. It is simple because it is easy to understand and clear. The fact that it includes an essay format implies that it would take a little more time to complete, but the number of essays is kept to a minimum. The form is also relevant, but only if the supervisor enters the correct job description and actual accountabilities. This form can be extremely descriptive due to its narrative nature. The form encourages the manager to give examples of relevant behavior. Next, the form is also adaptable, perhaps too adaptable; it would be hard to compare performance across employees because the manager can adapt the form to each employee. This form is comprehensive, but again only if the manager lists all of the expected accountabilities. This form does not have definition clarity. The competencies listed are not clearly defined, so ratings are likely to be inconsistent across raters. Next, this form can be communicated across the organization. Manager acceptance may be hard to gain, because of the amount of detail that the essay answers require. Finally, the form is time oriented. It asks for past and

TABLE 6.2   Desirable Features of All Appraisal Forms

Simplicity

Relevancy

Descriptiveness

Adaptability

Comprehensiveness

Clarity

Communication

Time orientation

future performance expectations and goals. In short, the following table summarizes which of the desirable characteristics are present in this form:

Desirable Features of All Appraisal Forms: Evaluation of Form in Figure 6.1	
X	Simplicity
X	Relevancy
X	Descriptiveness
X	Adaptability
X	Comprehensiveness
	Definitional clarity
X	Communication
X	Time orientation

Next, let's evaluate the form shown in Figure 6.2 in relation to the desirable features listed in Table 6.2. First, it is simple because it is easy to administer, quick to complete, clear, and concise. This form is easier to administer than the form in Figure 6.1 because it does not include an essay format. However, it scores low on the relevance dimension because it does not enumerate and specify the employee's tasks and responsibilities of the job. Third, this form is not descriptive. While the different levels of performance are described, the actual expectations of the individual employees are not clear. Fourth, the form is only somewhat adaptable. The beginning ratings regarding the competencies are exact, but the second half of the form can be adapted to each employee. This form is not comprehensive, because it does not include all the major components that indicate performance for a particular position for the entire review period. This form does not provide definitional clarity, because the competencies that are listed are not defined and there is no mention of the employee's key responsibilities. Each of the levels of performance are explained well, but they are not tailored to each individual employee. Next, the form could not be communicated throughout the organization. Since the competencies are not defined, it would be hard to explain the process to all stakeholders. Finally, the form makes no mention of time, so it does not focus on past or future expectations. In sum,

Desirable Features of All Appraisal Forms: Evaluation of Form in Figure 6.2	
X	Simplicity
	Relevancy
	Descriptiveness
X	Adaptability
	Comprehensiveness
	Definitional clarity
	Communication
	Time orientation

Many organizations use forms very similar to those presented in Figure 6.1 and 6.2. However, a careful analysis of these forms against the desired features indicates that the forms, particularly the one shown in Figure 6.2, could be improved substantially. An important point to consider regarding these and other forms is that they should include the critical components discussed here because such forms help organizations implement a performance-focused culture. An exclusive emphasis on the appraisal form should be avoided; it is just one component of the performance management system.

6.3 DETERMINING OVERALL RATING

Once the form is completed, there is usually a need to compute an overall performance score. This is particularly necessary for making administrative decisions such as the allocation of rewards. Computing overall performance scores is also useful to measure if employees, and groups of employees, are improving their performance over time.

There are two main strategies to obtain an overall performance score for each employee: judgmental and mechanical. The judgmental procedure consists of the consideration of every aspect of performance and then arriving at a defensible summary. This is basically a holistic procedure that relies on the ability of the rater to arrive at a fair and accurate overall score. The mechanical procedure consists of first considering the scores assigned to each section of the appraisal form and then adding them up to obtain an overall score. When adding scores from each section, weights are typically used based on the relative importance of each performance dimension measured.

Consider the performance evaluation form in Figure 6.3, which is used to evaluate the performance of sales associates at a supermarket chain.[3] This form includes the

FIGURE 6.3   Performance Appraisal Form Used by Grocery Retailer

Performance Appraisal Form Used by Grocery Retailer

Performance Evaluation Form
For use by Store Director; Co-Director; Meat, Seafood, Produce, Deli/Bakery, Floral and Grocery Managers

Name	Anthony Carmello	Review Period	2004
Position	Sales Associate	Store	#25
Evaluator	James LeBrown	Date	12/15/04

Competencies: Please rate the Associate on the following competencies. Determine the point total and multiply by the weight factor to achieve the point total for the competencies.

				1st	2nd	Wgt	Pts	Pts
Follow-Through/Dependability			Points:	4	3	0.7	2.8	2.1
4	3	2	1					
Work is completed correctly and on time without supervision. Anticipates needs. Extremely organized.	Work is usually completed correctly and on a timely basis with some supervision. Very organized.	Work is completed asassigned andresults can usually be relied upon with normal supervision. Organized.	Work can seldom be relied upon. Often fails to complete tasks correctly. Unorganized.					
Comments:								

FIGURE 6.3 Continued

Decision Making/Creative Problem Solving	Points:	1st	2nd	Wgt	Pts	Pts
		3	2	0.3	.9	.6

4	3	2	1
Anticipates, recognizes, and confronts problems with extraordinary skill. Perseveres until solution is reached. Extremely innovative and takes risks.	Defines and addresses problems well. Typically reaches useful solutions and decisions are sound. Innovative, with above-average risk taking.	Acknowledges and attempts to solve most problems when presented. Usually comes to conclusions on solving basic issues. Little innovation and sometimes takes risks.	Has difficulty recognizing problems and making decisions. Always needs guidance. No innovation and never takes risks.

Comments:

Total Score for Competencies Section	3.7	2.7

Key Results: Rate each area to the performance demonstrated in the achievement of budgeted numbers.

KR #1: Achieved Budgeted Sales (U.S. dollars)

	Budgeted	Actual	% of achievement (1, 2, 3, 4)	
1st half objective	$78,000	$77,000	2	Wgt 0.6
2nd half objective	$80,000	$83,000	3	Pts

4 = 108%+   3 = 107-103%   2 = 102-98%   1 = Below 97%

1.2	1.8

Comments:

KR #2: Margin Balance (gain/loss in U.S. dollars)

	Budgeted	Actual	% of achievement (1, 2, 3, 4)	
1st half objective	$30,000	$29,000	1	Wgt 0.4
2nd half objective	$31,000	$34,000	4	Pts

4 = 108%+   3 = 107-103%   2 = 102-98%   1 = Below 97%

.4	1.6

Comments:

FIGURE 6.3   Continued

TOTAL SCORE FOR KEY RESULTS:							1.6	3.4
	Comp. Score 1st half	Comp. Score 2nd half	KR Score 1st half	KR Score 2nd half			Subtotal	
Circle Rating:	3.7	2.7	1.6	3.4			11.4/4 = 2.85	
Excellent	**Above**	Average	Unsatisfactory					
3.6 – 4.0	**2.6 – 3.5**	1.6 – 2.5	1 – 1.5					
Associate						Date		
Store Director						Date		

hypothetical ratings obtained by a sales associate on just two competencies and just two key results (the complete form is likely to include more than just four performance dimensions). You can see that, in the Competencies section, each competency is weighted according to its value to the organization. Specifically, Follow-Through/Dependability is given a weight of .7 whereas Decision Making/Creative Problem Solving is given a weight of .3. So, for the competency Follow-Through/Dependability, Anthony Carmello obtained a score of 4 for the first half of the review period and a score of 3 for the second half of the review period. Consequently, the scores for this competency are $4 \times .7 = 2.8$ for the first half and $3 \times .7 = 2.1$ for the second half of the review period. Adding up the scores obtained for the first and second half in each competency leads to a total of 3.7 points for the first half and 2.7 for the second half of the review period.

The form also indicates that the key results have different weights. Specifically, KR #1 has a weight of .6 whereas KR #2 has a weight of .4. Consider KR #1. The objective for the first half was to achieve a sales figure of $78,000. The actual sales figure achieved by Carmello was $77,000, representing a 98.71% achievement, which is a score of 2. Multiplying this score times the weight of .6 yields 1.2 points for the first half of the review period. Similarly, for the second half, the goal was $80,000 and Carmello surpassed it by achieving a figure of $83,000, which represents a score of 3 (i.e., 103.75% achievement). Therefore, the score for the second half is $3 \times .6 = 1.8$. Finally, the form shows that the total score for the first half for all key results combined is 1.6, whereas the score for the second half is 3.4. These scores were computed by simply adding the scores obtained in each half.

Finally, the form shows the scores obtained for the competencies and the key results in each of the two halves of the review period. To obtain the overall performance score, we simply take an average of these four numbers: $(3.7 + 2.7 + 1/6 + 3.4)/4 = 2.85$. This puts Carmello in the 2.6 to 3.5 range, which represents a qualification of "above average."

Now, suppose that we do not follow a mechanical procedure to compute overall performance score and instead we use a judgmental method. That is, suppose raters have no information on weights. How would James LeBrown, Carmello's supervisor, compute the overall performance score? One possibility is that he may give equal weights to all competencies and would therefore consider that Follow-Through/Dependability is as important as Decision Making/Creative Problem Solving. This would lead to different scores compared to using weights of .7 and .3. Or, as an alternative, the supervisor may have his own ideas about what performance dimensions should be given more weight and decide to ignore how the work is done (i.e., behaviors) and instead assign an overall score based primarily on the key results (i.e., sales and margin balance).

The use of weights allows the supervisor to come to an objective and clear overall performance score for each employee. As this example illustrates, the use of clearly specified weights allows the supervisor to come to a verifiable score for each employee. Thus, the supervisor and the employees can be sure that the overall performance rating is reflective of the employee's performance in each category.

Which strategy is best, judgmental or mechanical? In most cases, the mechanical method is superior to the judgmental method.[4] A supervisor is more likely to introduce her own biases in computing the overall performance score when no clear rules exist regarding the relative importance of the various performance dimensions and there is no direction on how to combine the various performance dimensions in calculating the overall score.[5] As far as the computation of overall scores goes, the mechanical method is superior to the judgmental method.

6.4 APPRAISAL PERIOD AND NUMBER OF MEETINGS

How long should the appraisal period be? In other words, what period of time should be included in the appraisal form? Organizations with a performance management system typically conduct an annual review. However, others choose to conduct semiannual or even quarterly formal reviews. Conducting an annual review only may not provide sufficient opportunity for the supervisor and subordinate to discuss performance issues in a formal setting. The recommendation then is to conduct semiannual or quarterly reviews. For example, Colorado-based Hamilton Standard Commercial Aircraft uses a semiannual review system.[6] Twice a year, the company performs a modified 360-degree appraisal, meaning that performance information is collected from several sources. This type of system allows individuals to receive feedback and adjust goals or objectives if necessary in preparation for the more in-depth annual review. An example of a company implementing quarterly reviews is Synygy, Inc., a Philadelphia-based compensation software and services company.[7] Each quarter employees receive a summary of comments and specific examples from coworkers on how they are performing. Synygy states that the goal of the system is to encourage open communication. Employees are trained to write effective comments to their coworkers that will facilitate growth by pointing out positive and negative areas of performance. In areas that need improvement, coworkers are encouraged to suggest ways that an employee could improve his or her performance.

When is the best time to complete the reviews? Most organizations adopt one of two possibilities. First, the appraisal form could be completed on or around the annual anniversary date. In the case of semiannual reviews, the first review would be six months before the annual anniversary date and the second review would be on or around the anniversary date. The biggest advantage of this choice is that the supervisor does not have to fill out all forms at one time. However, the disadvantage of this choice is that, because results are not tied to a common cycle for all employees, resulting rewards cannot be tied to the fiscal year.

The second choice is to complete the appraisal forms toward the end of the fiscal year. In the case of a system including semiannual reviews, one review would be completed halfway through the fiscal year and the other one toward the end of the fiscal year. Adopting this approach leads to the completion of the appraisal form for all employees at about the same time, which facilitates cross-employee comparisons as well as the distribution of rewards. An additional advantage of following the fiscal year cycle is that individual goal setting can be more easily tied to corporate goal setting because most companies align their goal cycle with their fiscal year. This helps employees synchronize their work and objectives with those of their unit and organization. But what about the additional work imposed on the supervisors who need to evaluate all employees at once during a short period of time? This can be a major problem if the performance management system is not implemented using the best practices described in this book and performance appraisal is a once-a-year event. If there is ongoing communication between the supervisor and the employee about performance issues throughout the year, completing appraisal forms should not uncover any major surprises and filling out the appraisal form should not create a major time burden for the supervisors.

Performance management systems can include six formal meetings between the subordinate and the supervisor:[8]

- system inauguration
- self-appraisal
- classical performance review
- merit/salary review
- development plan
- objective setting

Recall that informal performance discussions take place throughout the year. In addition, however, there should be regularly scheduled formal meetings for the specific purpose of discussing the various aspects of performance and the performance management system. The fact that the supervisor allocates time to this activity sends a message that performance management is important.

The first meeting is the system inauguration and includes a discussion of how the system works and the identification of the requirements and responsibilities resting primarily on the employee and on the supervisor. This discussion includes the role of the self-appraisal and the dates when the employee and supervisor will meet formally to discuss performance issues. This meeting is particularly important for new employees, who should be introduced to the performance management system as soon as they become members of the organization.

The second meeting is the self-appraisal, and involves the employee's assessment of herself. This meeting is informational in nature and, at this point, the supervisor does not pass judgment on how the employee sees her own performance. This meeting provides an opportunity for the employee to describe how she sees her own performance during the review period. It is helpful if the employee is given the same form to be filled out later by the supervisor so that she can provide self-ratings using the same dimensions to be used by the supervisor.

The third meeting is the classical performance review meeting, during which employee performance is discussed, including both the perspective of the supervisor as well as that of the employee. Most performance management systems include this type of meeting only. No other formal meetings to discuss performance are usually scheduled. This meeting is mainly past oriented and typically does not focus on what performance should look like in the future.

The fourth meeting, the merit/salary review, discusses what, if any, compensation changes will result as a consequence of the period's performance. It is useful to separate the discussion of rewards from the discussion of performance so that the employee can focus on performance first and then on rewards. If these meetings are not separated, employees may not be very attentive during the discussion of performance and are likely to feel it is merely the price they must pay to move on to the part of the meeting that really matters: the discussion about rewards. Although these meetings are separate, supervisors should explain clearly the link between the employee's performance, discussed in detail in a previous meeting, and the rewards given. Rewards are not likely to carry their true weight if they are not linked directly to performance.

The fifth meeting, the development plan, discusses the employee's developmental needs and what steps will be taken so that performance will be improved during the following period. This meeting also includes information on what types of resources will be provided to the employee to facilitate the development of any required new skills.

The sixth and final meeting includes setting goals, both behavioral and result oriented, regarding the following review period. At this point, the employee has received very clear feedback about her performance during the past review period, knows what rewards will be allocated (if any), understands developmental needs and goals, and knows about resources available to help in the process of acquiring any required skills.

Although these six meetings are possible, not all six take place separately. For example, the self-appraisal, classical performance review, merit/salary review, developmental plan, and objective setting meetings may all take place during one umbrella meeting. However, it is best to separate the various types of information discussed so that the employee and supervisor focus on each of the components separately.

Take the case of Johnsonville Foods (www.johnsonville.com), a sausage-making plant in Wisconsin. Johnsonville Foods has a performance management system that includes the following meetings: self-appraisal, classical performance review, merit/salary review, development plan, and objective setting.[9] Team members (i.e., employees) and coaches (i.e., supervisors) write six-month contracts stating their goals for the following six months and how they plan to meet those goals (objective setting). This contract also has the employee state developmental goals for the upcoming six months (developmental plan). Some of these goals may include reading a book on leadership or learning a new computer software program. In addition, each month the employee writes up a contract with his goals for the month. That contract is posted on the company electronic bulletin board and sent to three internal customers, who evaluate that employee's performance over the month. The next month, employees and their coaches discuss how the goals were met (classical performance review) and how much bonus the employee should receive (merit/salary review), and set new goals for the upcoming month (objective setting). If the employee does not expect to meet his goals, then there is a meeting scheduled halfway through the month to discuss options.

In short, Johnsonville Foods includes all the formal meetings that can take place in a performance management system. However, it doesn't actually have six separate meetings. Instead, the company has only two formally scheduled meetings, but the system allows for the addition of more meetings if the need arises.

6.5 WHO SHOULD PROVIDE PERFORMANCE INFORMATION?

So far, we have assumed that the supervisor is the primary source for performance information. This is the case in most organizations because the supervisor observes employees directly and has good knowledge about performance standards. However, in addition to the direct supervisor, there are alternative sources of performance information. Let's consider the use of the direct supervisor as a source of performance information, followed by the use of other sources including peers, subordinates, self, and customers.[10]

6.5.1 Supervisors

An advantage of using supervisors as a source of performance information is that they are usually in the best position to evaluate performance in relation to strategic organizational goals. Supervisors are often those making decisions about rewards associated with performance evaluation. Therefore, supervisors are often the most important source of performance information and are usually in charge of managing employee performance.

Although supervisors are usually the most important, and sometimes only, source of performance, other sources should be considered as well. For example, we have already seen that self-appraisals are an important component in the performance review process. In addition to self-appraisals and supervisor appraisals, performance information can be collected from peers, customers, and subordinates (assuming there are any). Alternative sources are usually considered, because for some jobs, such as teaching, law enforcement, or sales, the supervisor may not observe her subordinates' performance on a regular basis. Also, performance evaluations given by the supervisor may be biased because the supervisor may evaluate performance based on whether the ratee is contributing to goals valued by the supervisor as opposed to goals valued by the organization as a whole.[11] For example, a supervisor may provide high performance ratings to employees who help the supervisor advance his career aspirations within the company, as opposed to those who engage in behaviors conducive to helping achieve organizational strategic goals.

6.5.2 Peers

Many organizations use performance evaluations provided by peers. Take, for example, the system implemented at a large international financial services bank.[12] Through acquisitions, the bank has been growing rapidly and has as its strategic goal the consolidation on of its offices. Change management is extremely important to the successful implementation of this consolidation. Therefore, the company is revising how it is assessing the competency "teamwork" at the senior and middle management levels, with the belief that successful teamwork is crucial to change management initiatives. Specifically, one-third of the score for this competency is determined by ratings provided by peers.

Peer evaluations suffer from two problems, however. First, such evaluations may not be readily accepted when employees believe there is friendship bias at work. In other words, if an employee believes that ratings provided by his peers will be lower than those provided for another employee because the other employee has more friends than he does, then performance evaluations will not be taken seriously. It is not likely that the employee will use the feedback received to improve his performance. The second problem with peer evaluations is that peers are less discriminating among performance dimensions than are to supervisors. In other words, if one is rated high on one dimension, one is also likely to be rated high on all the other dimensions, even though the performance dimensions rated may not be related to one other and may require very different knowledge, skills, and abilities.

Given these weaknesses of peer evaluations, it would not be wise to use them as the sole source of performance information. Peer evaluations can be part of the system, but information should also be obtained from other sources, including the supervisor.

6.5.3 Subordinates

Subordinates are good source of information regarding the performance of their managers.[13] For example, subordinates are in a good position to evaluate leadership competencies, including delegation, organization, and communication. In addition, subordinates may be asked to rate their managers' ability to (1) remove barriers that employees face, (2) shield employees from politics, and (3) raise employees' competence. Note that when implementing this type of system, subordinates may feel hesitant to provide upward feedback if put on the spot. However, if managers take the time to involve employees in the process by soliciting their input, employees are more likely to give honest feedback.[14]

Many organizations take upward feedback very seriously. Take the case of computer giant Dell., which employs over 55,000 individuals worldwide. In 1984 Michael Dell founded Dell based on the simple concept of selling computer systems directly to customers. In 2004, *Fortune* magazine ranked Dell the number 1 most admired company in the United States.[15] At Dell, all employees rate their supervisors, including Michael Dell himself, every six months, using "Tell Dell" surveys. Michael Dell said, "If you are a manager and you're not addressing [employee] issues, you're not going to get compensation. And if you consistently score in the bottom rungs of the surveys, we're going to look at you and say 'Maybe this isn't the right job for you.'"[16]

The intended purpose of the evaluation provided by subordinates has an impact on the accuracy of the information provided. Overall, performance information provided by subordinates is more accurate when the resulting ratings are to be used for developmental purposes rather than administrative purposes. When evaluation data are intended for administrative purposes (i.e., whether the manager should be promoted), subordinates are likely to inflate their ratings.[17] Most likely, this is because subordinates may fear retaliation if they provide low performance scores. So, confidentiality is key if subordinates are to be used as a source of performance information.

6.5.4 Self

As discussed earlier, self-appraisals are an important component of any performance management system. When employees are given the opportunity to participate in the performance management process, their acceptance of the resulting decision is likely to increase and their defensiveness during the appraisal interview is likely to decrease. An additional advantage associated with self-appraisals is that the employee is in a good position to keep track of activities during the review period, whereas a supervisor may have to keep track of the performance of several employees. On the other hand, self-appraisals should not be used as the sole source of information in making administrative decisions because they are more lenient and biased than are ratings provided by other sources, such as a direct supervisor.[18] This may explain why the vast majority of Fortune 500 companies do not include self-appraisals as part of their performance management systems.[19] Fortunately, self-ratings tend to be less lenient when they are used for developmental as opposed to administrative purposes. In addition, the following suggestions also improve the quality of self-appraisals:

- *Use comparative as opposed to absolute measurement systems.*   For example, instead of asking individuals to rate themselves using a scale ranging from "poor" to "excellent," provide a relative scale that allows them to compare their performance with that of others (e.g., "below average," "average," "above average"). Other options in terms of comparative systems were discussed in Chapter 5.
- *Allow employees to practice their self-rating skills.*   Provide multiple opportunities for self-appraisal, because the skill of self-evaluation may well be one that improves with practice.
- *Assure confidentiality.*   Provide reassurance that performance information collected from oneself will not be disseminated and shared with others besides the direct supervisor and other relevant parties (e.g., members of the same work group).
- *Emphasize the future.*   The developmental plan section of the form should receive substantial attention. The employee should indicate his plans for future development and accomplishments.

6.5.5 Customers

Customers provide yet another source of performance information. Collecting information from customers can be a costly and time-consuming process. However, performance information provided by customers is particularly useful for jobs that require a high degree of interaction with the public or with particular job-related individuals (e.g., purchasing managers, suppliers, sales representatives). Also, performance information can be collected from *internal* customers. For example, line managers may provide information regarding the performance of their HR representative. While the clients served may not have full knowledge of the organization's strategic direction, they can provide useful information. For example, consider how this is done at Federal Express (http://www.fedex.com/). Federal Express recently revised its performance management system to include measures of customer service.[20] Currently, the comany uses a six-item customer-satisfaction survey, which is evaluated by a representative sample of the employee's customers at the end of the year. As a result of adding customer input and customer-developed goals into the performance review process, employees are more focused on meeting customer expectations.

Although Federal Express is now considering external customer input in evaluating performance, organizations in other industries have some catch-up to do. For example, a recent study examining appraisal forms used to evaluate the performance of account executives in the largest advertising agencies in the United States found that there is much more emphasis on internal than on external customers.[21] Specifically, external client feedback was measured in only 12% of the agencies studied. About 27% of agencies do not evaluate the contributions that account executives make to client relationships and to growing the client's business. In short, advertising agencies might benefit from assessing the performance of account executives from the perspective of not only internal but also external customers.

6.5.6 Disagreement Across Sources: Is This a Problem?

If performance information is collected from more than one source, it is likely that there will be some overlap in the dimensions measured.[22] For example, a manager's peers and direct supervisor may rate him on the competency "communication." But in addition to the overlapping dimensions across sources, each source is likely to evaluate performance dimensions that are unique to each source. For example, subordinates may evaluate "delegation," but this competency may not be included on the form used by the direct supervisor. Once the competencies and results that need to be measured are identified for a particular position, a decision needs to be made regarding which source of information will be used to assess each dimension. Of course, it is likely that there will be some overlap and some dimensions will be rated by more than one source. Regardless of the final decision, it is important that employees take an active role in deciding which sources will rate which dimensions. Active participation in the process is likely to enhance acceptance of results and perceptions that the system is fair.

When the same dimension is evaluated across sources, we should not necessarily expect ratings to be similar.[23] Different sources disagreeing about an employee's performance is not necessarily a problem. Those rating the same employee may be drawn from different organizational levels, and they probably observe different facets of the employee's performance, even if they are evaluating the same general competency (e.g., "communication"). In fact, the behavioral indicators for the same competency may vary across sources. For example, an employee may be able to communicate very well with his superior, and not very well with his subordinates. The important issue to take into account is that, for each source, the behaviors and results to be rated must be defined clearly so that biases are minimized. In terms of feedback, however, there is no need to come up with one overall conclusion regarding the employee's performance. On the contrary, it is important that the employee receive information on how her performance was rated by each of the sources used. This is the crux of what are called 360-degree feedback systems, which are discussed in more detail in Chapter 8. When feedback is broken down by source, the employee can place particular attention and effort in the interactions involving the source that has detected performance deficiencies.

If disagreements are found, a decision must be made regarding the relative importance of the rating provided by each source. For example, is it equally important to please external and internal customers? Is communication an equally important competency regarding subordinates and peers? Answering these questions can lead to assigning differential weights to the scores provided by the different sources in computing the overall performance score used for administrative purposes.

6.6 A MODEL OF RATER MOTIVATION

Regardless of who rates performance, the rater is likely to be affected by biases that distort the resulting ratings. Performance ratings may be intentionally or unintentionally distorted or inaccurate. When this happens, incorrect decisions may be made, employees are likely to feel they are treated unfairly, and the organization is more prone to litigation. In other words, when performance ratings are distorted, the performance management system not only would not result in desired outcomes, but it is likely to lead to very negative consequences for the organization. To prevent these negative outcomes, we need to understand why raters are likely to provide distorted ratings. A useful model to understand the rater's motivation to provide accurate performance information is shown in Figure 6.4.

Figure 6.4 shows that rating behaviors are influenced by (1) the motivation to provide accurate ratings and (2) the motivation to distort ratings. The motivation to provide accurate ratings is determined by whether the rater expects positive and negative consequences of accurate ratings and by whether the probability of receiving these rewards and punishments will be high if accurate ratings are provided. Similarly, the motivation to distort ratings is determined by whether the rater expects any positive and negative consequences of rating distortion and by the probability of experiencing such consequences if ratings are indeed distorted. Consider a supervisor and his motivation to provide

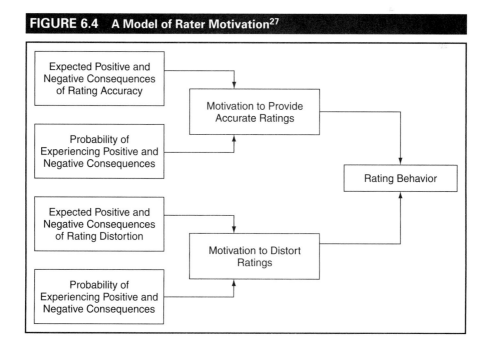

FIGURE 6.4   A Model of Rater Motivation[27]

accurate ratings. What will the supervisor gain if ratings are accurate? What will he lose? Will his own performance be rated higher and will he receive any rewards if this happens? Or will the relationship with his subordinates suffer? The answers to these questions provide information on whether this supervisor is likely to be motivated to provide accurate ratings. Similarly, are there any positive and negative consequences associated with rating distortion? What is the probability that this will indeed happen? The answers to these questions will determine the supervisor's motivation to distort ratings.

Figure 6.4 shows that there are motivational barriers that prevent raters from providing accurate performance information. Raters may be motivated to distort performance information and provide inflated or deflated ratings.[24] For example, a supervisor may be motivated to provide inflated ratings to:

- *Maximize the merit raise/rewards.*   A supervisor may want to produce the highest possible reward for his employees and he knows this will happen if he provides the highest possible performance ratings.
- *Encourage employees.*   A supervisor may believe that employees' motivation will be increased if they receive high performance ratings.
- *Avoid creating a written record.*   A supervisor may not want to leave a "paper trail" regarding an employee's poor performance because such documentation may eventually lead to negative consequences for the employee in question. This situation is likely if the supervisor and employee have developed a friendship.
- *Avoid confrontation with employees.*   A supervisor may feel uncomfortable providing negative feedback and, in order to avoid a possible confrontation with the employee, may decide to take the path of least resistance and give inflated performance ratings.
- *Promote undesired employees out of unit.*   A supervisor may believe that if an employee receives very high ratings she may be promoted out of the unit. In the view of the supervisor, this may be an effective way to get rid of undesired employees.
- *Make the manager look good to his/her supervisor.*   A supervisor may believe that if everyone receives very high performance ratings, the supervisor will be seen as an effective unit leader.

Once again, let's return to Figure 6.4. We can understand each of the reasons for a supervisor's choosing to inflate ratings using this model. For example, looking good in the eyes of one's own supervisor can be seen as a positive consequence of providing inflated ratings. Avoiding a possible confrontation with an employee can also be seen as a positive consequence of providing inflated ratings. Thus, given these anticipated positive consequences of rating inflation, the supervisor may choose to provide distorted ratings.

Supervisors may also be motivated to provide ratings that are artificially deflated. Some reasons for this are to:

- *Shock employees.*   A supervisor may believe that giving an employee a "shock treatment" and providing deflated performance ratings is a jolt to the employee, emphasizing that there is a problem.
- *Teach a rebellious employee a lesson.*   A supervisor may wish to punish an employee or force an employee to cooperate with the supervisor and so believes that the best way to do so is to provide deflated performance ratings.

- *Send a message to the employee that he should consider leaving.* A supervisor lacking communication skills may wish to convey the idea that an employee should leave the unit or organization. Providing deflated performance ratings can be seen as a way to communicate this message.
- *Build a strongly documented, written record of poor performance.* A supervisor may wish to get rid of a particular employee and so decides that the best way to do so is to create a paper trail of substandard performance.

We can also understand the psychological mechanisms underlying the decision to provide deflated ratings. Let's return to Figure 6.4. For example, if shocking employees and building strongly documented records about employees are seen as positive consequences of rating deflation, it is likely that the supervisor will choose to provide distorted ratings.

Fundamentally, this discussion should allow us to see that the process of evaluating performance can be filled with emotional overtones and hidden agendas that are driven by the goals and motivation of the person providing the rating.[25] If raters are not motivated to provide accurate ratings, they are likely to use the performance management system to achieve political and other goals, such as rewarding allies and punishing enemies or competitors, instead of using it as a tool to improve employee and, ultimately, organizational performance.[26]

What can be done to prevent conscious distortion of ratings? Considering the model in Figure 6.4, we need to provide incentives so that raters will be convinced that they have more to gain by providing accurate ratings than they do by providing inaccurate ratings. For example, if a supervisor is able to see the advantages of a well-implemented performance management system, as opposed to one dominated by office politics, then she will be motivated to help the system succeed.

In a nutshell, a supervisor asks herself, "What's in it for me if I provide accurate ratings versus inflated or deflated ratings?" The performance management system needs to be designed in such a way that the benefits of providing accurate ratings outweigh the benefits of providing inaccurate ratings. This may include assessing the performance of the supervisor in how she is implementing performance management within her unit and communicating that performance management is a key part of a supervisor's job. Also, supervisors need to have tools available to make their job of providing accurate ratings and feedback easier. This includes training on, for example, how to conduct the appraisal interview so that supervisors are able to provide both positive and negative feedback and are skilled at conveying both positive and, especially, negative news regarding performance.

In addition to conscious and intentional errors in the rating process, raters are also likely to make unintended errors. Observing information about performance, storing this information in memory, and then recalling it when it's time to fill out the appraisal form is a complex task. This task becomes more complex with more complex jobs that include several unrelated performance dimensions. Therefore, because of the cognitive complexity of the performance evaluation process, raters are likely to make not only intentional but also unintentional errors in evaluating performance. These errors are discussed in detail in Chapter 7. To a large extent, these errors can be minimized by improving the skills of those responsible for providing performance evaluations. These training programs, which target mostly supervisors, are discussed next.

6.7 PREVENTING RATING DISTORTION THROUGH RATER TRAINING PROGRAMS

Rater training programs have the overall objective of providing raters with tools that will allow them to implement the performance management system effectively and efficiently. Thus, such training programs also help prevent rating distortion. Table 6.3 provides a summary of the reasons discussed earlier for why raters are likely to inflate or deflate ratings.

How can training programs help mitigate the reasons causing intentional rating distortion listed in Table 6.3? To do so, such programs include content related to information, motivation, and skills. Recall that, in addition to intentional errors, raters are likely to also make unintentional errors in rating performance. So, training programs must address both types of errors. Specifically, training programs may cover the following topics:

- *Reasons for implementing the performance management system.* This includes an overview of the entire system, its purpose, and benefits for all employees.
- *How to identify and rank job activities.* This includes information on how to conduct a job analysis and understand the most important accountabilities and competencies.
- *How to observe, record, and measure performance.* This may include observational skills such as how to observe the behaviors that really matter and not be distracted by behaviors not related to the performance dimensions to be measured. It also includes skills needed to fill out the appraisal form.
- *Information on the appraisal form and system mechanics.* This includes a detailed description of the content of the appraisal form and what each section is intended to measure. It also includes information on the number of recommended meetings and the expectations regarding each participant.
- *How to minimize rating errors.* This includes steps that can be taken to minimize unintentional errors due to the cognitive demands associated with the observation and evaluation of performance.
- *How to conduct an appraisal interview.* This includes listening skills and communication skills and how to provide feedback during the appraisal interview. It also includes skills on how to help the employee create a development plan.
- *How to train, counsel, and coach.* This includes skills that the supervisor needs to help employees improve their performance on an ongoing basis.

TABLE 6.3 **Reasons for Rating Distortion**	
Rating Inflation	*Rating Deflation*
Maximize the merit raise/rewards	Shock employees
Encourage employees	Teach a rebellious employee a lesson
Avoid creating a written record	Send a message that employee should consider leaving
Avoid a confrontation with employees	
Promote undesired employees out of unit	Build a record of poor performance
Make manager look good to his or her supervisor	

For example, consider the training program used by the city of Aurora, Colorado. This program includes many of the issues listed here. First, it addresses general considerations about the performance management system, including the reasons performance management is important. Second, it covers the difference between results and job-oriented (i.e., behavior-based) performance dimensions. Third, the trainer discusses how to properly weight the various performance dimensions. Fourth, training includes a definition of the different levels of performance along a few sample job-oriented dimensions. For example, it includes an explanation of the dimension "problem solving" and examples of unacceptable, acceptable, and exceptional performance. Next, it teaches managers how to develop individual performance objectives and gives examples of good objectives. Finally, it teaches managers different ways to monitor performance and the benefits of doing so. Overall, Aurora's rater training program is fairly thorough and covers many of the subjects discussed here. However, it does not seem to include steps that can be taken to minimize unintentional errors; the way to conduct the appraisal interview; and the way to train, counsel, and coach employees. These are important components of rater training programs that are discussed in subsequent chapters.

In sum, raters are likely to make both intentional and unintentional errors in rating performance. However, training programs that address motivational issues, demonstrate how the system works, and provide a clear answer to the "What's in it for me?" question can help minimize intentional errors. In addition, training programs that include information on and skills regarding how to observe and rate performance can help minimize the presence of unintentional errors. We discuss the content of various types of training programs in more detail as we continue to describe the operational details of implementing a performance management system in Chapters 7, 8, and 9.

SUMMARY POINTS

- Appraisal forms are the key instruments used to measure performance. Care and attention are required to ensure that the forms include all the necessary components. Most forms include a combination of the following: (1) basic employee information; (2) accountabilities, objectives, and standards; (3) competencies and indicators; (4) major achievements and contributions; (5) developmental achievements; (6) developmental needs, plans, and goals; (7) stakeholder input; (8) employee comments; and (9) signatures. Note, however, that one size does not fit all and different components are appropriate based on the purposes of the appraisal.

- Regardless of the specific components included in the appraisal form, there are several characteristics that make appraisal forms particularly effective. These are (1) simplicity, (2) relevancy, (3) descriptiveness, (4) adaptability, (5) comprehensiveness, (6) definitional clarity, (7) communication, and (8) time orientation. Before it is used, each form needs to be evaluated based on the extent to which it complies with each of these characteristics.

- For administrative purposes, it is usually desirable to compute an employee's overall performance score. Two approaches are available: Judgmental and mechanical. The judgmental procedure consists of the consideration of every aspect of performance and then arriving at a fair and defensible summary. The mechanical procedure consists of combining the scores assigned to each performance dimension, usually taking into account the relative weight given to each dimension. The mechanical procedure is recommended over the judgmental procedure, which is more prone to biases.

- It is recommended that the period for review be six months (i.e., semiannual) or three months (i.e., quarterly). This provides fairly frequent opportunities for a formal discussion about performance issues between the subordinate and the supervisor. It is more convenient if the completion of the appraisal form coincides with the fiscal year so that rewards can be allocated shortly after the employee has received information on her performance during the period.

- Performance management systems can include up to six separate formal meetings between the supervisor and the subordinate: (1) system inauguration, (2) self-appraisal, (3) classical performance review, (4) merit/salary review, (5) development plan, and (6) objective setting. In practice, these meetings are usually condensed into two or so meetings during each review cycle. One point that should be emphasized is that these are *formal* meetings. *Informal* meetings involving a discussion of performance issues should take place on an ongoing basis.

- There are several sources that can be used to obtain performance information: supervisors, peers, subordinates, self, and customers. Before selecting a source, one needs to be sure that the source has first-hand knowledge of the employee's performance. Using each of these sources has advantages and disadvantages, none of them are foolproof, and not all may be available in all situations. However, it is important that employees take part in the process of selecting which sources will evaluate which performance dimensions. Active participation in the process is likely to enhance acceptance of results and perceptions that the system is fair.

- When multiple sources of performance information are used, it is likely that there will be disagreements about an employee's performance level, even if these multiple sources are rating the same performance dimension. This is because people rating the same employee may be drawn from different organizational levels and they may observe different facets of the employee's performance, even if they are evaluating the same general competency (e.g., "communication"). If an overall score is needed that considers all sources, then a weighting mechanism is needed. For example, a decision needs to be made regarding whether performance information provided by the supervisor has more or less relative importance than that provided by customers. But there is no need to summarize the information across the sources for feedback purposes. In fact, it is beneficial for the employee to receive feedback broken down by source so the employee can place particular attention and effort in the interactions involving any source that has detected performance deficiencies.

- In providing performance information, raters may make intentional errors. These errors may involve inflating or deflating performance scores. For example, a supervisor may want to avoid a confrontation with his employees and inflate ratings. A peer may believe that providing accurate ratings may jeopardize the relationship with a colleague and may, consequently, provide inflated ratings. When raters provide performance ratings, they are faced with providing either accurate or inaccurate ratings. They weigh costs and benefits of choosing one or the other path.

If the cost/benefit equation does not favor providing accurate ratings, it is likely that ratings will be distorted. When this happens, incorrect decisions may be made, employees are likely to feel they have been treated unfairly, and the organization is more prone to litigation. In other words, when performance ratings are distorted because raters are not motivated to provide accurate scores, the performance management system not only would not result in desired outcomes but it is likely to lead to very negative consequences for the organization.

- In addition to intentional errors, raters may make unintentional errors in providing performance ratings. This is because observing information about performance, storing this information in memory, and then recalling it when it's time to fill out the appraisal form is a complex cognitive task.

- Intentional and unintentional distortion in performance ratings can be minimized by providing raters with extensive training. Such training programs include content related to information, motivation, and skills. For example, regarding information, training programs address an overview of the entire performance management system. Regarding motivation, raters are given information on how rating employees accurately will provide them with direct and tangible benefits. Training programs can show how to conduct an appraisal interview. No performance management system is foolproof and performance ratings are inherently subjective. However, the implementation of such training programs, together with rewards associated with accurate ratings, provides raters with the needed motivation and skills to minimize rating errors.

Case Study 6.1 Evaluating the Appraisal Form Used by a Grocery Retailer

Consider the appraisal form shown here, which is adapted from a form used by a grocery retailer based in the United States. First, use the table to place check marks next to each component if the component is present. Second, in the Comments section, please write (1) for those components that are present, whether any changes or revisions are needed in the form and why; and (2) for those components that are absent, why they should be added and what are the possible negative consequences of not doing so. ■

Major Components of Appraisal Forms	Comments
Basic employee information	
Accountabilities, objectives, and standards	
Competencies and indicators	
Major achievements and contributions	
Developmental achievements	
Developmental needs, plans, and goals	
Stakeholder input	
Employee comments	
Signatures	

Performance Evaluation Form
For use by Store Director; Co-Director; Meat, Seafood, Produce, Deli/Bakery, Floral and Grocery Managers

Name _____   Review Period _____

Position _____   Store _____

Evaluator _____   Date _____

Competencies: Please rate the Associate on the following competencies. Determine the point total and multiply by the weight factor to achieve the point total for the competencies.

				1st	2nd	Wgt	Pts	Pts
Follow-Through/Dependability			Points:			0.5		
4	3	2	1					
Work is completed correctly and on time without supervision. Anticipates needs. Extremely organized.	Work is usually completed correctly and on a timely basis with some supervision. Very organized.	Work is completed as assigned and results can usually be relied upon with normal supervision. Organized.	Work can seldom be relied upon. Often fails to complete tasks correctly. Unorganized.					
Comments:								

				1st	2nd	Wgt	Pts	Pts
Decision Making/Creative Problem Solving			**Points:**			0.5		
4	3	2	1					
Anticipates, recognizes, and confronts problems with extraordinary skill. Perseveres until solution is reached. Extremely innovative and takes risks.	Defines and addresses problems well. Typically reaches useful solutions and decisions are sound. Innovative, with above-average risk taking.	Acknowledges and attempts to solve most problems when presented. Usually comes to conclusions on solving basic issues. Little innovation and sometimes takes risks.	Has difficulty recognizing problems and making decisions. Always needs guidance. No innovation and never takes risks.					

Comments:

Total Score for Competencies Section [ ] [ ]

Key Results: Rate each area to the performance demonstrated in the achievement of budgeted numbers.

KR #1: Achieved Budgeted Sales (U.S. dollars)

	Budgeted	Actual	% of achievement (1, 2, 3, 4)	
1st half objective				Wgt 0.80
2nd half objective				Pts
	4 = 108%+	3 = 107-103%	2 = 102-98% 1 = Below 97%	0

Comments:

KR #2: Targeted Margin Gain/Loss (shrink)(%)

	Budgeted	Actual	% of achievement (1, 2, 3, 4)	
1st half objective				Wgt 0.20
2nd half objective				Pts
	4 = 108%+	3 = 107-103%	2 = 102-98% 1 = Below 97%	

Comments:

TOTAL SCORE FOR KEY RESULTS:

	0	0	0		0
	Comp. Score 1st half	Comp. Score 2nd half	Key Resp Score		Subtotal
Circle Rating:					
Excellent	Above	Average	Unsatisfactory		
3.6 – 4.0	2.6 – 3.5	1.6 – 2.5	1 – 1.5		

Objectives from Last Review/Results (Associate completes this section with Supervisor)
List objectives set for last review period and indicate performance results:

Program for Developing Career Success
What development will benefit the individual's performance? List specific programs and timetable to complete in order to move the Associate's performance forward. List personal development objectives as well as project objectives:

Career Goal
What does the Associate ultimately want to do in his or her career?

Associate Comments: This is to be completed by the Associate. It should be used for comments related to this evaluation. (Attach additional sheet if necessary.)

Associate _____ Date _____

Store Director _____ Date _____

Case Study 6.2 Judgmental and Mechanical Methods of Assigning Overall Performance Score at *The Daily Planet*

The form here shows performance ratings obtained by David Kuhn, a hypothetical reporter at a major newspaper in the United States.[1] First, use the judgmental method to come up with his overall performance score. What is Kuhn's overall performance score?

The form on page 143 actually omitted weight information for the various competencies. The weights are the following:

Competency	Weight
Productivity	.25
Quality of work	.40
Dependability and adherence to company values and policies	.15
Contribution to effectiveness of others/unit	.20

Now compute Kuhn's overall performance score using the weights in the table. Is there a difference between the score computed using a subjective rather than the mechanical method? If yes, what are the implications of these differences for the employee being rated, for the supervisor, and for the organization? ■

---

[1] Adapted from R. J. Greene, "Contributing to Organizational Success Through Effective Performance Appraisal," SHRM Online. (2003), http://www.shrm.org/hrresources/whitepapers_published/2CMS_005421.asp#P-4_0. Retrieval date: August 15, 2005.

Name: David Kuhn	Job Title: Reporter				
Dept.: International	Supervisor: John DuBoss				
Performance Period:	from Jan 06	to Dec 06			

Job Description: Researches and writes news, features, analyses, human interest stories. Develops and cultivates news sources and contacts. Completes assignments by deadlines, ensuring accuracy by verifying sources. Attends newsworthy events and interviews key sources. Respects confidentiality as appropriate.

	Unacceptable	Does not fully meet standards	Fully meets standards	Significantly exceeds standards	Outstanding
Productivity—Production is high relative to time and resources consumed; develops expected number of stories and covers beat adequately to ensure stories are detected as they break; stories are developed within time frame that enables deadlines to be met and appropriate reviews are performed as they are refined.	1	②	3	4	5
Quality of work—Work meets quality standards and established editorial standards; stories are written in clear and appropriate manner, are consistent with editorial policy, and are fair and balanced; research is thorough and encompasses all relevant sources, which are verified to ensure accuracy; works with editors to revise and improve content; develops and maintains network of contacts who can provide early notification of breaking stories.	1	2	3	④	5
Dependability and adherence to company values and policies— Consistently meets deadlines; conforms to attendance policies; adapts to work demands; conforms					

to established values and policies; adheres to ethical standards of the paper and the profession; respects confidentiality as appropriate; behaves in manner that enhances the image of the paper.	1	2	3	4	⑤
<u>Contribution to effectiveness of others/ unit</u>—Works with others within and outside the unit in a manner that improves their effectiveness; shares information and resources; develops effective working relationships; builds consensus; constructively manages conflict; contributes to the effectiveness of own unit/group and the paper.	1	②	3	4	5

Case Study 6.3 Minimizing Intentional and Unintentional Rating Errors

Consider the areas typically covered by rater training programs (Section 6.7). Use the table to identify which of these content areas address intentional errors and which unintentional errors. Please place a check mark where appropriate. Fill in the Comments section to describe the rationale that guided each of your responses. ■

Intentional Errors	Unintentional Errors	Content Area	Comments
		Reasons for implementing the performance management system. This includes an overview of the entire system, its purpose, and benefits for all employees.	
		How to identify and rank job activities. This includes information on how to conduct a job analysis and understand the most important accountabilities and competencies.	

		How to observe, record, and measure performance. This may include observational skills such as how to observe the behaviors that really matter and not be distracted by behaviors not related to the performance dimensions to be measured. It also includes skills needed to fill out the appraisal form.	
		Information on the appraisal form and system mechanics. This includes a detailed description of the content of the appraisal form and what each section is intended to measure. It also includes information on number of meetings and the expectations regarding each participant.	
		How to minimize rating errors. This includes steps that can be taken to minimize unintentional errors due to the cognitive demands associated with the observation and evaluation of performance.	
		How to conduct an appraisal interview. This includes listening skills and communication skills and how to provide feedback during the appraisal interview. It also includes skills on how to help the employee create a development plan.	
		How to train, counsel, and coach. This includes skills that the supervisor needs to help employees improve their performance on an ongoing basis.	

END NOTES

1. Adapted from D. Grote, *The Complete Guide to Performance Appraisal* (New York: AMACOM, 1996), chap. 10.
2. Grote, D. (1996). *The Complete Guide to Performance Appraisal* (New York: AMA-COM).
3. Adapted from Workforce Research Center, (2003, April), "Busch Performance Evaluations," *Workforce Online.* Available online at http://www.workforce.com/archive/article/23/42/03.php.
4. Ganzach, Y., Kluger, A. N., & Klayman, N. (2000). Making decisions from an interview: Expert measurement and mechanical combination. *Personnel Psychology*, 53, 1–20.
5. Kraiger, K., & Aguinis, H. (2001). Training effectiveness: Assessing training needs, motivation, and accomplishments. In M. London (Ed.), *How people evaluate others in organizations* (pp. 203–220). Mahwah, NJ: Lawrence Erlbaum.

6. Milliman, J. F., Zawacki, R. A., Schulz, B., Wiggins, S., & Norman, C. A. (1995). Customer service drives 360-degree goal setting. *Personnel Journal, 74,* 136–142.

7. Workforce Research Center. The new thinking in performance appraisals: Writing effective co-worker comments. *Workforce Online.* Available online at http://www.workforce.com/archive/feature/22/28/68/223579.php. Retrieval date: August 15, 2005.

8. Adapted from D. Grote, *The Complete Guide to Performance Appraisal* (New York: AMACOM, 1996), chap. 10.

9. Talbott, S. P. (1994). Peer review drives compensation at Johnsonville. *Personnel Journal, 73,* 126–132.

10. The discussion of the various sources of performance information is based, in part, on W. F. Cascio, and H. Aguinis, *Applied Psychology in Human Resources Management,* 6th ed. (Upper Saddle River, NJ: Prentice Hall, 2005).

11. Hogan, R., & Shelton, D. (1998). A socioanalytic perspective on job performance. *Human Performance,* 11, 129–144.

12. Workforce Research Center. Dear workforce: How are peer reviews used for compensation? *Workforce Online.* Available online at http://www.workforce.com/archive/article/22/13/94.php. Retrieval date: August 15, 2005.

13. Antonioni, D. (1994). The effects of feedback accountability on upward appraisal ratings. *Personnel Psychology, 47,* 349–356.

14. Jelley, R. B., & Goffin, R. D. (2001). Can performance-feedback accuracy be improved? Effects of rater priming and rating-scale format on rating accuracy. *Journal of Applied Psychology, 86,* 134–145.

15. Useem, J. (2005). America's most admired companies. *Fortune, 151*(5), 66–70.

16. Serwer, A. (2005). The education of Michael Dell. *Fortune, 151*(5), 76.

17. Greguras, G. J., Robie, C., Schleicher, D. J., & Goff, M. (2003). A field study of the effects of rating purpose on the quality of multisource ratings. *Personnel Psychology, 56,* 1–21.

18. Atkins, P. W. B., & Wood, R. E. (2002). Self- versus others' ratings as predictors of assessment center ratings: Validation evidence for 360-degree feedback programs. *Personnel Psychology, 55,* 871–904.

19. Wells, B., & Spinks, N. (1990). How companies are using employee self-evaluation forms. *Journal of Compensation & Benefits, 6,* 42–47

20. Milliman, J. F., Zawacki, R. A., Schulz, B., Wiggins, S., & Norman, C. A. (1995). Customer service drives 360-degree goal setting. *Personnel Journal, 74,* 136–142.

21. Franke, G. R., Murphy, J. H., & Nadler, S. S. (2003). Appraising account executive performance appraisals: Current practices and managerial implications. *Journal of Current Issues & Research in Advertising, 25,* 1–11.

22. Facteau, J. D., & Craig, S. B. (2001). Are performance appraisal ratings from different rating sources comparable? *Journal of Applied Psychology, 86,* 215–227.

23. Viswesvaran, C., Schmidt, F. L., & Ones, D. S. (2002). The moderating influence of job performance dimensions on convergence of supervisory and peer ratings of job performance: Unconfounding construct-level convergence and rating difficulty. Journal of *Applied Psychology, 87,* 345–354.

24. Longenecker, C. O., Sims, H. P., & Gioia, D. A. (1987). Behind the mask: The politics of employee appraisal. *Academy of Management Executive, 1,* 183–193.

25. Fletcher, C. (2001). Performance appraisal and management: The developing research agenda. *Journal of Occupational and Organizational Psychology, 74,* 473–487.

26. Murphy, K. R., Cleveland, J. N., Skattebo, A. L., & Kinney, T. B. (2004). Raters who pursue different goals give different ratings. *Journal of Applied Psychology, 89,* 158–164.

27. Adapted from Murphy, K. R. and Cleveland, J. N. Understanding performance appraisal: Social, organizational, and Goal-based perspectives (Thousand Oaks, CA: Sage, 1995).

7

Implementing a Performance Management System

Training is everything.
—MARK TWAIN

Learning Objectives

By the end of this chapter, you will be able to do the following:

- Understand that there are crucial steps that must be taken before the performance management system is launched, including implementing a communication plan, an appeals process, training programs for raters, and pilot testing the system to fix any glitches.

- Design a communication plan that answers the key critical questions: What is performance management? How does performance management fit in the organization's strategy? How does everyone benefit from the system? How does the performance management system work? What are employees' and supervisors' key roles and responsibilities in implementing the system? How is performance management related to other key organizational initiatives?

- Design a communication plan that will include features aimed at reducing the effect of cognitive biases on how the performance management system is perceived and help minimize the impact of intentional rating errors.

- Be aware of cognitive biases that affect how people take in, use, and recall information, including selective exposure, selective perception, and selective retention.

- Understand that setting up an appeals process helps gain support for the performance management system.

- Design an appeals process including two levels: Level 1, which involves the HR department in the role of mediator, and Level 2, which involves a panel of managers and peers and, possibly, a senior-level manager in the role of arbitrator and final decision maker.

- Describe unintentional and intentional types of errors that raters are likely to make in evaluating performance.

■ Implement training programs such as rater error, frame of reference, and behavior observation that will minimize the impact of unintentional rating errors.

■ Implement a self-leadership training program that will allow supervisors to increase confidence in their skills to manage the performance management process and, consequently, allow them to minimize rating errors.

■ Understand the importance of conducting a pilot test before the performance system is implemented organization-wide.

■ Conduct a pilot test of the performance management system using a selected group of employees and managers from the organization.

■ Once the performance management system is in place, collect various measurements that will provide information regarding the system's effectiveness and the extent to which it is working the way it should and whether it is producing the expected results.

Chapters 4 and 5 described operational details about how to measure performance. Chapter 6 described operational details about appraisal forms and the process of providing performance ratings. This chapter, the last one in Part II, continues to address operational issues in implementing a performance management system. Specifically, it addresses the steps needed before the system is put in place, such as setting good communication and appeals procedures that will gain system acceptance, implementing training programs to minimize rating errors, and pilot testing the system. Finally, the chapter describes how to monitor the system once it is in place to make sure it is working properly.

7.1 PREPARATION: COMMUNICATION, APPEALS PROCESS, TRAINING PROGRAMS, AND PILOT TESTING

As should be evident by now, the implementation of a performance management system requires the involvement of many players. Specifically, the successful implementation of the system requires a clear understanding of how the system works and a clear understanding of its benefits from the different perspectives of all involved. In other words, successful implementation requires wide organizational support and acceptance. Initially, it may be that each organizational layer and unit includes one or just a handful of individuals who are knowledgeable and supportive of the system. These "champions" are likely to serve as advocates and resources for the system. Eventually, however, the system cannot be implemented successfully if only a handful of organizational members are on board.

Before the system is launched, a successful communication plan must be implemented that will gain system acceptance. Part of the communication plan includes a description of the appeals process. Then, as part of the preparation phase before the system is actually launched, raters are trained to observe and evaluate performance as well as to give feedback. The system should then be tested and the results of a pilot test used to fix any glitches. Only after these presystem implementation steps are taken can the system be launched with confidence. Finally, once the system has been tested and is launched, there is a need to monitor and evaluate the system on an ongoing basis to understand if it is working properly and what adjustments may be needed to make it work. The ongoing monitoring of the system is crucial because the system may eventually lose support if no data are provided to show the system's benefits.

Next, let's discuss what needs to be done before the system is actually implemented, including a communication plan, an appeals process, training raters, and pilot testing the system.

7.2 COMMUNICATION PLAN

In general, having more and better knowledge of the performance management system leads to greater employee acceptance and satisfaction.[1] Organizations often design a communication plan to ensure that information regarding the performance management system is widely disseminated in the organization. A good communication plan answers the following questions:[2]

- *What is performance management?* Answering this question involves providing general information about performance management, how performance management systems are implemented in other organizations, and the general goals of performance management systems.
- *How does performance management fit in our strategy?* To answer this question, we should provide information on the relationship between performance management and strategic planning. Specifically, information is provided on how the performance management system will help accomplish strategic goals.
- *What's in it for me?* A good communication plan describes the benefits of implementing performance management for all those involved.
- *How does it work?* Answering this question entails giving a detailed description of the performance management process and time line, for example, when meetings will take place, what the purposes of each meeting are, when decisions about rewards will be made, and so forth.
- *What are my responsibilities?* The communication plan should include information on the role and responsibilities of each person involved at each stage of the process. For example, it includes a description of the employees' and supervisors' main responsibilities in the performance management process.
- *How is performance management related to other initiatives?* The communication plan should include information on the relationship between performance management and other initiatives and systems, such as training, promotion, succession planning, and so forth.

Consider the performance management system for the position of Senior Executive Service (SES) in the United States Department of Justice.[3] SES members serve in key leadership positions directly below the top presidential appointees. SES members link the appointees to the rest of the federal government and they are charged with overseeing various government activities in 75 federal agencies.

The communication plan that the Department of Justice implemented for this performance management system is described in a document divided into three chapters, Chapter 1, "General Information," Chapter 2, "Performance Appraisal for the Senior Executive Service," and Chapter 3, "Actions Based on Less Than Fully Successful Performance." This is how their plan answered each of the questions discussed in the previous list:[4]

- *What is performance management?*   Chapter 1 states why the department is implementing a performance management system, and what it is expected to accomplish. For example, some of this information notes that performance management aims at promoting efficient and effective attainment of the department's mission, program objectives, and strategic planning initiatives, and also aims at motivating high levels of achievement and accountability. This chapter also includes definitions of several key terms, including *performance management system, performance, progress review, rating levels*, and *annual summary rating*.
- *How does performance management fit in our strategy?*   Chapter 2 begins with a list of principles that guide the system, including, "The Department of Justice federal leaders and managers create a climate for excellence by communicating their vision, values and expectations clearly. . . ." It goes on to detail all of the ways that leaders in the agency do this. In addition, in a memorandum that was sent with the chapters, the director of the Office of Personnel Management (OPM) included this quote from President George W. Bush: "We are not here to mark time, but to make progress, to achieve results, and to leave a record of excellence." The director then described how the system would be used to implement the key principles of the president's administration.
- *What's in it for me?*   Throughout the memo, there is clear information on how the performance management system will help the SES members be more effective leaders so that the president's mission can be achieved.
- *How does it work?*   Chapter 2 outlines the steps in a performance management process, detailing the managers' responsibilities at each step. For example, it outlines the performance dimensions, the rating categories, and how to assign an overall rating.
- *What are my responsibilities?*   The communication plan outlines the responsibilities of the SES members as well as their rating official, the person in charge of rating their performance. The plan emphasizes that leaders must create a culture performing at a high level by continually communicating expectations and rewarding high-achieving performers.
- *How is Performance Management Related to other initiatives?*   The communication plan touches briefly on the importance of linking system outcomes to performance-based pay. The importance of training to maximizing performance is also touched on.

In summary, the communication plan implemented by the Department of Justice is extremely detailed and provides answers to most, if not all, of the key questions that should be addressed by a good plan. However, even if a communication plan answers all or most of the important questions, the fact that the information has been made available does not necessarily mean the communication plan will be successful in gaining acceptance. This is because people have cognitive biases that affect what information is taken in and how it is processed. Specifically, there are three types of biases that affect the effectiveness of a communication plan, regardless of how well it has been implemented. These are *selective exposure, selective perception*, and *selective retention*.

First, selection exposure is a tendency to expose our minds only to ideas with which we already agree. Those employees who already agree that performance management is a good idea may become involved in the communication plan activities, including reading about the system and attending meetings describing how the system works. On the other hand, those who do not see much value added in performance management may choose not to read information about it and not to attend meetings related to performance management. Second, selective perception is a tendency to perceive a piece of information as meaning what we would like it to mean even though the information, as intended by the communicator, may mean the exact opposite. Someone who believes performance management is about only rewards and punishments may incorrectly interpret that receiving formal performance feedback at the end of each quarter translates into receiving a pay or bonus. Third, selective retention is a tendency to remember only those pieces of information with which we already agree. If an employee perceives his employer as vindictive, that employee is not likely to remember information about how the appeals process works or about other fair and equitable aspects of the system.

Selective exposure, selective perception, and selective retention biases are pervasive and could easily render the communication plan ineffective. Fortunately, there are several ways to minimize the negative impact of these biases and, therefore, help gain support for the system. Consider the following:[5]

- *Involve employees.* Involve employees in the design of the system. People support what they help create. Thus, the higher the level of participation in designing the system, the greater the support for the system.[6]
- *Understand employee needs.* Understand the needs of the employees and identify ways in which these needs can be met through performance management. Basically, provide a personal, clear, and convincing answer to the "What's in it for me?" question.
- *Strike first.* Create a positive attitude toward the new performance system before any negative attitudes and rumors are created. Make communications realistic and don't set up expectations you can't deliver. Discuss some of the arguments that might be used against the system and provide evidence to counter them.
- *Provide facts and consequences.* Because of the employee biases, facts don't necessarily speak for themselves. Clearly explain facts about the system and also explain what they mean or what the consequences are. Don't let users draw their own conclusions because they may differ from yours.
- *Put it in writing.* In Western cultures, written communications are usually more powerful and credible than spoken communications because they can be carefully examined and challenged for accuracy. Create documentation, which can be made available online, describing the system.
- *Use multiple channels of communication.* Use multiple methods of communication, including meetings, e-mail, and paper communication. In other words, allow employees to be exposed repeatedly to the same message delivered using different communication channels. Of course, make sure all channels convey consistent information.
- *Use credible communicators.* Use credible sources to communicate the performance management system. In companies where the human resources (HR) department members are perceived as "HR cops" because they continually emphasize what cannot be done as opposed to how one's job can be done better, it may be better to use a different department or group. Instead, in such situations,

communication should be delivered by people who are trusted and admired within the organization. It also helps if those delivering the communication and endorsing the system are seen as key and powerful organizational players.
- *Say it, and then say it again.* Repeat the information frequently. People can absorb only a small amount of information at a time, so the information needs to be repeated frequently.

Table 7.1 summarizes what can be done to minimize cognitive biases including selective exposure, selective perception, and selective retention. Consider the Department of Justice communication process, described earlier in this chapter. The plan attempts to minimize negative biases and gain support for the performance management system. For example, while it is a government agency and the performance management system is a federal mandate, the OPM offered to help managers tailor the systems to their specific agencies. This is likely to help employees become more involved and is also helpful in addressing the specific needs of the employees in the various agencies. The memorandum from the director of the OPM, who is also a credible source of information on both the performance management system and the president's policies, sets an extremely positive tone and appeals to employees' patriotism by including a message from the president reminding them of the importance of serving the "American people." The communication plan also provides facts and conclusions about the system. For example, it explains the reasoning for realigning the performance management system with the fiscal year, how to carry out this time line, and the importance of doing so. The communication plan is also posted on the department's Web site. There are also links to other Web sites with information on performance management. It is not clear whether the Department of Justice distributed this memorandum and accompanying system information using other media. Finally, the information presented in the memorandum and in the chapter is repeated and clarified. The memorandum gives an overview of the importance of the performance management system; the first chapter in the document gives an overview of PM systems, and then the second chapter gives details of the system. All in all, the plan implemented by the Department of Justice is a good example of a communication plan that attempts to minimize the impact of the various communication barriers.

In addition to implementing a communication process, support for the performance management system can be gained by implementing an appeals process. This topic is discussed next.

TABLE 7.1   Considerations to Minimize the Effects of Communication Barriers

Involve employees
Understand employee needs
Strike first
Provide facts and consequences
Put it in writing
Use multiple channels of communication
Use credible communicators
Say it, and then say it again

7.3 APPEALS PROCESS

The inclusion of an appeals process is important in gaining employee acceptance for the performance management system because it allows employees to understand that if there is a disagreement regarding performance ratings or any resulting decisions; then such disagreements can be resolved in an amicable and nonretaliatory way. In addition, the inclusion of an appeals process increases perceptions of the system's fairness.[7]

When an appeals process is in place, employees have the ability to question two types of issues: judgmental and administrative.[8] Judgmental issues center on the validity of the performance evaluation. For example, an employee may believe that a manager's performance ratings for that employee do not reflect his actual performance. Administrative issues involve whether the policies and procedures were followed. For example, an employee may argue that her supervisor did not meet with her as frequently as he has with other coworkers and that the feedback she is receiving about her performance is not as thorough as that received by her coworkers.

Typically, when an appeal is first filed, the HR department serves as a mediator between the employee and the supervisor. An appeal sent to the HR department is usually called a Level 1 or Level A appeal. The HR department is in a good position to judge whether policies and procedures have been implemented correctly and also has good information about the various jobs, levels of performance expected, and levels of performance of other employees within the unit and organization. The HR department gathers the necessary facts and brings them either to the attention of the rater to encourage reconsideration of the decision that caused the appeal or to the complainant to explain why there have been no biases or violations. In other words, the HR department either suggests corrective action to the supervisor or informs the employee that the decision or procedures were correct.

If the supervisor does not believe corrective action should be taken and the appeal continues, then an outside and unbiased arbitrator makes a final and binding resolution. This is usually called a Level 2 or Level B appeal. This arbitrator can consist of a panel of peers and managers. The panel reviews the case, asks questions, interviews witnesses, researches precedents, and reviews policy. Then, they simply take a vote to make the decision. In some cases, the vote represents the final decision. In other cases, the vote is forwarded to a high-level manager (vice president or higher level) who takes the panel's vote into consideration in making the final decision.

The box "Selected Excerpts from the University of North Carolina Performance Management Appeals Process" shows some of the key sections of the performance management appeals process for employees at the University of North Carolina.[9] The appeals process is intended to air concerns and to resolve disagreements. The purpose of this specific policy is to provide employees and management a means for resolving disagreements involving performance evaluations and performance pay issues.

The information shown in the box describing the appeals process at the University of North Carolina spells out the steps involved, the time line that should be followed, and the various outcomes that could be expected. Given that such a policy is in place, employees are given assurances that, if there is an appeal, the case will be treated fairly and as objectively as possible. Once again, this should help gain support for the performance management system.

BOX 7.1

**Selected Excerpts from the University of North Carolina
Performance Management Appeals Process**

GENERAL PROVISIONS

Under State policy neither party in the Appeals Process may be represented by an attorney. State law and policy provide that the Chancellor's decision on an appeal is final and cannot be appealed further.

The Appeals Process has jurisdiction over the following issues only:

- the overall evaluation received as part of the Annual Review
- the rating on one or more principal functions
- the explanatory remarks included in the evaluation

Depending on the actions taken by the General Assembly regarding salary increases related to the performance evaluation process, the following issues also may be appealed:

- failure to receive a performance increase and/or performance bonus when eligible
- the amount of the increase or bonus received

An employee is limited to one appeal for any work cycle, regardless of the number of issues involved. The employee should describe the complete remedy desired should the appeal be decided in his/her favor. For example, an employee who appeals the overall evaluation should specify the overall evaluation requested. If such an overall evaluation would result in eligibility for a performance increase, an increase percentage should be stated as part of the remedy requested in the appeal.

By request (and with management approval) an employee may be granted a maximum of 12 hours off from regular duties for processing an appeal under this Appeals Process without any loss of pay and without charge to leave.

PERFORMANCE MANAGEMENT REVIEW BOARD

The Chancellor appoints the Chair of the Performance Management Review Board (Board Chair) and the other members of the Review Board. When a Level B appeal is received, the Board Chair selects a three-member Panel and appoints a Panel Leader. The Board Chair notifies the employee of the name, job title and department of each proposed Panel member. The employee has the right to disqualify up to two proposed members by notifying the Board Chair before the date stated in the letter of notification.

Each panel will have one member with supervisory responsibility and two members with no supervisory responsibility. No member of the Panel will be from the employee's own department. Any member may be designated as Panel Leader. The Panel determines what information is needed. The involved parties must provide the information requested by the Panel.

The Panel Leader notifies the employee and the department head in writing of the hearing date and location. Every effort must be made to arrange for a timely hearing. The Level B hearing is confidential. It is not open to the media or other persons whose attendance is not approved in advance by the Panel Leader. The employee, the department head, and supervisors involved in the performance review are allowed to appear in person at the hearing. However, any party may elect not to appear and to have the Panel's Level B recommendation based only on documentation presented to the Panel. The chair must receive advance notification if anyone other than the employee and department head are to provide information to the Review Board. The employee and management must request approval in advance for witnesses to address the Panel. Only witnesses approved in advance may appear at the hearing.

After the hearing, the Panel decides whether additional information is needed. Any information requested and received after the hearing is shared with the employee and the department head. After considering all of the information presented, the Panel makes its recommendation by majority vote and submits its written recommendation through the Board Chair to the Chancellor. The Chancellor either accepts, modifies, or rejects the Panel's recommendation and issues the University decision within 15 calendar days of receiving the Panel recommendation. If the Chancellor rejects the Panel recommendation, the written decision will state the reason(s) for rejection. The Chancellor sends the written decision to the employee.

Source: Performance management appeals process. Available online at http://hr.unc.edu/Data/SPA/perfmgt/perf-appeal. Retrieval date: August 15, 2005.

7.4 TRAINING PROGRAMS FOR THE ACQUISITION OF REQUIRED SKILLS

Training the raters is another step necessary in preparing for the launching of the performance management system. Training not only provides participants in the performance management system with needed skills and tools to do a good job implementing it, but training also helps increase satisfaction with the system.[10]

In Chapter 6 we discussed the general content of such training programs. Specifically, the content areas that can be included in rater training programs are listed in Table 7.2.

Consider the list of content areas included in Table 7.2. The first two content areas are not unique to rater training programs. In fact, these are usual components of the communication plan in which all organizational members participate, and not just the raters. However, given the suggestion that the same information should be presented many times and through different communication channels, it does not hurt to

---

TABLE 7.2 Content Areas That Can Be Included in Rater Training Programs

1. Reasons for implementing the performance management system
2. Information on the appraisal form and system mechanics
3. How to identify and rank job activities
4. How to observe, record, and measure performance
5. How to minimize rating errors
6. How to conduct an appraisal interview
7. How to train, counsel, and coach

---

include this content area as part of a rater training program. Content areas 3–5 involve the general issue of identifying, observing, recording, and evaluating performance. Content areas 6 and 7 involve the general issue of how to interact with the employee receiving performance information. Next, we address various choices in terms of implementing training programs specific to content areas 3–5. The development of skills related to content areas 6 and 7 is addressed in detail in Chapter 9.

7.4.1 Rater Error Training

The goal of rater error training (RET) is to make raters aware of what the rating errors are that they are likely to make and to help them develop strategies to minimize those errors. The goal of RET is to increase rating accuracy by making raters aware of the unintentional errors they are likely to make.

RET programs typically include definitions of the most typical errors and a description of possible causes for those errors. Such programs also allow trainees to view examples of common errors and to review suggestions on how to avoid making errors. This can be done by showing videotaped vignettes designed to elicit rating errors and asking trainees to fill out appraisal forms regarding the situations that they observed on the videotapes. Finally, a comparison is made between the ratings provided by the trainees and the correct ratings. The trainer then explains why the errors took place, which specific errors were made, and ways to overcome the errors in the future.

RET does not guarantee increased accuracy. Raters do become aware of the possible errors they can make but, because many of the errors are unintentional, simple awareness of the errors does not mean that errors will not be made. Nevertheless, it may be useful to expose raters to the range of possible errors. These errors include the following:

- *Similar to me error.* Similarity leads to attraction, so we tend to favor those who are similar to us. Consequently, in some cases supervisors are more likely to give higher performance ratings to those employees who are perceived to be more similar to them in terms of attitudes, preferences, personality, and demographic variables including race and gender.
- *Contrast error.* Contrast error occurs when, even when an absolute measurement system is in place, supervisors compare individuals with one another instead of against predetermined standards. For example, when a supervisor rates an individual of only average performance, the rating may actually be higher than deserved if the other individuals rated by the same supervisor display substandard performance levels: the average performer may seem to be better in comparison to others. This error is most likely to occur when supervisors complete multiple appraisal forms at the same time, because in such situations it is difficult to ignore the ratings given to other employees.
- *Leniency error.* Leniency error occurs when raters assign high (lenient) ratings to most or all employees. In other words, leniency involves artificial rating inflation. As discussed in Chapter 6, leniency is mostly an intentional error caused by a desire to maximize the merit raise/rewards, to encourage employees, to avoid creating a written record of poor performance, to avoid a confrontation with employees, to promote undesired employees out of unit,

or to make the manager look good to his supervisor. Also, recent research has uncovered that individuals with certain personality traits are more likely to be more lenient: those low on conscientiousness (i.e., individuals who do not always strive for excellence) and high on agreeableness (i.e., individuals who are more trustful, cooperative, and polite).[11]

- *Severity error.*   Severity error occurs when raters assign low (severe) ratings to most or all employees. That is, severity involves artificial rating deflation. As discussed in Chapter 6, severity is mostly an intentional type of error caused by the supervisor's desire to shock employees, to teach employees a lesson, to send a message that the employee should consider leaving, or to build a record of poor performance.

- *Central tendency error.*   Central tendency error occurs when raters use only the middle points on the rating scales and avoid using the extremes. The result is that most or all employees are rated as "average." This is also an intentional type of error and is mainly caused by a supervisor's desire to play it safe. One negative consequence of this error is that it is hard to make performance-based distinctions among employees rated by the same rater.

- *Halo error.*   Halo error occurs when raters fail to distinguish among the different aspects of performance being rated. If an employee receives a high score on one dimension, she also receives a high score on all other dimensions, even though performance may not be even across all dimensions. For example, if an employee has a perfect attendance record, then the rater may give her a high mark on dedication and productivity. However, the perfect attendance record may be caused by the fact that the employee has large loan payments to make and cannot afford to miss work and not because the employee is actually an excellent overall performer. In other words, being present at work is not the same as being a productive employee. This error is typically caused by the supervisor's assigning performance ratings based on an overall impression about the employee instead of evaluating each performance dimension independently.

- *Primacy error.*   Primacy error occurs when performance evaluation is influenced mainly by information collected during the initial phases of the review period. For example, in rating communication skills, the supervisor gives more weight to incidents involving communication that took place toward the beginning of the review period as opposed to incidents taking place at all other times.

- *Recency error.*   Recency error occurs when performance evaluation is influenced mainly by information gathered during the last portion of the review period. This is the opposite of the primacy error: raters are more heavily influenced by behaviors taking place toward the end of the review period instead of giving equal importance and paying attention to incidents occurring throughout the entire review period.

- *Negativity error.*   Negativity error occurs when raters place more weight on negative information than on positive or neutral information. For example, a rater may have observed one negative interaction between the employee and a customer and several positive interactions in which customers' expectations were surpassed. However, the rater may focus on the one negative incident in rating the "customer service" dimension. The negativity error explains why most people have a tendency to remember negative as opposed to positive news that they read in the newspaper or watch on television.

- *First impression error.* First impression error occurs when raters make an initial favorable or unfavorable judgment about an employee and then ignore subsequent information that does not support the initial impression. This type of error can be confounded with the "similar to me error" because first impressions are likely to be based on the degree of similarity: the more similar the person is to the supervisor, the more positive the first impression will be.
- *Spillover error.* Spillover error occurs when scores from previous review periods unjustly influence current ratings. For example, a supervisor makes the assumption that an employee who was an excellent performer in the previous period ought also to be an excellent performer during the current period and provides performance ratings consistent with this belief.
- *Stereotype error.* Stereotype error occurs when a supervisor has an oversimplified view of individuals based on group membership. That is, a supervisor may have a belief that certain groups of employees (e.g., women) are unassertive in their communication style. Then, in rating women, he may automatically describe communication as being "unassertive" without actually having any behavioral evidence for the rating.[12] This type of error can also lead to biased evaluations of performance when an individual (e.g., woman) violates stereotypic norms by working in an occupation that does not fit the stereotype (e.g., assembly of airplane parts).[13]

Table 7.3 includes a summary list of possible errors that raters may make in assigning performance ratings. These errors can be classified as intentional or unintentional.

As described in Chapter 6, to minimize the intentional errors shown in Table 7.3, we must focus on the rater's motivation. In other words, we must demonstrate to the raters that the benefits of providing accurate ratings outweigh the benefits of intentionally distorting ratings either by inflation, deflation, or central tendency. Once again, this goes back to the "What's in it for me?" question. For example, the communication program should include a clear description of the benefits that supervisors can expect to receive if their performance ratings lack intentional distortion.

TABLE 7.3 Errors Likely to Be Made in Providing Performance Ratings	
Unintentional	*Intentional*
Similar to me	Leniency
Contrast	Severity
Halo	Central tendency
Primacy	
Recency	
Negativity	
First impression	
Spillover	
Stereotype	

Regarding unintentional errors, RET exposes raters to the different errors and their causes. However, being aware of the unintentional errors does not mean that supervisors will no longer make these errors.[14] Awareness is certainly a good first step, but we need to go further if we want to minimize unintentional errors. One fruitful possibility is the implementation of frame of reference training.

7.4.2 Frame of Reference Training

Frame of reference (FOR) training helps improve rater accuracy by thoroughly familiarizing raters with the various performance dimensions to be assessed. The overall goal is to give raters skills so that they can provide accurate ratings of each employee on each dimension by developing a common frame of reference.

A typical FOR training program includes a discussion of the job description for the individuals being rated and the duties involved. Then, raters are familiarized with the performance dimensions to be rated by reviewing the definitions for each dimension and a discussion of examples of good, average, and poor performance. Then, raters are asked to use the appraisal forms to be used in the actual performance management system to rate fictitious employees usually shown in written or videotaped practice vignettes. The trainees are also asked to write a justification for the ratings. Finally, the trainer informs trainees of the correct ratings for each dimension and the reasons for such ratings and discusses differences between the correct ratings and those provided by the trainees. Typically, FOR training programs include the following formal steps:[15]

1. Raters are told that they will evaluate the performance of three employees on three separate performance dimensions.
2. Raters are given an appraisal form and instructed to read it as the trainer reads aloud the definition for each of the dimensions and the scale anchors.
3. The trainer discusses various employee behaviors that illustrate various performance levels for each rating scale included in the form. The goal is to create a common performance theory (frame of reference) among raters so that they will agree on the appropriate performance dimension and effectiveness level for different behaviors.
4. Participants are shown a videotape of a practice vignette, including behaviors related to the performance dimensions being rated, and are asked to evaluate the employee's performance using the scales provided.
5. Ratings provided by each participant are shared with the rest of the group and discussed. The trainer seeks to identify which behaviors participants used to decide on their assigned ratings, and to clarify any discrepancies among the ratings.
6. The trainer provides feedback to participants, explaining why the employee should receive a certain rating (target score) on each dimension and shows discrepancies between the target score and the score given by each trainee.

Consider how the Canadian military uses FOR training.[16] First, the training program includes a session regarding the importance of performance management systems in the military. In the next session, raters are told that they will be evaluating the performance of four subordinates. They are given the appraisal form to be used and information on each of the scales included in the form. As the trainer reads through each of the scales, participants are encouraged to ask questions. At the same time, the trainer gives examples of behaviors associated with each level of performance. The trainer thus makes sure the trainees come to a common frame of reference concerning what behaviors constitute the different levels of performance. Then, participants are shown a videotape of a soldier and they are asked to evaluate the performance using the appraisal form explained earlier. Next, the ratings are discussed as a group, focusing on the behaviors exhibited in the videotape and the ratings that would be most appropriate in each case. This process is repeated several times. Finally, the participants are given three more samples of behavior to rate, as displayed by three hypothetical soldiers, and they receive feedback on how well they evaluate each soldier.

It should be evident by now that FOR training can take quite a bit of time and effort to develop and administer, but it's worth it. Specifically, as a consequence of implementing this type of training, raters not only are more likely to provide consistent and more accurate ratings, but they are also more likely to help employees design effective development plans. This is because sharing a common view of what constitutes good performance allows supervisors to provide employees with better guidelines to employ to reach such performance levels.[17]

7.4.3 Behavioral Observation Training

Behavioral observation (BO) training is another type of program implemented to minimize unintentional rating errors. BO training focuses on how raters observe, store, recall, and use information about performance. Fundamentally, this type of training improves raters' skills at observing performance.

For example, one type of BO training involves showing raters how to use observational aids such as notes or diaries. These observational aids help raters record a preestablished number of behaviors on each performance dimension. Using these aids helps raters increase the sample of incidents observed and recorded during a specific time period. In addition, an aid such as a diary is an effective way to standardize the observation of behavior and record critical incidents throughout the review period. In addition, it also serves as a memory aid when filling out evaluation forms. Memory aids are beneficial because ratings based on memory alone, without notes or diaries, are likely to be distorted due to factors of social context (e.g., friendship bias) and time (i.e., duration of supervisor-subordinate relationship).[18]

Consider how BO training is implemented by the Canadian military. The Canadian military has found that a combination of FOR and BO training works best. Earlier, we described how the Canadian military uses FOR training. BO training is added to the FOR training program. In addition to FOR training, there are sessions on the importance of behavioral observation and common behavioral observation errors, including first impression, stereotypes, and halo effects. Finally, the participants are trained in the importance of keeping diaries and taking notes on their subordinates throughout the year. Furthermore, the trainer explains the criteria for each performance dimension and provides written descriptions of the different levels of performance. The participants are given a chance to practice keeping a diary while watching the vignettes used in the FOR training section of the training program. After watching each vignette, participants are given tips on note taking and recording behaviors as well as the resulting outcomes.

7.4.4 Self-Leadership Training

The goal of self-leadership (SL) training is to improve a rater's confidence in her ability to manage performance. SL training techniques include positive self-talk, mental imagery, and positive beliefs and thought patterns.[19] The assumption is that if there is increased self-direction, self-motivation, and confidence, there will be increased accuracy. Overall, SL emphasizes intrinsic (i.e., internal) sources of behavioral standards and emphasizes doing things for their intrinsic value.

SL training has become a popular tool in the context of performance management systems, and as a type of training program beneficial for supervisors even when they are not necessarily involved in a performance management system. Several studies have shown that SL training can be effective in enhancing mental processes and increasing self-efficacy (i.e., the belief that one can do something if one tries). Designing an SL training program involves the following steps:[20]

1. Observe and record existing beliefs and assumptions, self-talk, and mental imagery patterns. For example, what are the beliefs about the performance management system? How do managers visualize their role in the performance management system? Do they believe they have the capacity to observe and record performance accurately?
2. Analyze the functionality and constructiveness of the beliefs, self-talk, and imagery patterns uncovered in step 1. For example, are the beliefs about the system detrimental to the system's expected success?
3. Identify or develop more functional and constructive beliefs and assumptions, self-verbalizations, and mental images to substitute for dysfunctional ones, for example, develop images of employees being satisfied, as opposed to defensive and confrontational, after receiving performance feedback from their supervisors.
4. Substitute the more functional thinking for the dysfunctional thoughts experienced in actual situations. For example, more constructive assumptions, ways of talking to oneself, and mental images of the likely outcome of a performance discussion with an employee can be worked out and written down on paper.
5. Continue monitoring and maintaining beliefs, self-verbalizations, and mental images over time.

In summary, raters are likely to make both intentional and unintentional errors when providing performance information. Intentional errors are largely due to motivational issues: in some cases, raters see more benefit in distorting ratings than in providing accurate information. Unintentional errors are largely due to cognitive biases that are the product of the complex tasks of observing, encoding, storing, and retrieving performance information. Through the combined use of a good communication plan and various training programs, ratings errors can be substantially minimized. Regarding the communication plan, it is important that it include convincing reasons it is more advantageous to provide accurate than inaccurate performance information. Regarding training programs, these often focus on describing the errors that raters usually make (i.e., RET programs). However, in addition, they should allow raters to come up with a common frame of reference to be used to evaluate performance as well as offer raters tools to improve observation and memory skills. FOR training is particularly beneficial when performance measurement emphasizes behaviors. On the other hand, BO training is particularly beneficial when performance measurement emphasizes results because raters learn not only how to observe behaviors but also how these behaviors are linked to results.

Thus far, this chapter has described how to prepare for the implementation of a performance management system by designing a communication plan and an appeals process, and by delivering training programs. Next, we turn to the final set of activities required before the performance management system is put into practice: pilot testing.

7.5 PILOT TESTING

Before the performance management system is implemented formally, it is a good idea to test a version of the entire system so that adjustments and revisions can be made as needed.[21] In this pilot test of the system, evaluations are not recorded in employee files. However, the system is implemented in its entirety from beginning to end, including all the steps that would be included if the system were to be implemented for real. In other words, meetings take place between supervisor and employee, performance data are gathered, developmental plans are designed, and feedback is provided. The most important aspect of the pilot test is that all participants should maintain records noting any difficulties they encountered, ranging from problems with the appraisal form and how performance is measured to the feedback received. The pilot test allows for the identification and early correction of any flaws before the system is implemented organization-wide.

We should not assume that the performance management system will necessarily be executed and that it will produce the results that are anticipated. The pilot test allows us to gain information from the perspective of the system's users on how well the system works, to learn about any difficulties and unforeseen obstacles, to collect recommendations on how to improve all aspects of the system, and to understand personal reactions to it. In addition, conducting a pilot test is yet another way to achieve early acceptance from a small group who can then act as champions for the performance management system, rather than putting the burden on the HR department to sell the idea. Finally, another good reason to conduct a pilot test is that end users are likely to have a higher system acceptance rate knowing that stakeholders in the company had a say in its design, rather than feeling that the system was created by the HR department alone.

An important decision to be made is the selection of the group of employees with whom the system will be tested. In choosing this group, we need to understand that the managers who will be participating should be willing to invest the resources required to do the pilot test. In addition, this group should be made up of managers who are flexible and willing to try new things. Thus, managers should know what the system will look like and receive a realistic preview before they decide to participate in the pilot test.

In selecting the group, we must also consider that the group should be sufficiently large and representative of the entire organization so that reactions from the group will be generalizable to the rest of the organization. Thus, in selecting the group, we should select jobs that are similar to those throughout the company, and the group selected should not be seen as an exception in either a positive or a negative way. Specifically, the group should not be seen as particularly productive, loose, hard, lazy, and so forth.

Pilot tests provide crucial information to be used in improving the system before it is actually put in place. Pilot testing the system can provide huge savings and identify potential problems before they become irreversible and the credibility of the system is ruined permanently. For example, consider the case of the Washington State Patrol.[22] In 1997, it realized that there were several changes occurring in its department, as well as in patrol departments in other states, that prompted the revision of its performance management system. It established a committee to develop the new appraisals. Before implementing the system, the state patrol pilot tested it in two districts. First, the committee prepared a training chapter that included a preappraisal work group meeting. In this meeting, employees discussed their roles and expectations surrounding the performance management system and applied those discussions to a common goal. The training also focused on how new developments in the patrol led to the new elements in the performance management system. During the training, the trainers encouraged the participants to ask questions regarding the shift to the new approach. The trainers then used the feedback received in these sessions to fix specific operational issues before introducing the training to the entire agency. After the appraisal process was fine-tuned, it was submitted for the approval of the troopers' and sergeants' associations. Then a select number of individuals across the districts received "train the trainer" training. Finally, the system was instituted agency-wide. Each of these steps allowed for the identification of potential barriers that could have prevented the system from being successful.

7.6 ONGOING MONITORING AND EVALUATION

When the testing period is over and the performance management system is implemented organization-wide, it is important to use clear measurements to monitor and evaluate the system.[23] In a nutshell, a decision needs to be made about how to evaluate the system's effectiveness, how to evaluate the extent to which the system is being implemented as planned, and how to evaluate the extent to which it is producing the intended results.

Evaluation data should include reactions to the system and assessments of the system's operational and technical requirements. For example, a confidential survey could be administered to all employees asking about perceptions and attitudes about the system. This survey can be administered during the initial stages of implementation and then at the end of the first review cycle to see if there have been any changes. In addition, regarding the system's results, one can assess performance ratings over time to see what positive effects the implementation of the system is having.

There are additional measures that can be used on a regular basis to monitor and evaluate the system:

- *Number of individuals evaluated.*   One of the most basic measures is to assess the number of employees who are actually participating in the system. If performance evaluations have not been completed for some employees, then we need to find out who they are and why a performance review has not been completed.
- *Distribution of performance ratings.*   An indicator of quality of the performance assessments is whether all or most scores are too high, too low, or clumped around the center of the distribution. This may indicate intentional

errors such as leniency, severity, and central tendency. Distributions of performance ratings can be broken down by unit and supervisor to see if any trends exist regarding rating distortion and whether these distortions are localized in particular units. Note that there may be exceptional units in which most employees are outstanding performers and units in which most employees are poor performers. However, this is the exception to the rule and such distributions usually indicate intentional errors on the part of raters.

- *Quality of information.*   Another indicator of quality of the performance assessments is the quality of the information provided in the open-ended sections of the forms. For example, how much did the rater write? What is the relevance of the examples provided?
- *Quality of performance discussion meeting.*   A confidential survey can be distributed to all employees on a regular basis to gather information on how the supervisor is managing the performance discussion meetings. For example, is the feedback useful? Has the supervisor made resources available so the employee can accomplish the developmental plan objectives? How relevant was the performance review discussion to one's job? To what degree have developmental objectives and plans been discussed?[24]
- *System satisfaction.*   A confidential survey could also be distributed to assess the perceptions of the system's users, both raters and ratees. This survey can include questions about satisfaction with equity, usefulness, and accuracy.
- *Overall cost/benefit ratio.*   A fairly simple way to address the overall impact of the system is to ask participants to rate the overall cost versus benefit ratio for the performance management system. This is a type of bottom-line question that can provide convincing evidence for the overall worth of the system.
- *Unit-level and organization-level performance.*   Another indicator that the system is working well is provided by the measurement of unit- and organization-level performance. Such performance indicators might be customer satisfaction with specific units and indicators of the financial performance of the various units or the organization as a whole. We need to be aware that it may take some time for changes in individual and group performance level to be translated into unit- and organization-level results. We should not expect immediate results as soon as the system is implemented. However, we should start to see some tangible results at the unit level a few months after the system is in place.

Returning to the performance management system at the Washington State Patrol, we can examine how it has evaluated effectiveness since the system was implemented.[25] The patrol has several measures in place for continual evaluation of the effectiveness of the program. First, before all employees were reviewed using the system, they were surveyed regarding their satisfaction with the new system. This input was then used to further improve the appraisal process. In addition, the patrol also uses the results of a biyearly citizen's survey conducted by Washington State University. The results of this survey are used to determine if the state patrol's customers are satisfied with its performance and the data are also used to adjust and reprioritize performance objectives. In addition, the data are used to measure division-level performance, one indicator of the success of the performance management process. The Washington State Patrol collects other types of data as well. For example, every six months division managers give presentations regarding performance management to their peers and to several executives. Initially, the meetings have been focused on efforts to implement the new performance management system and increasing quality, but this will change as new issues arise. The presentation is 30–40 minutes long, followed by 20–30 minutes of questions from peers and executives. The feedback from these presentations is used to measure how well the system is being implemented, and feedback on the success of the meetings will be used to make any necessary changes to the system.

The Washington State Patrol may also want to consider measuring how many people are participating in the system. The patrol would also benefit from assessing whether the new system is distinguishing high- from low-level performers, and the overall cost/benefit ratio of implementing the system.

SUMMARY POINTS

- Some important steps need to be taken before the performance management system is implemented. These include implementing a communication plan and an appeals process, which will help gain system acceptance, training programs for raters, which will help minimize errors in performance ratings, and pilot testing the system, which will allow for revisions and changes before the system is actually implemented. Careful attention to these presystem implementation steps will help improve the success of the system.

- The main goal of the communication plan is to gain support for the system. A good communication plan addresses the following questions:

  - What is performance management? What are its general goals? How have performance management systems been implemented in other organizations?

  - How does performance management fit with the organizational strategy?

  - What are the tangible benefits of the performance management system for all parties involved?

  - How does the system work? what are the various steps in the process?

  - What are the roles and responsibilities of each organizational member?

  - How does performance management relate to other initiatives and programs such as training, promotion, compensation, and so forth?

Including detailed, convincing, and clear answers for each of these questions is likely to help increase support for the system.

- People have biases in how they take in and process information. Thus, even though there may be a good communication plan in place, these biases may distort the information presented. Biases to take into account are selective exposure, selective perception, and selective retention. Selective exposure is a tendency to expose our minds only to ideas with which we already agree. Selective perception is a tendency to perceive a piece of information as meaning what we would like it to mean even though the information, as intended by the communicator, may mean the exact opposite. Finally, selective retention is a tendency to remember only those pieces of information with which we already agree.

- The negative effects of cognitive biases can be minimized by involving employees in system design, considering employees' needs in designing and implementing the system, delivering the communication plan before negative attitudes are established and rumors start circulating, putting information concerning the system in writing, providing facts and consequences and not just facts, using multiple channels of communication to present information on the system, using credible and powerful communicators, and repeating the information frequently. A good communication plan includes as many of these features as possible.

- In addition to a communication plan, setting up an appeals process also helps gain system acceptance. An appeals process allows employees to understand that, if there is a disagreement regarding performance ratings or any resulting decisions, such disagreements can be resolved in an amicable and nonretaliatory way.

- The appeals process begins with an employee filing an appeal with the HR department, which serves as a mediator between the employee and her supervisor. This is a Level 1 appeal. If the appeal is not resolved, then an outside and unbiased arbitrator makes a final and binding resolution. This is a Level 2 appeal. The arbitrator for a Level 2 appeal is usually a panel that includes peers and managers.

- In rating performance, raters may make intentional or unintentional errors. Intentional errors take place when raters believe it will be more beneficial to them to provide distorted as opposed to accurate ratings. For example, a supervisor may not want to give a low rating to avoid a possible confrontation with an employee. Intentional errors include leniency (giving better scores than warranted), severity (giving worse scores than warranted), and central tendency (giving scores around the midpoint of the scales only). Motivation is the key to minimize intentional errors. In other words, we must demonstrate to the raters that the benefits of providing accurate ratings outweigh the benefits

of intentionally distorting ratings either by inflation, deflation, or central tendency. The communication plan takes care of this; by addressing the "What's in it for me?" question, including the "What's in it if I provide accurate ratings?" question.

- Unintentional errors are caused by the fact that observing, encoding, storing, and retrieving performance information is a complex cognitive task. Unintentional errors include the following: (1) similar to me, (2) contrast, (3) halo, (4) primacy, (5) recency, (6) negativity, (7) first impression, (8) spillover, and (9) stereotype. Unintentional errors can be minimized by implementing rater training programs.

- Rater error training (RET) is a type of program that exposes raters to the different errors and their causes. RET does not guarantee rating accuracy, but becoming aware about what types of errors are likely to occur and the reasons for these errors is a very good first step in minimizing them.

- Frame of reference (FOR) training is a type of program that familiarizes raters with the various performance dimensions to be assessed. The goal is that raters will develop a common frame of reference in observing and evaluating performance. This type of training is most appropriate when performance measurement focuses on behaviors.

- Behavioral observation (BO) training is a type of program that focuses on how raters observe, store, recall, and use information about performance. For example, this type of program teaches raters how to use aids such as diaries to standardize performance observation. This type of training is most appropriate when performance measurement focuses on counting and recording how frequently certain behaviors and results take place.

- Self-leadership (SL) training is a type of program that aims at improving raters' confidence in their ability to manage performance. SL training includes positive self-talk, mental imagery, and positive beliefs and thought patterns.
- Pilot testing the system before it is instituted fully is useful because it allows for the discovery of potential problems and glitches and then take corrective action, before the system is put in place. Pilot testing consists of implementing the entire system, including all of its components, but only with a select group of people, and results are not recorded in employees' records. Instead, the goal is that people participating in the pilot test provide feedback on any possible problems and on how to improve the system.
- The group participating in the pilot test needs to take into account that the test will take time and resources. A representative group should be selected so that conclusions drawn from the group can be generalized to the organization as a whole. The group should not be seen as an exception in either a positive or negative way.
- After the system is implemented, there should be a measurement system to evaluate the extent to which it is working the way it should and producing the results that were expected. Such measures include confidential employee surveys assessing perceptions and attitudes about the system and whether there is an upward trend in performance scores over time. In addition, other measures include number of individuals evaluated, distribution of performance ratings, quality of performance information gathered, quality of performance discussion meetings, user satisfaction with the system, overall cost/benefit ratio, and unit- and organization-level performance indicators. Taken together, these indicators are a powerful tool to demonstrate the value that is added by the performance management system.

Case Study 7.1 Implementing a Performance Management Communication Plan at Accounting, Inc.[1]

Accounting, Inc., is a consulting and accounting firm headquartered in Amsterdam, the Netherlands. Recently, Accounting, Inc., implemented a performance management system. The first step in the implementation of the new system was the development of a set of core competencies that would be used to evaluate most employees regardless of function or level. In addition, each employee was evaluated using more job-specific performance dimensions.

As the first step in the communication plan, the employees received individual e-mail messages asking them to define what the core competencies meant to them and to give descriptions and examples of how each of the core competencies played out in their specific positions. Next, the company held meetings, handed out frequently asked questions (FAQs) sheets, and placed posters around the company detailing how the core competencies were related to the organization's strategic priorities and how performance scores would be related to monetary rewards. In these communications, Accounting, Inc., detailed how the performance system worked, how the raters were chosen, how performance feedback was used, and other details about the system. The information also outlined the benefits employees could expect from the new system as well as employees' responsibilities regarding the system.

Please evaluate Accounting, Inc.'s communication plan. Specifically, does it answer all of the questions that a good communication plan should answer? Which questions are left unanswered? How would you provide answers to the unanswered questions (if any)? ■

Case Study 7.2 Implementing an Appeals Process at Accounting, Inc.

Following up on Case Study 7.1, when the system was implemented many employees were not happy with the scores and the type of performance feedback information they received from their supervisors. If you were to design an appeals process to handle these complaints well, what would the appeals process be like? (Hint: Use the appeals process shown in the box on pages 154–155 as a model.) ■

---

[1]Adapted from P. Brotherton, "Meyners Pays for Performance: Changing a Compensation System Is a Sensitive Undertaking; Here's How One Firm Handled It," *Journal of Accountancy, 196*(2003): 41–46.

Case Study 7.3   Evaluation of Performance Management System at Accounting, Inc.

This is a follow-up to Case Study 7.1 and Case Study 7.2. Once the performance system was in place, Accounting, Inc., implemented several measures to evaluate the system. First, the company distributed an employee survey to assess employee satisfaction with the new system. In addition, the HR department examined the distribution of ratings to see if scores were influenced by leniency, central tendency, or severity biases. Finally, the HR department also kept track of the allocation of rewards in the various departments to examine if there were any departments that stood out. From your perspective, what other types of data can be collected to assess the effectiveness of the system? What kind of information would each measure provide? What is the rationale for implementing each type of measure? ■

End Notes

1. Williams, J. R., & Levy, P. (2000). Investigating some neglected criteria: The influence of organizational level and perceived system knowledge on appraisal reactions. *Journal of Business and Psychology, 14*, 501–513.
2. Grote, D. (1996). *The complete guide to performance appraisal.* New York: AMACOM.
3. U.S. Department of Justice, Human Resources. (2004, April 30) http://www.usdoj. gov/jmd/ps/sespmsplan.htm.
4. U.S. Department of Justice, Senior Executive Service, Performance management system for SES employees. Available online at http://www.usdoj.gov/jmd/ps/sespmsplan.htm. Retrieval date: August 15, 2005.
5. Morhman, A. M., Resnick-West, S. M., & Lawler, E. E. (1989). *Designing performance appraisal systems* (p. 133). San Francisco, CA: Jossey-Bass.
6. Kleingfeld, A., van Tuijl, H. & Algera, J. A. (2004). Participation in the design of performance management systems: A quasi-experimental field study. *Journal of Organizational Behavior, 25*, 831–851.
7. Greenberg, J. (1986). Determinants of perceived fairness of performance evaluations. *Journal of Applied Psychology, 71*, 340–342.
8. Grote, D. (1996). *The complete guide to performance appraisal* (pp. 263–269). New York: AMACOM.
9. University of North Caroline at Chapel Hill, Office of Human Resources, *Performance management appeals process.* Available online at http://hr.unc.edu/Data/SPA/perfmgt/perf-appeal. Retrieval date: August 15, 2005
10. Spears, M. C., Parker, D. F. (2002). A probit analysis of the impact of training on performance appraisal satisfaction. *American Business Review, 20*, 12–16.
11. Bernardin, H. J., Cooke, D. K., & Villanova, P. (2000). Conscientiousness and aggreableness as predictors of rating leniency. *Journal of Applied Psychology, 85*, 232–234.
12. Aguinis, H., & Adams, S. K. R. (1998). Social-role versus structural models of gender and influence use in organizations: A strong inference approach. *Group and Organization Management, 23*, 414–446.
13. Heilman, M. E., Wallen, A. S., Fuchs, D., & Tamkins, M. M. (2004). Penalties for success: Reactions to women who succeed at male gender-typed tasks. *Journal of Applied Psychology, 89*, 416–427.
14. London, M., Mone, E. M., & Scott, J. C. (2004). Performance management and assessement: Methods for improved rater accuracy and employee goal setting. *Human Resource Management, 43*, 319–336.
15. Pulakos, E. D. (1986). The development of training programs to increase accuracy with

different rating tasks. *Organizational Behavior and Human Decision Processes, 38,* 76–91.

16. Noonan, L. E., & Sulsky, L. M. (2001). Impact of frame-of-reference and behavioral observation training on alternative training effectiveness criteria in a Canadian Military Sample. *Human Performance, 14,* 3–26.

17. Stamoulis, D. T., & Hauenstein, N. M. A. (1993). Rater training and rating accuracy: Training for dimensional accuracy versus training for rate differentiation. *Journal of Applied Psychology, 78,* 994–1003.

18. Duarte, N. T., Goodson, J. R., & Klich, N. R. (2004). Effects of dyadic quality and duration on performance appraisal. *Academy of Management Journal, 37,* 499–521.

19. Neck, C. P., Stewart, G. L., & Manz, C. C. (1995). Thought self-leadership as a framework for enhancing the performance of performance appraisers. *Journal of Applied Behavioral Science, 31,* 278–302.

20. Neck, C. P., Smith, W. J., & Godwin, J. L. (1997). Thought self-leadership: A self-regulatory approach to diversity management. *Journal of Managerial Psychology, 12,* 190–203.

21. Grote, D. (1996). *The complete guide to performance appraisal* (pp. 254–256). New York: AMACOM.

22. Cederblom, D., & Pemerl, D. E. (2002). From performance appraisal to performance management: One agency's experience. *Public Personnel Management, 31,* 131–140.

23. Grote, D. (1996). *The complete guide to performance appraisal* (pp. 260–263). New York: AMACOM.

24. Dipboye, R. L, and de Pontbriand, R. (1981). Correlates of employee reactions to performance appraisal and appraisal systems. *Journal of Applied Psychology, 66,* 248–251.

25. Cederblom, D., & Pemerl, D. E. (2002). From performance appraisal to performance management: One agency's experience. *Public Personnel Management, 31,* 131–140.

C H A P T E R

Performance Management and Employee Development

One of the tests of leadership is the ability to recognize a problem before it becomes an emergency.

—Arnold H. Glasow

Learning Objectives

By the end of this chapter, you will be able to do the following:

- Describe the importance and benefits of including a developmental plan as part of the performance management system.

- Describe the various short-term and long-term objectives of a developmental plan.

- Design a high-quality developmental plan.

- Learn about the key activities that will help the successful implementation of a developmental plan.

- Understand the role that the direct supervisor plays in the design and implementation of a developmental plan.

- Implement a 360-degree feedback system with the goal of providing feedback on and improving performance.

- Implement an online 360-degree feedback system.

- Understand the advantages, as well as the risks, of implementing a 360-degree feedback system.

- Evaluate the quality of a 360-degree feedback system.

Part I of this text described strategic and macro-organizational issues in designing a performance management system. Part II described operational details on how to implement the system. Part III includes two chapters dealing with employee developmental issues. There are two key stakeholders in the developmental process: (1) the employees of the organization who are improving their own performance, and (2) the managers who help guide the process of employee development for their staff, and support it so that it can successfully occur. Developmental planning is a joint activity entered into by both the employee and the manager. Chapter 8 addresses how to use a performance management system to help employees develop and improve their performance. Chapter 9 addresses skills needed by managers so that they can best manage the performance of their employees. Let's begin this chapter by discussing personal developmental plans.

8.1 PERSONAL DEVELOPMENTAL PLANS

Personal developmental plans specify courses of action to be taken to improve performance. Achieving the goals stated in the developmental plan allows employees to keep abreast of changes in their field or profession. Such plans highlight an employee's strengths and the areas in need of development, and provide an action plan to develop areas of weaknesses and further develop areas of strength.[1] In a nutshell, personal developmental plans allow employees to answer the following questions:

- How can I continually learn and grow in the next year?
- How can I do better in the future?
- How can I avoid performance problems faced in the past?

Developmental plans can be created for every job, ranging from entry level to the executive suite. No matter how high up the position within the organization and how simple or complex the nature of the job in question, there is always room for improvement. Information to be used in designing developmental plans comes from the appraisal form. Specifically, a developmental plan can be designed based on each of the performance dimensions evaluated. So, for example, if the performance dimension "communication" is rated as substandard, then this would be an area targeted by the developmental plan. In addition, however, developmental plans also focus on knowledge and skills needed for more long-term career aspirations.

8.1.1 Developmental Plan Objectives

The overall objective of a developmental plan is to encourage continuous learning, performance improvement, and personal growth. In addition, developmental plans have more specific objectives. These are to:

- *Improve performance in current job.* A good developmental plan helps employees meet performance standards. Thus, a developmental plan includes suggested courses of action to address each of the performance dimensions that are deficient. This is an important point given that recent surveys have shown that about 25% of federal employees and between 11%–16% of private sector employees in the United States are not performing up to standards.[2]
- *Sustain performance in current job.* A good developmental plan provides tools so that employees can continue to meet and exceed expectations regarding the current job. Thus, the plan includes suggestions about how

to continue to meet and exceed expectations for each of the performance dimensions included in the appraisal form.

- *Prepare employees for advancement.*   A good developmental plan includes advice and courses of action that should be taken so that employees will be able to take advantage of future opportunities and career advancement. Specifically, a good plan indicates which new competencies and behaviors should be learned to help career advancement.
- *Enrich the employee's work experience.*   Even if career opportunities within the organization are not readily available, a good plan provides employees with growth opportunities and opportunities to learn new skills. These opportunities provide employees with intrinsic rewards and a more challenging work experience, even if the new skills learned are not a formal part of their jobs. Such opportunities can make jobs more attractive and serve as a powerful employee retention tool. In addition, the new skills can be useful in case of lateral transfers within the organization.

Consider the employee developmental plan used by Texas A&M University in College Station Texas (http://hr.tamu.edu/ed/forms.html). The developmental plan is a formal component of the university's performance management system, so the developmental plan is included within the appraisal form. The appraisal form used by Texas A&M first lists the five objectives of the performance management system, which are to:

1. Provide employees with feedback to improve or maintain job performance
2. Outline areas for employee development
3. Set performance standards for the next review period
4. Recognize job-related accomplishments
5. Enhance communication and working relationships

Based on objective 2, the employee developmental plan is described as an important component of the performance management system. The inclusion of this objective up front sets the tone for the developmental process by helping managers understand that this is an important issue.

After the sections in the form in which the manager rates employee performance, the following material is included:

SECTION B: PROFESSIONAL DEVELOPMENTAL PLAN

Please list professional developmental activities to be completed and resources needed to support these activities, if applicable (link to examples of suggested employee development: http://hr.tamu.edu/ed/suggest.pdf)

Professional Development Needs | Resources/Support Needed | Time Frame

_____ _____ _____

_____ _____ _____

_____ _____ _____

_____ _____ _____

The inclusion of this information after performance ratings allows the manager and employee to focus on developmental areas identified as weaknesses in the performance review process. In this way, the developmental plans created for employees at Texas A&M are directly related to performance dimensions important for the unit and the overall organization. In addition, including the developmental plan at the end of the review and after setting annual performance goals allows the employee to determine if there are areas he or she needs to develop in order to attain the specified goals.

Why does goal setting work? In other words, in studies of over 40,000 people in eight countries, why have "stretch" goals led to better performance than "do your best" or easy goals?[3] There are four basic reasons. First, when an employee commits to a goal, he or she diverts attention away from activities that are not relevant to the goal and toward activities that are relevant. Second, challenging goals are energizing and lead to higher levels of effort. Third, stretch goals lead to persistence (e.g., tight deadlines lead to a faster pace than do loose deadlines). Finally, stretch goals motivate employees to use the knowledge they have to reach the goal or to search for new knowledge that they may need.[4]

8.1.2 Content of Developmental Plan

What does a developmental plan look like? Plans should include a description of specific steps to be taken and specific objectives to reach. In other words, what is the new skill or knowledge that will be acquired and how will this happen? This includes information on the resources and strategies that will be used to achieve the objectives. For example, will the employee learn the skill from a coworker through on-the-job training? Will the company reimburse the employee for expenses associated with taking an online course?

The plan's objectives should include not only the end product, such as the new skill to be learned, but also the completion date and how the supervisor will know whether the new skill has indeed been acquired. For example, in the case of the online course, the objective could state that the course will be completed by July 23, 2007, and the employee is expected to receive a grade of B+ or better. Overall, objectives included in the developmental plans should be practical, specific, time oriented, linked to a standard, and developed jointly between the supervisor and the employee.

An additional important feature of developmental plans is that they should keep the needs of both the organization and the employee in mind. The choice for what specific skills or performance areas will be improved is dictated by the needs of the organization, especially when the organization is investing in the plan. In addition, the plan created is dictated by the needs of the individual. The supervisor and the employee need to agree on what development or new skills will help enrich the employee's work experience, and will help accomplish organizational goals at present or in the near future.

As an example, consider the content of the developmental plan at Texas A&M. First, employees are directed to a Web site that includes examples of possible developmental activities (http://hr.tamu.edu/ed/suggest.pdf). This list includes workshops, certifications, local, state, and national conferences, on-the-job training, and other activities. This is good information because it presents employees and managers with various options they need to achieve the developmental objectives. Second, the form includes space so that each professional developmental need is paired with a description of resources or support needed and a time frame for completion. For example, the developmental plan for an administrative assistant in the Business School may look like this:

SECTION B: PROFESSIONAL DEVELOPMENTAL PLAN

Please list professional developmental activities to be completed and resources needed to support these activities, if applicable (link to examples of suggested employee development: http://hr.tamu.edu/ed/suggest.pdf)

Professional Development Needs	Resources/Support Needed	Time Frame
1. Knowledge of Excel (spreadsheet program)	Reimbursement for online course	Course to be completed by August 1, 2007
2. Customer service skills in dealing with students and faculty	Reimbursement for 1-day workshop. Time to receive on-the-job training from administrative assistant in Psychology Department.	Workshop to be completed by Oct. 15, 2007. On-the-job training completed by November 1, 2007.

Overall, the Texas A&M plan includes all of the required components. There is a description of developmental objectives, activities that will be conducted to reach these objectives, and dates of completion. However, an important piece is missing. The plan does not include specifics of how the accomplishment of each objective will be measured. Specifically, how will the supervisor know if the administrative assistant has good knowledge of Excel after she completes the online course? How will the supervisor know if the administrative assistant's customer service skills have improved after attending the workshop and undergoing on-the-job training? Regarding the Excel training, this could be measured by the administrative assistant's performance in the course. In addition, this could be measured by examining answers to questions about knowledge of Excel that faculty and others giving Excel assignments to the administrative assistant answer in filling out appraisal forms. Regarding customer service skills, the accomplishment of the objective might be measured by questioning those customers served by the administrative assistant (i.e., faculty and students).

8.1.3 Developmental Activities

There are several ways through which employees can reach the objectives stated in their developmental plans. These include the following:

- *On-the-job-training.*   Employees are paired with a coworker or supervisor who designs a formal on-the-job training course. The design of these mini-training programs includes how many hours a day or week training will take place and specific learning objectives.
- *Courses.*   Some large organizations, such as McDonald's, Motorola, Capgemini, Ernst & Young, and others, offer in-house courses given at their own corporate universities. Other organizations may provide tuition reimbursement. Given the proliferation of online courses, employees have a wide variety of options from which to choose.
- *Self-guided reading.*   An employee can read books and other resources on her own. Once again, it is important that an objective be set regarding what

will be read and within what time frame, as well as what measure(s) will be used to assess whether learning has taken place.

- *Mentoring.* Many organizations have mentoring programs. In general terms, mentoring is a developmental process that consists of a one-on-one relationship between a senior (mentor) and junior (protégé) employee. For such programs to be successful, it is best to allow the mentor and protégé to choose each other rather than arbitrarily assigning who will be mentoring whom. In general, mentors serve as role models and teach protégés what it takes to succeed in the organization. In more specific terms, mentors can help protégés gain targeted skills.

- *Attending a conference.* Another way to acquire required knowledge and skills is to sponsor an employee's attendance at a conference or trade show. It is useful to require that the employee provide a written report, or even deliver a presentation, upon returning from the conference. In this way, it is easier to assess what has been learned and, in addition, the knowledge gained can be shared with other organizational members.

- *Getting a degree.* Some organizations will provide tuition reimbursement benefits so their employees can obtain additional degrees or certifications. For example, the organization can sponsor an employee's MBA program or an employee's taking a course with the goal of earning a certification designation (e.g., Certified Novell Administrator, Professional in Human Resources). In most cases, employees commit to continuing the relationship with their employer for a prespecified amount of time after completing the degree. If the employee leaves the organization before this time frame, he may have to reimburse the organization for the cost of his education.

- *Job rotation.* Another way to gain necessary skills is to be assigned to a different job on a temporary basis. This is the model followed in the medical profession in which residents have to rotate across specialty areas for several months (e.g., OB-GYN, psychiatry, pediatrics). For example, residents may be required to rotate across the various emergency medicine services for a 19-month period.

- *Temporary assignments.* A less systematic rotation system includes the opportunity to work on a challenging temporary assignment. This allows employees to gain specific skills within a limited time frame.

- *Membership or leadership role in professional or trade organizations.* Some employers may sponsor membership in professional or trade organizations. Such an organization distributes publications to its members and also allows for informal and formal meetings in which employees have an opportunity to learn about best practices and other useful information for their jobs. For example, this could include the Society for Human Resource Management (www.shrm.org) or the Chartered Institute of Personnel and Development (http://www.cipd.co.uk/) for human resources (HR) professionals. Also, presentation, communication, planning, and other skills can be learned while serving in a leadership role in a volunteer organization outside of work.

Table 8.1 includes a summarized list of developmental activities that may be available to achieve goals included in a developmental plan. Based on your own preferences

---

TABLE 8.1   Summary List of Developmental Activities

On-the-job-training

Courses

Self-guided reading

Mentoring

Attending a conference

Getting a degree

Job rotation

Temporary assignments

Membership in professional or trade organizations

---

and learning style, which of these activities do you believe would be most beneficial to you? Please rank these activities in terms of your preference.

An example of a developmental plan is included in Figure 8.1. The developmental plan can be part of the appraisal form, or be included in a separate form. The form

---

FIGURE 8.1   Example of a Developmental Plan Form[5]

Update Date:
Name:
Job Title/Job Code:
Department:
Primary Reviewer:
Education:
Prior Training:
Job History:
Career Goals:
      Next 1 year
      Next 2 years
      Next 3 years
      Next 5 years

Dev. Options	Description	Type of Development	When	How Long	Completed Hours (this Qtr.)	Comments— Approx. Cost —Other	Objectives/ Evaluation
OJT (on the job) training							
Classes	Current Qtr.						
Conferences							
Online							
Self-study							
Job rotation	Next. Qtr.						
Videos							
Books							
Temp. assignment							
Mentorship	Current +2						
Other (specify)							
	Current +3						

included in Figure 8.1 shows that employees have several choices in terms of developmental activities. Note that the form includes space so that information can be inserted regarding what activities will take place when, what the objectives are, and whether the objective has been met or not.

Consider your future career expectations and developmental needs. Then fill out the form included in Figure 8.1, assuming your current or future employer is willing to provide any developmental opportunities of your choosing. What does your plan look like? What did you discover about what you would like to learn in the future? What does this information tell you about your level of aspirations and future prospects for your career advancement?

8.2 DIRECT SUPERVISOR'S ROLE

The direct supervisor or line manager has an important role in the creation and completion of the employee's developmental plan. First, the supervisor needs to explain what would be required for the employee to achieve the desired performance level, including the steps that an employee must take to improve her performance. This information needs to be provided together with information on the probability of success if the employee completes the suggested steps. Second, the supervisor has a primary role in referring the employee to appropriate developmental activities that can assist the employee in achieving her goals. This includes helping the employee select a mentor, appropriate reading resources, courses, and so forth. Third, the supervisor reviews and makes suggestions about the developmental objectives. Specifically, the supervisor helps assure the goals are achievable, specific, and doable. Fourth, the supervisor has primary responsibility for checking on the employee's progress toward achieving the developmental goals. For example, the supervisor can remind the employee of due dates and revise goals if needed. Finally, the supervisor needs to provide reinforcements so the employee will be motivated to achieve the developmental goals. Reinforcements can be extrinsic and include rewards such as bonuses and additional benefits. However, reinforcements can also include the assignment of more challenging and interesting work that takes advantage of the new skills learned.

Supervisors themselves need to be motivated to perform functions that will support the employees' completion of their developmental objectives. For this to happen, supervisors must be rewarded for doing a good job in helping their employees develop. Consider how this is done at KLA-Tencor Corporation (www.kla-tencor.com), one of the world's top 10 manufacturers of semiconductor equipment. At KLA-Tencor, between 10%–30% of supervisors' bonus pay is directly tied to employee development. Employee development is measured in terms of employee training and certification levels. Managers are given at least quarterly updates on the status of their staff development. In addition, employees themselves are rewarded for engaging in developmental activities. In fact, only employees with up-to-date training and certification levels are eligible for bonuses. Thus, employee development is successful at KLA-Tencor because both employees and managers are directly rewarded for employee development. After several years of implementing these practices, employee development has become the norm and is part of the KLA-Tencor's culture.[6]

TABLE 8.2	**Factors Promoting Successful Implementation of Personal Developmental Plans**[7]

All employees have a plan (including managers from all levels in the organization).

All employees are entitled to developmental opportunities on an ongoing basis.

Managers are involved with the assessment of objective accomplishment and monitor progress toward accomplishing developmental objectives.

Managers are committed to the development of their employees and to helping their employees fulfill their career aspirations.

The developmental plan becomes an integral part of the performance management system.

The performance of managers is evaluated, in part, based on how well they manage the developmental process for their employees.

In short, the direct supervisor plays a key role in the success of the developmental plan. Table 8.2 summarizes many of the points we have discussed thus far that will promote successful implementation of personal developmental plans.

8.3 360-DEGREE FEEDBACK SYSTEMS

The 360-degree feedback system has become a preferred tool for helping employees, particularly those in supervisory roles, improve performance by gathering information from different groups. These systems are called 360-degree because information is gathered from individuals all around the employee. Specifically, information on what performance dimensions could be improved is gathered from superiors, peers, customers, and subordinates. This information is usually collected anonymously to minimize rating inflation. Employees also rate themselves on the various performance dimensions and compare self-perceptions with the information provided by others. A gap analysis is conducted to examine the areas for which there are large discrepancies between self-perceptions and the perceptions of others. Also, a 360-degree feedback system report usually includes information on dimensions for which there is agreement that further development is needed. Then, this information is used in creating a developmental plan as described earlier in the chapter. For example, a study including over 2,000 managers demonstrated that the objectives included in personal developmental plans were driven by performance dimensions that received low scores in 360-degree feedback systems.[8]

The 360-degree feedback system is most helpful when it is used for developmental purposes only and not for administrative purposes.[9] This is because people are more likely to be honest if they know the information will be used to help the individual improve and not just to punish or to reward him or her. The 360-degree feedback system is usually implemented for individuals who have supervisory roles, but these systems can be used for all positions within the organization.

Many organizations take advantage of technology to minimize the amount of paperwork and time involved in collecting such data. The Internet is becoming a pervasive medium by which to administer 360-degree feedback systems. The service provider, usually an outside consulting firm, sends an e-mail message with instructions and time frames for assessment to each employee to be rated. Then, employees can access a secure Web site and, after entering their personal IDs and passwords, create individual lists of raters who will be asked to provide feedback about their performance. To make things easier, the employee can even select names from a drop-down menu that includes company managers and employees. Allowing employees to select the raters who will provide information on their performance is likely to increase acceptance of the results.[10] Then, raters selected are asked to visit the Web site and to provide performance feedback within a certain time period. Once data are collected electronically, it is fairly easy to compile the results and e-mail a report to the employee who has been evaluated.

Some Internet-based systems also provide online training for raters in how to complete the feedback forms in helpful and constructive ways. Some systems even include features that allow for the detection of rating errors. For example, a window may pop up if a rater gives the maximum score to an employee on all dimensions. Raters can see a graph on the screen that shows the extent to which the ratings they have provided agree with the ratings provided by other people rating the same employee. Finally, some systems include an online virtual feedback coach to help create developmental plans. The final plan, however, must be consensually decided upon in a meeting between the employee and his supervisor. Unless the developmental plan has complete acceptance from the employee, it is likely to become another inconsequential HR-mandated task.[11]

Feedback reports can include graphs showing the areas for which employees' perceptions differ the most from the perceptions of other raters. They can also show average scores, across sources of information, so that areas that need improvement are readily identified. The resulting report can be e-mailed automatically to the employee and his supervisor so that both have an opportunity to review the results before meeting to create a developmental plan.

Table 8.3 includes a nonexhaustive list of vendors that offer Internet-based 360-degree feedback systems and a brief description of their products. This table also includes information on whether there is a demonstration of it available online. As can be seen by the information included in this table, there are many such systems available.

As an illustration, consider the system offered by CheckPoint (http://ourworld. compuserve.com/homepages/gately/chkpoint.htm). This system is designed for employees in supervisory roles and includes information on the following competencies:

- Communication (listens to others, processes information, communicates effectively)
- Leadership (instills trust, provides direction, delegates responsibility)
- Adaptability (adjusts to circumstances, thinks creatively)
- Relationships (builds personal relationships, facilitates team success)
- Task management (works efficiently, works competently)
- Production (takes action, achieves results)
- Development of others (cultivates individual talent, motivates successfully)
- Personal development (displays commitment, seeks improvement)

TABLE 8.3   Examples of Vendors Offering 360-Degree Feedback Systems

Vendor	Description from Web Site
Panoramic Feedback http://www.panoramicfeedback.com/ (demo available online)	Internet-based 360-degree feedback, supports more than 20 languages (more on the way soon!), HRIS integration, aggregate reporting to guide strategy, excellent for larger and/or multilingual organizations.
Halogen Software http://www.halogensoftware.com/ products/e360open.php (demo available online)	Halogen e360 is a sophisticated Web-based 360-degree feedback software that simplifies the entire multirater process. It's a simple approach to employee performance management that significantly reduces resource demands. Creating an evaluation, monitoring the process, and generating reports are all as easy as point and click. Participating is equally simple.
The Booth Company http://www.boothco.com/home.html (demo available online)	Fifteen unique surveys customized to organizational roles. Psychometrically sound instrumentation. Web-based developmental programs for each survey.
Personnel Decisions International http://www.personneldecisions.com/ offerings/multitrater.asp	We know how to design and deliver 360-degree feedback for insight, behavior change, and improved performance. Whether you choose a standard or customized model, you can trust that you're using the best tool on the market.
Development Dimensions International http://www.ddiworld.com/default.asp	Seven standard survey options—available in English, French, German, and Spanish—and a listing of 72 competencies enable you to assess different skill sets and job levels, or we can customize a system that is specifically aligned with the key factors your organization views as critical to job success. Comprehensive reports can be used to monitor the developmental process, prioritize learning and developmental approaches, evaluate training effectiveness, identify trends, and measure organizational performance or success over time.
IRI Consultants to Management http://www.irisolutions.com/default.asp	IRI's 360-degree feedback includes a standard set of questions, or we can use a set of questions developed by the client. This provides the client the flexibility of linking items to organizational efforts already begun, or to organizational efforts planned for future deployment.
Center for Creative Leadership www.ccl.org (demo available online)	360 BY DESIGN is a robust, fully Internet-based feedback and developmental process that can be tailored to match the competencies important to your organization. It provides online assessment and feedback, as well as developmental planning, featuring 360 best practices pioneered by the Center for Creative Leadership (CCL®).

(Continued)

TABLE 8.3 Continued	
Vendor	*Description from Web Site*
MindSolve www.mindsolve.com (demo available online)	MVP's Multi-Source Feedback provides every advantage of 360 assessment, but stands out from other methods due to MindSolve's patented drag-and-drop technology. Drag-and-drop's elegantly simple yet powerful, automated process dramatically reduces time and cost, offering the only system in the world that lets employees simultaneously rate multiple people and add supporting comments all within a single screen.
2020 Insight Gold www.2020insight.net (demo available online)	20/20 Insight GOLD is the world's first fully integrated family of feedback and individual developmental planning software, making it the complete feedback solution. This software can be used for 360 surveys, 360 feedback, organizational surveys, customer feedback, and training evaluation. 2020 Insight is easy to install and is customizable at any step for no extra charge.
Right Management Consultants www.right.com (demo available online)	They offer three different 360 packages: Compass®: A feedback tool and workshop focusing on effective leadership. Matrixsm: Our 360° survey that provides feedback on people's power and influence. eCustom 360sm: Focus on the competencies people need to succeed in a specific company, function, or job.

The CheckPoint system includes self-evaluations as well as evaluations provided by the direct supervisor, direct subordinates, and peers. Once performance information is collected from all these sources, the manager evaluated receives feedback in the form of the graph included in Figure 8.2. This graph shows discrepancies between self- and others' ratings as well as the scores obtained for each competency. For example, this graph shows that this particular manager has the greatest gap for the competency "development of others." Specifically, the manager assigned a score of about 4.5 to herself, whereas the average score provided by her direct supervisor, direct subordinates, and peers is only 2.55. The CheckPoint system uses the following scale to rate competencies:

0 Not applicable (not averaged into scores)
1 Never demonstrates this
2 Seldom demonstrates this
3 Sometimes demonstrates this
4 Usually demonstrates this
5 Always demonstrates this

In this particular illustration, the manager believes that she displays behaviors indicating the competency "development of others" somewhere between "usually" and "always." In contrast, her boss, employees, and peers believe that she demonstrates

FIGURE 8.2   CheckPoint 360-Degree Competency System: Executive Overview

Executive Overview
Overview of Self vs. All Observers

Favorable Zone
(3.50 to 4.25)

Total CheckPoint Scores

All Observers \ Self

Differential
0.34

Color Key: ⬤ Self Ⓐ All Observers (combined scores of Boss, Direct Reports and Peers)
◀—Gap—▶ Self perception varies from All Observers by 1 point or more.

Copyright © 2005 Profiles International, Inc., Waco, Texas USA

Courtesy of Bob Gately, PE, MBA, Gately Consulting Strategic Business
Partner of Profiles International, Inc., 508-634-7748,
GATELY@COMPUSERVE.COM, http://go.ourworld.nu/gately

these behaviors somewhere between "seldom" and "sometimes." In other words, the self-rating falls within the favorable zone whereas the ratings provided by others do not.

To explore this gap further, the report provided to the manager also includes more detailed information on the scores provided by each source of information. The Reference Group Comparison chart included in Figure 8.3 shows this information. An examination of the scores provided for the competency "development of others" indicates that all sources, except for the manager herself, agree that work is needed regarding this competency because all scores are between the "seldom" and "sometimes" categories.

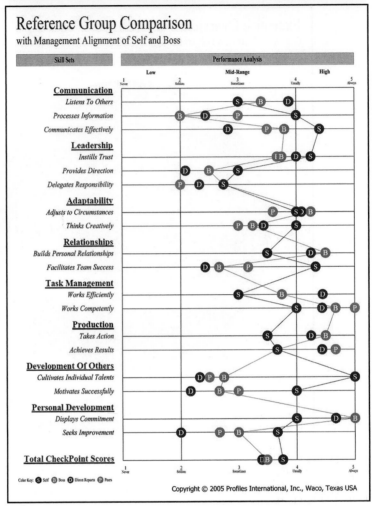

FIGURE 8.3 CheckPoint 360-Degree Competency System: Reference Group Comparison

Courtesy of Bob Gately, PE, MBA, Gately Consulting Strategic Business Partner of Profiles International, Inc., 508-634-7748, *GATELY@COMPUSERVE.COM*, *http://go.ourworld.nu/gately*

In contrast, the manager believes she is doing an exceptional job regarding cultivating individual talent (score of 5) and motivating successfully (score of 4).

However, it is not sufficient to provide scores regarding each of the competencies. Becoming aware that there is a problem with a competency is a very good first step, but a good 360-degree feedback system also provides concrete suggestions about what to do to improve competencies.[12] The CheckPoint system does this by providing what is called a *development summary*. The development summary describes strengths and areas that should be developed further. An example of this is included in Figure 8.4. This graph shows that this particular manager does have several strengths, but also that there are some areas that deserve further development. For example, there is a need to work

FIGURE 8.4   CheckPoint 360-Degree Competency System: Development Summary

Development Summary
for Darcy Walker

Skill Set	All Observers Rating
	1 Never 2 Seldom 3 Sometimes 4 Usually 5 Always

Strengths

A consensus of your reference group ratings shows these competencies are clear strengths, as they fall in or above the Favorable Zone.

S Displays Commitment	4.73
Works Competently	4.60
SE Achieves Results	4.33
Takes Action	4.15
Builds Personal Relationships	4.15
Works Efficiently	4.12
S Adjusts to Circumstances	4.00
Instills Trust	3.88
Listens To Others	3.79

Development Areas

A consensus of your reference group ratings shows these competencies (which fall below the Favorable Zone) as in need of improvement and should be considered a top priority for your career development.

Thinks Creatively		3.31
B Communicates Effectively		3.24
SE Facilitates Team Success	Critical Development Area!	2.65
S Processes Information		2.53
B Seeks Improvement	Critical Development Area!	2.45
Motivates Successfully		2.45
Cultivates Individual Talents		2.45
B Provides Direction	Critical Development Area!	2.40
SE Delegates Responsibility	Critical Development Area!	2.35

The critical development areas are determined by input from Boss and Self and the relationship of the Favorable Zone.

Color Key: S or B Chosen by Self or Boss as a Critical Skill Set   SE Chosen by both Self and Boss as a Critical Skill Set

1 Never   2 Seldom   3 Sometimes   4 Usually   5 Always

Copyright © 2005 Profiles International, Inc., Waco, Texas USA

Courtesy of Bob Gately, PE, MBA, Gately Consulting Strategic Business Partner of Profiles International, Inc., 508-634-7748, *GATELY@COMPUSERVE.COM*, *http://go.ourworld.nu/gately*

on the "facilitates team success" dimension of the competency "relationships." Consequently, the report also includes specific suggestions on how to improve. This is shown in Figure 8.5. Specifically, the manager is given tips and advice regarding concrete steps to be taken to improve performance. For example, in terms of learning to collaborate on team decisions, the manager is given advice on how to compromise and reach win-win decisions and how to gain support for decisions.

Are 360-degree feedback systems beneficial for all organizations? Not necessarily. These systems work best in organizations that have cultures that support open and honest feedback. Also, these systems work best in organizations that have a participatory, as opposed to authoritarian, leadership style in which giving

FIGURE 8.5 **CheckPoint 360-Degree Competency System: Suggestions for Improvement**

Development Summary
for Darcy Walker

The following suggestions will help direct your development efforts:

Facilitates Team Success

Handle Conflict in a Direct and Effective Manner.

- Don't ignore conflict, thinking it will disappear. It won't. And don't expect a conflict-free workplace. Some discord is inevitable and constructively dealing with it will create a more productive work environment.
- Listen carefully to all viewpoints in a disagreement. Define the problem. Then begin the process of resolution.
- Explore multiple options. Then resolve differences with solutions that are acceptable to all involved parties.

Encourage Cooperation in Order to Reap the Benefits of a Strongly Unified Group Effort.

- When recognizing outstanding performance, go beyond the acknowledgment of individual successes. Give equal emphasis to team achievements and effective cooperation among teams.
- Validate the importance of each and every team member's contribution.

Learn to Collaborate on Team Decisions.

- Practice the art of compromise when making decisions, creating win/win situations.
- To gain support for decisions, involve the team in considering alternative approaches. Strive for consensus in order to increase commitment to the final decision.

Establish Team Objectives.

- As much as possible involve the team in formulating goals consistent with, and supportive of, the overall mission of your business. Also solicit input when planning the implementation of the goals.
- Make sure everyone understands the team's goals, as well as their role in attaining the goals.
- Keep everyone apprised of team progress.

Develop Group Dynamics That Bring Out the Best in Everyone.

- Recruit individuals with talents that will complement the skills of other team members.
- Capitalize on each person's strengths and experiences to create a potent team effort.

Courtesy of Bob Gately, PE, MBA, Gately Consulting Strategic Business Partner of Profiles International, Inc., 508-634-7748, *GATELY@COMPUSERVE.COM, http://go.ourworld.nu/gately*

and receiving feedback is the norm and is seen as valuable. Answering the following questions can give a good indication as to whether implementing a 360-degree system would be beneficial in a specific organization:

1. Are decisions that are made about rewards and promotion fairly free of favoritism?
2. Are decisions made that take into account the input of people affected by such decisions?
3. Do people from across departments usually cooperate with each other and help each other out?
4. Is there little or no fear of speaking up?
5. Do people believe that their peers and subordinates can provide valuable information about their performance?
6. Are employees trusted to get the job done?
7. Do people want to improve their performance?

In sum, the successful implementation of a 360-degree feedback system is heavily dependent on the culture of the organization and the work context.[13] If the answer to most of these questions is yes, then the implementation of a 360-degree feedback system is likely to be successful and lead to performance improvement.

8.3.1 Advantages of 360-Degree Feedback Systems

Organizations and individuals can gain several advantages as a consequence of implementing a 360-degree feedback system. These include the following:

- *Decreased possibility of biases.*   Because these systems include information from more than one source, there is a decreased possibility of biases in the identification of employees' weaknesses.
- *Increased awareness of expectations.*   Employees become very aware of others' expectations about their performance. This includes not only the supervisor's expectations but also the expectations of other managers, coworkers, and customers.
- *Increased commitment to improve.*   Employees become aware of what others think about their performance, which increases their commitment to improve. This is because information about performance is no longer a private matter.
- *Improved self-perceptions of performance.*   Employees' distorted views of their own performance are likely to change as a result of the feedback received from other sources. In other words, it is difficult to continue to have distorted views of one's own performance in the presence of overwhelming evidence that these perceptions may not be correct.
- *Improvement of performance.*   Although receiving information about one's performance is not sufficient cause to improve, it is certainly a very important step. Thus, having information on one's performance, if paired with a good developmental plan, is likely to lead to performance improvement.
- *Reduction of "undiscussables."*   360-degree feedback systems provide an excellent opportunity to coworkers, superiors, and subordinates to give information on performance in an anonymous and nonthreatening way. Many supervisors may feel uncomfortable providing negative feedback, but a 360-degree system makes providing such feedback easier.
- *Help employees take control of their careers.*   By receiving detailed and constructive feedback on weaknesses and strengths in various areas, employees can gain a realistic assessment of where they should go with their careers.

Table 8.4 includes a summarized list of benefits that organizations can obtain from implementing a 360-degree feedback system. Consider how some of these benefits were realized when a system was implemented at Sonoco Products, a supplier of industrial and consumer packaging.[14] First, two-thirds of respondents to a survey indicated expectations about performance were clearer and they were able to more clearly understand the link between individual performance and organizational goals. Second, respondents to this same survey also felt more responsible for managing their performance, which the company took as an indication that individuals also had a better understanding of their jobs and self-perceptions of performance. Overall, while we do not have evidence that all of the benefits listed in Table 8.4 were realized with this system, there is sufficient documentation to show that several important benefits resulted from implementing it.

TABLE 8.4 Summary List of Benefits Resulting from a 360-Degree Feedback System
Decreased possibility of biases
Increased awareness of expectations
Increased commitment to improve
Improved self-perceptions of performance
Improvement of performance
Reduction of "undiscussables"
Help employees take control of their careers

8.3.2 Risks of Implementing 360-Degree Feedback Systems

Although we have discussed the many advantages of 360-degree feedback systems, we should also consider that there are some risks involved.[15] For example, negative feedback can hurt, particularly if those giving feedback do not offer their comments in a constructive way. Second, the system is likely to lead to positive results only if individuals feel comfortable with the system and believe they will be rated honestly and treated fairly. User acceptance is an important determinant of the system's success. Third, when there are very few raters that provide information, say, two or three, it may be easy for the employee being rated to identify who the raters are. When anonymity is compromised, raters are more likely to distort the information they provide. Fourth, an additional risk of 360-degree feedback systems is that raters may become overloaded with forms to fill out because they need to provide information on so many individuals (peers, superiors, and subordinates). Finally, implementing a 360-degree feedback system should not be a one-time-only event. The system should be in place and data collected over time on an ongoing basis. The implementation of ongoing 360-degree feedback systems is sometimes labeled a 720-degree feedback system, referring to the fact that the collection of 360-degree data takes place at least twice. In short, administering the system only once will not be as beneficial as administering the system repeatedly.

The risks associated with implementing a 360-degree system can be illustrated by the Watson Wyatt's 2001 Human Capital Index (HCI).[16] This is an ongoing study of the effects that HR practices have on the stock value of over 700 publicly traded companies. One particular result was especially alarming. Of the companies surveyed, those that implemented 360-degree feedback had lower stock value! For example, those companies that used peer reviews had 4.9% lower market value than did similar companies that did not implement peer reviews. Furthermore, companies that implemented upward feedback, where employees rated managers, had a 5.7% lower stock value than did similar companies that did not implement upward feedback. Does this necessarily mean that implementing 360-degree feedback systems causes the stock price to decrease? Based on the data collected, there is no definitive answer to this question. It could be that organizations that are not performing well financially decide to implement 360-degree feedback systems precisely to help improve their performance. Nevertheless, these results highlight the importance of following best practices in implementing 360-degree feedback systems in order to avoid any negative consequences of implementing such a system.

8.3.3 Characteristics of a Good System

Fortunately, there are several things that can be done to maximize the chance that the system will work properly. First, in general terms, consider the following advice:[17]

> 360-degree feedback systems . . . are always work in progress—subject to vulnerabilities, requiring sensitivity to hidden conflicts as much as to tangible results, but nevertheless responsive to thoughtful design and purposeful change. Companies that have success with these programs tend to be open to learning and willing to experiment. They are led by executives who are direct about the expected benefits as well as the challenges. . . . By laying themselves open to praise and criticism from all directions and inviting others to do the same, they guide their organizations to new capacities for continuous improvement.

Second, in more specific terms, when systems have the following characteristics, they are most likely to be successful:[18]

- *Anonymity.*   In good systems, feedback is anonymous and confidential. When such is the case, raters are more likely to provide honest information regarding performance, particularly when subordinates are providing information about superiors.
- *Observation of employee performance.*   Only those with good knowledge and first-hand experience with the person being rated should participate in the process. There is no point in asking for performance feedback from people who are not able to observe performance.
- *Feedback interpretation.*   Good systems allow the person being rated to discuss the feedback received with a person interested in the employee's development. In most cases, feedback is discussed with the direct supervisor. In other cases, the discussion can involve a representative of the HR department or a superior to whom the person does not report directly.
- *Follow-up.*   The information gathered has little value if there is no follow-up action. Once feedback is received, it is essential that a developmental plan is created right away.
- *Used for developmental purposes only.*   When 360-degree feedback systems are used for administrative purposes such as promotions and compensation, raters are likely to distort the information provided. Make it clear that the purpose of the system is developmental and developmental only. The information collected should not be used for making reward allocations or any other administrative decisions.
- *Avoidance of survey fatigue.*   Survey fatigue can be avoided if individuals are not asked to rate too many employees at the same time. For example, data collection can be staggered so that not all surveys are distributed at the same time.
- *Emphasis on behaviors.*   Although systems can include feedback on both behaviors (competencies) and results, it is better to emphasize behaviors. Focusing on behaviors can lead to the identification of concrete actions that the person being rated can take to improve performance.

TABLE 8.5	Characteristics of a Good 360-Degree Feedback System
Anonymity	
Observation of employee performance	
Feedback interpretation	
Follow-up	
Used for developmental purposes only	
Avoidance of survey fatigue	
Emphasis on behaviors	
Raters go beyond ratings	
Raters are trained	

- *Raters go beyond ratings.*   In addition to providing scores on the various dimensions, raters should also provide written descriptive feedback that gives detailed and constructive comments on how to improve performance. It is helpful if this information also includes specific examples that help support the ratings and recommendations provided.
- *Raters are trained.*   As in the case of providing evaluations for administrative purposes, raters should be trained. Mainly, this includes skills to discriminate good from poor performance and how to provide feedback in a constructive manner.

Table 8.5 includes a summarized list of characteristics of good 360-degree feedback systems. Consider the Compass system, which is offered by Right Management Consultants (www.right.com). This 360-degree feedback tool has many of the ideal characteristics found in Table 8.5. Compass is a tool based on leadership competencies. It allows raters to assess how well the leader executes each of the behaviors associated with various competencies such as "communication." The survey raters are anonymous. Right Management Consultants offers tailored feedback programs where coaching is given in individual or group sessions to help interpret the information collected. Right can also certify internal organizational employees to give the feedback. After the assessment, a developmental plan is constructed, based on each individual's strengths and weaknesses. Furthermore, an online leadership developmental suite is available that includes a self-initiated online 6-month and 12-month follow-up. Given the availability of Compass, and other systems such as those described in Table 8.3, there is little excuse to implement a system that does not include most of the characteristics listed in Table 8.5.

SUMMARY POINTS

- Personal developmental plans are a key component of a performance management system because they specify courses of action to be taken to improve performance. A performance management system that lacks information about how to improve performance will not help employees go beyond what they do and know. In a nutshell, a good developmental plan allows employees to answer the following two questions: How can I do better in the future? How can I avoid performance problems faced in the past?

- Developmental plans focus on both the short term and the long term. Specifically, developmental plans address how to improve performance in the current job, how to sustain good levels of performance in the current job, and how to prepare employees for future advancement. In addition, developmental plans provide employees with growth opportunities so that, even if advancement within the organization is not clear, employees are able to enrich their daily work experiences.

- Good developmental plans include a description of the specific steps to be taken and specific developmental objectives. So, a good plan includes information on (1) developmental objectives, (2) how the new skills or knowledge will be acquired, (3) a time line regarding the acquisition of the new skills or knowledge, and (4) standards and measures that will be used to assess whether the objectives have been achieved. Learning objectives should be designed to take into account both the needs of the individual and those of the organization.

- Developmental objectives can be achieved by one or more of the following activities: (1) on-the-job training, (2) courses, (3) self-guided reading, (4) mentoring, (5) attending a conference, (6) getting a degree, (7) job rotation, (8) temporary assignments, and (9) membership in professional or trade organizations. Developmental activities for specific objectives are chosen by the employee and his or her direct supervisor. This choice is guided by taking into account the employee's learning preferences, the developmental objective in question, and the organization's available resources.

- The direct supervisor has a key role in helping the employee define the scope of the developmental plan and in explaining the relationship between the developmental objectives and strategic priorities for the unit and the organization. The direct supervisor also has direct responsibility for checking on the employee's progress toward achieving the developmental objectives and providing resources so that the employee will be able to engage in the appropriate activities (e.g., courses, mentoring). Supervisors must reinforce an employee's accomplishments toward completing a developmental plan so that the employee remains motivated. Finally, supervisors themselves must be motivated to perform all these functions in support of their employees' developmental plans. To do so, supervisors' performance regarding how well they help their employees develop should be measured and rewarded appropriately.

- 360-degree feedback systems are tools that help employees build new skills and improve their performance in general by gathering and analyzing performance information from several sources, including peers, superiors, subordinates, and oneself. Performance information gathered from oneself is compared to information gathered by other sources to perform a gap analysis showing discrepancies between how one sees one's own performance in relation to how others see one's performance. These types of systems are also used to identify performance dimensions for which all, or most, performance information sources agree there is little or great room for improvement. Accordingly, this information can be used in creating a developmental plan.

- Many organizations implement 360-degree feedback systems electronically because doing so facilitates data collection and analysis. There are many vendors that offer systems that can be implemented online. Some systems are comprehensive and include rater training, data analysis, and detailed feedback reports for those evaluated.

- The implementation of 360-degree feedback systems can produce many benefits including (1) decreased possibility of biases, (2) increased awareness of performance expectations, (3) increased commitment to improve, (4) improved performance, (5) reduction of undiscussables, and (6) increased career control on the part of employees.

- In spite of the many advantages associated with implementing 360-degree feedback systems, there are some risks involved. For example, negative feedback can hurt, individuals may not be ready to receive such feedback and may therefore not participate willingly, anonymity may be compromised and therefore information may be distorted, and raters may be overloaded with forms to fill out. These risks, and the associated failure of the system, are particularly high when the organization does not value participation in decision making, there is little cooperation among employees, there is favoritism, employees do not value the opinion of others (i.e., peers, subordinates), decisions are based on hearsay, and employees are not trusted to get the job done.

- There are some features that will enhance the success rate of a 360-degree feedback system. These are anonymity, that raters have first-hand knowledge of the performance of the person evaluated, that feedback is interpreted by a person interested in the development of the person evaluated, that there is follow-up after receiving feedback, that the system is used for development purposes only, that raters do not become fatigued, that there is an emphasis on behaviors instead of results, that raters provide information beyond performance ratings only, and that raters are trained. The presence of these characteristics is likely to lead to the successful design and implementation of the system.

Case Study 8.1   Developmental Plan Form at Old Dominion University

Consider the following developmental plan form used for employees at Old Dominion University in Norfolk, Virginia.[19]

What are some positive features of this form? What are some features that could be improved? ■

CONFIDENTIAL

OLD DOMINION UNIVERSITY/221

EMPLOYEE WORK PROFILE
PERFORMANCE PLANNING & EVALUATION

Parts V, VI, VII, VIII, and X are written or reviewed by the supervisor and discussed with the employee at the end of the evaluation cycle.

The following pages are printed separate from the remainder of the EWP because they contain confidential employee information.

Part III – Position Identification Information	
26. Position Number:	27. Department:
28. Employee Name:	29. Social Security or Employee ID Number.

Part IV – Employee Development Plan
30. Professional development goals:
31. Steps to be taken by the supervisor to assist employee to enhance job performance and in furthering professional development:
32. Steps to be taken by the employee toward enhancing job performance and in furthering professional development:

Case Study 8.2   Evaluation of a 360-Degree Feedback System Demo

Visit Hr-survey.com and click on the following link to see the demo: http://www.hr-survey.com/sd36023.htm. Please view the demo questionnaire and results. Then, answer the following questions:

1. What are the good features of this system?
2. What are the features that could be improved? ■

Case Study 8.3   Implementation of 360-Degree Feedback System at Ridge Intellectual

When Ridge Intellectual, a graphics design firm, implemented 360-degree feedback in its organization two years ago, it was met with resistance and was eventually discontinued. Ron Bartlett, the president of Ridge Intellectual, had seen a demonstration by a 360-degree vendor at a trade conference and decided to use the system at Ridge. Subsequently, Bartlett worked with the consultant to implement the system. Specifically, he sent out a company-wide e-mail stating the reasons for changing to the new system, how the ratings collected using the new system would be linked to bonuses, and the

importance of completing the online training course on the system. The consultants provided online rater training for those who were interested as well as links to documents on how to observe, assess, and record performance behaviors. Once the surveys were made available, individuals were encouraged to contact HR if they had any problems.

Based on the information here what could Ridge have done to implement the 360-degree feedback system more successfully? Please refer to the characteristics of a good system listed in Table 8.4 in answering this question. ■

END NOTES

1. Reyna, M., & Sims, R. R. (1995). A framework for individual management development in the public sector. *Public Personnel Management, 24*, 53–65.
2. Tyler, K. (2004). One bad apple: Before the whole bunch spoils, train managers to deal with poor performance. *HR Magazine, 49*(12), 77–86.
3. Locke, E. A. (2004). Goal-setting theory and its applications to the world of business.

Academy of Management Executive, 18, 124–125.
4. Latham, G. (2004). The motivational benefits of goal-setting. *Academy of Management Executive, 18*, 126–129.
5. Adapted from Information Systems and Technology Development Plan. Available on-line at <http://web.mit.edu/is/competency/devplan.html>.

6. Ellis, K. (2003). Developing for dollars. *Training, 40*(5), 34–38.

7. Hgigson, M., & Wilson, J.P. (1995). Implementing personal development plans: A model for trainers, managers and supervisors. *Industrial & Commercial Training, 27,* 25–29.

8. Brutus, S., London, M., & Martineau, J. (1999). The impact of 360-degree feedback on planning for career development. *Journal of Management Development, 18,* 676–693.

9. Toegel, G., & Conger, J. A. (2003). 360-Degree assessment: Time for reinvention. *Academy of Management Learning & Education, 2,* 297–311.

10. Becton, J. B., & Schraeder, M. (2004). Participant input into rater selection: Potential effects on the quality and acceptance of ratings in the context of 360-degree feedback. *Public Personnel Management, 33,* 23–32.

11. Stringer, R., & Cheloha, R. (2003). The power of a development plan. *Human Resource Planning, 26,* 10–17.

12. Luthans, F., & Peterson, S. J. (2003). 360-Degree feedback with systematic coaching: Empirical analysis suggests a winning combination. *Human Resource Management, 42,* 243–256.

13. Maurer, T. J., Barbeite, F. G., & Mitchell, D. R. (2002). Predictors of attitudes toward a 360-degree feedback system and involvement in post-feedback management development activity. *Journal of Occupational & Organizational Psychology, 75,* 87–107.

14. Maloney, R. Competency-based integrated HR systems Sonoco Products. DDI client successes. Available online at www.ddiworld.com (retrieved on May 20, 2004).

15. Frisch, M. H. (2001). Going around in circles with "360" tools: Have they grown too popular for their own good? *Human Resource Planning, 24,* 7–8.

16. Pfau, B., & Kay, I. (2002). Does 360-degree feedback negatively affect company performance? *HR Magazine, 47*(6), 54–59.

17. Peiperl, M. A. (2001, January). Getting 360 degree feedback right. *Harvard Business Review, 79,* 147.

18. Some of these recommendations are adapted from A. S. DeNisi, and A. N. Kluger, "Feedback Effectiveness: Can 360-degree Appraisals Be Improved?" *Academy of Management Executive, 14*(2000): 129–139, and A. M. McCarthy, and T. N. Garavan, "360° Feedback Process: Performance, Improvement and Employee Career Development," *Journal of European Industrial Training, 25*(2001): 5–32.

19. The EWP - Employee Development Plan. Available online at http://www.odu.edu/af/humanresources/performance/Performance%20Planning%20-%20Dream/EWP%20-%20Part%203-4%20-%20Employee%20Development%20Plan.htm. Retrieval date: August 15, 2005.

Performance Management Skills

Selecting the right person for the right job is the largest part of coaching.
—Philip Crosby

Learning Objectives

By the end of this chapter, you will be able to do the following:

- Understand that managers need several key skills to manage the performance of their employees effectively, including skills regarding coaching, giving feedback, and conducting performance review meetings.

- Define coaching and describe its major functions, including giving advice, providing guidance and support, and enhancing employee confidence and competence.

- Identify behaviors that managers need to display to perform the various coaching functions.

- Understand that a manager's personality and behavioral preferences determine his or her coaching style.

- Understand your own coaching style and the need to adapt one's coaching style to the situation and your subordinates' preferences.

- Describe the coaching process and its components including setting developmental goals, identifying developmental resources and strategies, implementing strategies, observing and documenting developmental behavior, and giving feedback.

- Understand the time, situational, and activity constraints involved in observing and documenting an employee's progress toward the achievement of developmental goals and good performance in general.

- Implement a communication plan and training programs that will minimize the impact of constraints present when observing and documenting performance.

- Describe the benefits of accurate documentation of an employee's developmental activities and performance.

- Implement several recommendations that will lead to documenting performance in a useful and constructive manner.

■ Understand the purposes served by feedback on performance regarding the achievement of developmental goals and performance in general.

■ Implement several recommendations that will lead to creating useful and constructive feedback systems.

■ Understand why people do not feel comfortable giving negative feedback and recognize what happens when managers refuse to give negative feedback.

■ Understand the various purposes served by performance review meetings and the various types of meetings that can be conducted.

■ Understand the signs of employee defensiveness, implement suggestions to minimize employee defensiveness before a performance review meeting takes place, and deal with defensiveness during the performance review meeting.

Chapter 8 addressed issues about employee development. Specifically, Chapter 8 discussed how to use a performance management system to help employees develop and improve their performance and also to address more long-term career goals and aspirations. Performance management systems are not likely to help employees develop and improve their performance if managers do not have the necessary skills to help employees accomplish these goals. Such skills include being able to serve as coaches, to observe and document performance accurately, to give both positive and negative feedback, and to conduct useful and constructive performance review discussions. This chapter addresses each of these topics. Let's begin with the first of these issues: coaching.

9.1 COACHING

Coaching is a collaborative ongoing process in which the manager interacts with his employees and takes an active role and interest in their performance.[1] In general, coaching involves directing, motivating, and rewarding employee behavior. Coaching is a day-to-day function that involves observing performance and complimenting good work, as well as helping correct and improve performance that does not meet expectations and standards. Coaching is also concerned with long-term performance and involves making sure the developmental plan is being achieved. In more specific terms, coaching involves the following functions:[2]

• Giving *advice* to help employees improve their performance. In other words, coaching involves not only describing what needs to be done, but also how things need to be done. Coaching is concerned with both results and behaviors.
• Providing employees with *guidance* so that employees can develop their skills and knowledge appropriately. Coaching involves providing both information about what skills and knowledge are necessary to do the work right, and also information about how the employee can acquire these skills and knowledge.
• Providing employees *support* and being there only when the manager is needed. Coaching involves being there when the employee needs it, but it also involves not monitoring and controlling an employee's every move. In the end, coaching is about facilitation. The responsibility for improving performance ultimately rests on the shoulders of the employee.

- Giving employees *confidence* that will enable them to enhance their performance continuously and to increase their sense of responsibility for managing their own performance. Coaching involves giving positive feedback that allows employees to feel confident about what they do, but it also involves giving feedback on things that can be improved.
- Helping employees gain greater *competence* by guiding them toward acquiring more knowledge and sharpening skills that can prepare them for more complex tasks and higher-level positions. Coaching involves a consideration of both short-term and long-term objectives, including how the employee can benefit from acquiring new skills and knowledge that could be useful in future positions and in performing novel tasks.

Based on this list of the various functions of coaching, it is evident that coaching requires that managers contribute quite a lot. For example, consider the case of NCCI Holdings, Inc., a company based in Boca Raton, Florida, that manages the largest database of workers' compensation insurance information in the United States (www.ncci.com). NCCI analyzes industry trends, prepares workers' compensation insurance rate recommendations, assists in pricing proposed legislation, and provides a variety of data products to maintain a healthy workers' compensation system and reduce the frequency of employee injuries. At NCCI Holdings, supervisors undergo extensive coaching training, including learning how to listen and to be empathic. Managers also attend monthly roundtables where they can learn from one other's coaching experiences. At these roundtables, managers can solicit feedback from other managers regarding their own coaching performance.[3]

Coaching helps turn feedback into results. For this to happen, coaches need to:

- *Establish development objectives.* The manager works jointly with the employees in creating the developmental plan and its objectives.
- *Communicate effectively.* The manager maintains regular and clear communication with employees about their performance, including both behaviors and results.
- *Motivate employees.* Managers must reward positive performance. When positive performance is rewarded, employees are motivated to repeat the same level of positive performance in the future.
- *Document performance.* Managers observe employee behaviors and results. Evidence must be gathered regarding instances of good and poor performance.
- *Give feedback.* Managers measure employee performance and progress toward goals. They praise good performance and point to instances of substandard performance. Managers also help employees avoid poor performance in the future.
- *Diagnose performance problems.* Managers must listen to employees and gather information on whether performance deficiencies are the result of a lack of knowledge and skills, abilities, motivation, or stem from situational factors beyond the control of the employee. Diagnosing performance problems is important because such a diagnosis dictates whether the course of action should be, for example, providing the employee with resources so she can acquire more knowledge and skills, or addressing contextual issues that

may be beyond the control of the employee (e.g., the employee is usually late in delivering the product because he receives the parts too late).

- *Develop employees.*　Managers provide financial support and resources for employee development (e.g., funding training, allowing time away from the job for developmental activities), by helping employees plan for the future, and by giving challenging assignments that force employees to learn new things.

Not all coaches perform all the coaching functions by engaging in all of the behaviors described here. But, managers who do so are highly effective. In fact, some have become legendary leaders. Consider Table 9.1, which summarizes the critical functions served by coaching and the behaviors that coaches use to perform these functions. Now, consider the case of Jack Welch, who was extremely dedicated to developing his employees by engaging in several of the coaching behaviors described here when he was CEO of General Electric (GE).[4] One of the things that Welch did to get involved with his employees was to speak during a class held at a three-week developmental course for GE's high-potential managers. Over the course of his career, he attended more than 750 of these classes, engaging over 15,000 GE managers and executives. During this presentation, he expected to answer hard questions and communicated honestly and candidly to his employees. After the class, he would invite all the participants to come talk with him after the course concluded. In addition to attending these sessions, he also held meetings with his top 500 executives every January. While these examples do not constitute formal coaching, Welch used the opportunities to communicate his expectations and receive feedback from the various business groups at GE.

Welch also conducted formal performance reviews in which he engaged in several of the behaviors included in Table 9.1, including establishing developmental objectives, motivating employees, documenting performance, giving feedback, and diagnosing performance problems. He set performance targets and monitored them throughout the year. Each year the operating heads of GE's 12 businesses received individual two-page, hand-written notes about their performance. Welch attached the previous year's comments to the new reviews with comments in the margin about the progress the individual managers had made toward the goal or work that each manager still needed to do to reach the goal. Then, he distributed bonuses and reiterated the goals for the upcoming year. This process then cascaded through the organization,

TABLE 9.1　Coaching	
Major Functions	*Key Behaviors*
Give advice	Establish developmental objectives
Provide guidance	Communicate effectively
Give support	Motivate employees
Give confidence	Document performance
Promote greater competence	Give feedback
	Diagnose performance problems
	Develop employees

as other operating heads engaged in the same performance review discussions with their subordinates.

Another example of Welch's coaching behaviors occurred after he had heard customer complaints about a specific product. Welch charged the manager of the division with improving the productivity of that product fourfold. The manager sent Welch detailed weekly reports over the course of the next four years. Welch would send the reports back every three or four weeks with comments congratulating successes or pointing out areas in which the manager needed to improve. The manager stated that the fact that the CEO took the time to read his reports each week and send back comments motivated him to reach the lofty goal that Welch had set for him.

In addition to this, Jack Welch took the time to recognize hourly workers and managers who impressed him. For example, after one high-ranking leader turned down a promotion and transfer because he did not want his daughter to change schools, Welch sent him a personal note stating that he admired the man for many reasons and he demonstrated it again with his decision to put his family first. The employee explained later that this incident proved that Welch cared about him both as a person and as an employee.

In short, Jack Welch was a legendary leader who developed his employees by setting expectations, communicating clearly, documenting and diagnosing performance, motivating and rewarding his employees, and taking an interest in their personal development. In fact, he engaged in virtually all the behaviors and performed most of the coaching functions listed in Table 9.1. How does Jack Welch compare to the CEO of your current company, or a CEO you have known or heard about?

We can see that Jack Welch was an extremely effective coach. In general, however, how do we know whether a manager is doing a good job at coaching her employees? From a results point of view, we could simply measure how many of a manager's employees go on to become successful on their own. But, as in the case of evaluating performance in general, we should also consider behaviors in evaluating coaching performance. Consider the good coach questionnaire included in Table 9.2. If you are or have been in a management position, answer the questions about yourself. Otherwise, think about your current or latest supervisor or someone you know. How many of these questions can you answer "yes" to? How many would you answer "no" to? Overall, given your responses, what is the evaluation of this person (yourself or someone else) as a coach from a behavioral point of view?

TABLE 9.2 The Good Coach Questionnaire

1. Do you listen to your employees?
2. Do you understand the individual needs of your employees?
3. Do you encourage employees to express their feelings openly?
4. Do you provide your employees with tangible and intangible support for development?
5. Do your employees know your expectations about their performance?
6. Do you encourage open and honest discussions and problem solving?
7. Do you help your employees create action plans that will solve problems and create changes when needed?
8. Do you help your employees explore potential areas of growth and development?

9.2 COACHING STYLES

A manager's personality and behavioral preferences are more likely to influence his or her coaching style. There are four main coaching styles: driver, persuader, amiable, and analyzer. First, coaches can adopt a driving style in which they tell the employee being coached what to do. Assume that the coach wants to provide guidance regarding how to deal with a customer. In this situation, the preference for a *driver* is to say to the employee, "You must talk to the customer in *this* way." Such coaches are assertive, speak quickly and often firmly, usually talk about tasks and facts, are not very expressive, and expose a narrow range of personal feelings to others. Second, coaches can use a persuading style in which they try to sell what they want the employee to do. Someone who is a *persuader* would try to explain to the employee why it is beneficial for the organization, as well as for the employee himself, to talk to a customer in a specific way. Similar to drivers, persuaders are also assertive, but tend to use expansive body gestures, talk more about people and relationships, and expose others to a broad range of personal feelings. Third, other coaches may adopt an *amiable* style and want everyone to be happy. Such coaches are likely to be more subjective than objective and direct employees to talk to customers in a certain way because it "feels" like the right thing to do or because the employee feels it is the right way to do it. Such coaches tend not to be very assertive and to speak deliberately and pause often, they seldom interrupt others, and make many conditional statements. Finally, coaches may have a preference for analyzing performance in a logical and systematic way and then follow rules and procedures when providing a recommendation. To use the same example, such *analyzer* coaches may tell employees to talk to a customer in a specific way "because this is what the manual says." Analyzers, then, are not very assertive but, similar to drivers, are likely to talk about tasks and facts than personal feelings.

Which of these four styles is best? Which coaches are most effective? Drivers, persuaders, amiable coaches, or analyzers? The answer is that no style is necessarily superior to the others. Good coaching should be seen as a learning opportunity and as an opportunity to set clear goals and delegate action. Coaching involves sometimes providing direction, sometimes persuading employees how to do things a certain way, sometimes showing empathy and creating positive effects, and sometimes paying close attention to established rules and procedures. One thing is for sure, however: an exclusive emphasis on one of these four styles is not likely to help employees develop and grow. Ineffective coaches stick to one style only and cannot adapt to use any of the other styles. On the other hand, adaptive coaches, who are able to adjust their style according to an employee's needs, are most effective. In fact, 56% of participants in a survey of employees who had a coach at work reported that coaching was not helping them because there was a mismatch between coaching style and employee need.[5] In sum, a combination of styles is needed.

9.3 COACHING PROCESS

The coaching process is shown in Figure 9.1. We have already discussed many of the process's components in previous chapters. The first step involves setting developmental goals. As discussed in Chapter 8, these developmental goals are a key component of the developmental plan. These goals must be reasonable, attainable, and derived from a careful analysis of the areas where an employee needs to improve. In addition, goals should take into account both short- and long-term career objectives.

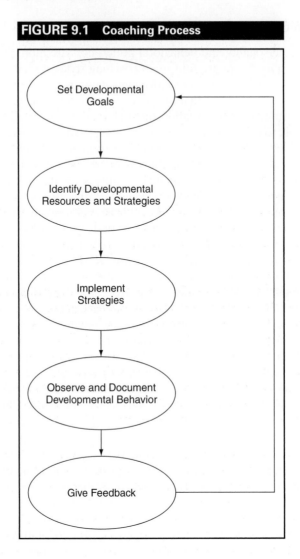

FIGURE 9.1 Coaching Process

The second step in the coaching process is to identify resources and strategies that will help the employee achieve the developmental goals. As discussed in Chapter 8, these can include on-the-job training, attending courses, self-guided reading, mentoring, attending a conference, getting a degree, job rotation, a temporary assignment, and membership in a professional or trade organization.

The third step involves implementing the strategies that will allow the employee to achieve the developmental goals. The employee may begin her job rotation plan or take a course online.

The next step in the process is to collect and evaluate data to assess the extent to which each of the developmental goals has been achieved. Finally, the coach provides feedback to the employee and, based on the extent to which each of the goals has been achieved, the developmental goals are revised and the entire process begins again.

Chapter 8 included a discussion of developmental goals and developmental resources and strategies. Let's discuss the two remaining components of the coaching model that have not yet been addressed: observing and documenting developmental behavior data and giving feedback.

9.3.1 Observation and Documentation of Developmental Behavior and Outcomes

Chapter 6 addressed the fact that people are likely to make intentional and unintentional errors in observing and evaluating performance. Managers may make similar errors in observing and evaluating behaviors related to developmental goals. For example, a manager may make a halo error and assume that if the employee does a good job at working toward one developmental goal (i.e., improving her typing skills), she is also doing a good job at working toward a different developmental goal (i.e., improving customer service). As is the case for performance in general, it is important to observe and document behaviors specifically related to developmental activities. Documentation can include memos, letters, e-mail messages, hand-written notes, comments, observations, descriptions, and evaluations provided by colleagues.[6] The discussion presented in this section complements information given in previous chapters because, although it is specifically related to behaviors related to developmental activities, it can be easily generalized to behaviors related to performance in general. In other words, the discussion that follows applies to the observation of all performance behaviors and not just those related to behaviors displayed in attempting to achieve developmental goals.

Observing an employee's progress toward the achievement of developmental goals is not as easy as it may seem. Consider the following constraints that managers may experience in attempting to observe an employee's performance regarding developmental activities:

- *Time constraints.*   Managers may be too busy to gather information on an employee's progress toward his developmental goals. Consequently, too much time may elapse between the assignment of the activity and the manager's checking on the employee's progress.
- *Situational constraints.*   Managers are often unable to observe employees as they engage in developmental activities and therefore may not have first-hand knowledge regarding their performance. For example, managers do not observe the extent to which an employee enrolled in an online course is an active participant and contributor or is a passive learner.
- *Activity constraints.*   When the developmental activity is highly unstructured, such as an employee reading a book, the manager may have to wait until the activity is completed to assess whether the activity has been beneficial.

How can we address these constraints and make sure that a manager will be able to observe and evaluate an employee's performance regarding developmental activities? The same recommendations provided in Chapter 7 regarding the observation and evaluation of performance in general apply. Specifically, a good communication plan should explain the benefits of implementing a developmental plan effectively. This helps managers to accept the plan. Also, managers should be trained so that they minimize errors (i.e., rater error training), share notions of what it means to complete developmental activities successfully (i.e., frame-of-reference training), are able to observe performance accurately (i.e., behavioral observation training), and are confident and comfortable managing employees' developmental activities (i.e., self-leadership training). Finally, we should understand managers' motivational forces that may direct them to invest time and effort, or not, in the development of their employees. In other words, what's in it for the manger if her employee's developmental activities are supervised appropriately?

The importance of documenting an employee's progress toward the achievement of developmental goals cannot be overemphasized. Similarly, it is critical to document employee performance in general. Why is this so important? Consider the following reasons:

- *Minimize cognitive load.*   Observing and evaluating developmental activities, and performance in general, is a complex cognitive task. Thus, documentation helps prevent memory-related errors.
- *Create trust.*   When documentation exists to support evaluations, there is no mystery regarding the outcomes. This, in turn, promotes trust and acceptance of decisions based on the evaluation provided.
- *Plan for the future.*   Documenting developmental activities and their outcomes allows for a discussion about specific facts and not assumptions or hearsay. A careful examination of these facts allows for better planning of developmental activities for the future.
- *Legal protection.*   There are specific laws that prohibit discrimination against members of various classes (e.g., based on sex or religion) in how developmental activities are allocated. For example, it is prohibited to provide male employees with better developmental opportunities than for female employees. In addition, some court rulings have determined that employees working under contract may challenge a dismissal. Thus, keeping accurate records of what developmental activities employees complete and to what degree of success, and of performance in general, is a good line of defense in case of litigation based on discrimination or wrongful termination.

The importance of keeping thorough performance documentation and taking actions consistent with this documentation are illustrated by the outcome of several cases. For example, in one such case John E. Cleverly, an employee at Western Electric Co., was discharged after 14 years of good service.[7] Western Electric Co. was found guilty of age discrimination and Cleverly was awarded back pay because the documentation indicated that Cleverly was given adequate performance ratings and increases to his salary over a course of 14 years. Upon his discharge, six months before his pension vested, Cleverly was informed that one reason for his discharge was to make room for younger employees. As illustrated by this case, documentation of performance should be taken seriously. In this case, the documentation available indicated the employee had a valid claim. In other cases, documentation could be used to discount charges of discrimination. If Cleverly had alleged age discrimination, but the company could show that his performance was deteriorating over time, then the company would have won the case.

What can managers do to document performance regarding developmental activities, and performance in general, in a useful and constructive way? Consider the following recommendations:[8]

- *Be specific.*   Document specific events and outcomes. Avoid making general statements such as "He's lazy." Provide specific examples to illustrate your point, for example, "He turns in memos after deadlines at least once a month."

- *Use adjectives and adverbs sparingly.*   The use of evaluative adjectives (e.g., good, poor) and adverbs (e.g., speedily, sometimes) may lead to ambiguous interpretations. In addition, it may not be clear whether the level of achievement has been average or outstanding.
- *Balance positives with negatives.*   Document instances of both good and poor performance. Do not focus on only the positives or only the negatives.
- *Focus on job-related information.*   Focus on information that is job related and, specifically, related to the developmental activities and goals at hand.
- *Be comprehensive.*   Include information on performance regarding all developmental goals and activities and cover the entire review period as opposed to a shorter time period. Also, document performance for all employees and not only those not achieving their developmental goals (or those who do).
- *Standardize procedures.*   Use the same method and format to document information for all employees.
- *Describe observable behavior.*   Phrase your notes in behavioral terms and avoid statements that would imply subjective judgment or prejudice.

Obviously, not all managers do a good job at documenting performance regarding the accomplishment of developmental goals or performance in general. Table 9.3 includes a summarized list of recommendations to follow in the documentation process.

Now, consider the recommendations listed in Table 9.3 in evaluating a set of quotes in Table 9.4 reportedly taken from actual employee performance evaluations in a large corporation in the United States.[9]

We can be sure that employees at the receiving end of these quotes were not too happy with them. It also goes without saying that this type of documentation is extremely detrimental to the performance management system. In fact, this organization has serious problems beyond the scope of its performance evaluation system.

Now, let's turn to another important component of the coaching process: giving feedback.

9.3.2 Giving Feedback

Giving feedback to the employee regarding her progress toward achieving her goals is a key component of the coaching process.[10] Feedback is information about past behavior that is given with the goal of improving future performance. Feedback

TABLE 9.3   Documentation of Performance and Performance in Developmental Activities: Some Recommendations

Be specific.

Use adjectives and adverbs sparingly.

Balance positives with negatives.

Focus on job-related information.

Be comprehensive.

Standardize procedures.

Describe observable behavior.

TABLE 9.4   Individual Quotes Taken from Actual Employee Performance Evaluations

Since my last report, this employee has reached rock bottom . . . and has started to dig.

I would not allow this employee to breed.

This employee is really not so much of a has-been, but more of a definitely won't be.

Works well when under constant supervision and cornered like a rat in a trap.

He would be out of his depth in a parking lot puddle.

He sets low personal standards and then consistently fails to achieve them.

This employee is depriving a village somewhere of an idiot.

This employee should go far, . . . and the sooner he starts, the better.

He's been working with glue too much.

He would argue with a signpost.

He has a knack for making strangers immediately detest him.

He brings a lot of joy whenever he leaves the room.

If you see two people talking and one looks bored, . . . he's the other one.

Donated his brain to science before he was done using it.

Gates are down, the lights are flashing, but the train isn't coming.

If he were any more stupid, he'd have to be watered twice a week.

If you give him a penny for his thoughts, you'd get change.

If you stand close enough to him, you can hear the ocean.

One neuron short of a synapse.

Some drink from the fountain of knowledge; . . . he only gargled.

Takes him 2 hours to watch *60 Minutes.*

The wheel is turning, but the hamster is dead.

includes information about both positive and negative aspects of job performance and lets employees know how well they are doing with respect to meeting the established standards.[11] Feedback is important in the context of performance regarding development activities and goals. However, our discussion of feedback goes beyond that and includes feedback about performance in general. Feedback is not a magic bullet for performance improvement.[12] However, it serves several important purposes:

- *Helps build confidence.*   Praising good performance builds employee confidence regarding future performance. It also lets employees know that their manager cares about them.
- *Develops competence.*   Communicating clearly about what has been done right and how to do the work correctly is valuable information that helps employees become more competent and improve their performance. In addition, communicating clearly about what has not been done right also provides useful information so that past mistakes are not repeated.
- *Enhances involvement.*   Receiving feedback and discussing performance issues allows the employee to understand his role in the unit and organization as a whole. This in turn helps employees become more involved in the unit and organization.

Unfortunately, however, the mere presence of feedback, even if it is delivered correctly, does not necessarily mean that all of these purposes are fulfilled. For example, a review of 131 studies that examined the effects of feedback on performance concluded that 38% of the feedback programs reviewed had a *negative* effect on performance.[13] In other words, in many cases the implementation of feedback led to *lower* performance levels. This can happen when, for example, feedback does not include useful information or is not delivered in the right way. For example, feedback can have detrimental effects if it focuses on the employee as a whole as opposed to specific behaviors at work. This is precisely the case of a very successful woman who made many personal sacrifices, such as not starting a family, to reach the top echelons of the organizational hierarchy.[14] She received feedback including information that she had failed to retain a valued client. The feedback was accurate and delivered in the correct manner. However, after receiving the feedback, she began to question her life choices in general, instead of focusing specifically on how to not lose valued clients in the future. In this example, feedback was not instrumental in improving performance. Instead, the feedback created self-doubt and questions about identity.

Although some feedback systems do not work well, the advantages of providing feedback generally outweigh any disadvantages. Also, consider the possible cost of *not* providing feedback. First, organizations would be depriving employees of a chance to improve their performance. Second, organizations may be stuck with chronic poor performance because employees may not recognize any performance problems and may feel justified in continuing to perform at substandard levels. Finally, employees may develop inaccurate perceptions of how their performance is regarded by others.

So, given that, overall, feedback systems are beneficial, what can we do so that we make the most of them? Consider the following suggestions to enhance feedback:[15]

- *Timeliness.*   Feedback should be delivered as close to the performance event as possible. For feedback to be most meaningful, it must be given immediately after the event.
- *Frequency.*   Feedback should be provided on an ongoing basis, daily if possible. If performance improvement is an ongoing activity, then feedback about performance should also be provided on an ongoing basis.
- *Specificity.*   Feedback should include specific work behaviors, results, and the situation where these behaviors and results were observed.[16] Feedback is not about the employee and how the employee "is," but about behaviors and results and situations in which these behaviors and results took place.
- *Verifiability.*   Feedback should include information that is verifiable and accurate. It should not be based on inferences or rumors. Using information that is verifiable leads to more accurate feedback and subsequent acceptance.
- *Consistency.*   Feedback should be consistent. In other words, information on specific aspects of performance should not vary unpredictably between overwhelming praise and harsh criticism.
- *Privacy.*   Feedback should be given at a place and time that avoids any potential embarrassment. This applies to both criticism and praise, because some employees, due to personality or cultural background, may not wish to be rewarded in public.

- *Consequences.* Feedback should include contextual information that allows the employee to understand the importance and consequences of the behaviors and results in question. For example, if an employee has become frustrated and behaved inappropriately with an angry customer and the customer's complaint has not been addressed satisfactorily, feedback should explain the impact of these behaviors (i.e., behaving inappropriately) and results for the organization (i.e., the customer's problem was not resolved, the customer was upset, and likely to not give repeat business to the organization).
- *Description first, evaluation second.* Feedback should first focus on describing behaviors and results rather than on evaluating and judging behaviors and results. It's better first to report what has been observed and, once there is agreement on what happened, to evaluate what has been observed. If evaluation takes place first, employees may become defensive and feedback may be rejected.
- *Performance continuum.* Feedback should describe performance as a continuum, going from less to more in the case of good performance and from more to less in the case of poor performance. In other words, feedback should include information on how to display good performance behaviors more often and poor performance behaviors less often. Thus, performance is a matter of degree, and even the worst performer is likely to show nuggets of good performance that can be described as a starting point for a discussion on how to improve performance.
- *Pattern identification.* Feedback is most useful if it is about a pattern of poor performance rather than isolated events or mistakes. Identifying a pattern of poor performance also allows for a better understanding of the causes leading to poor performance.
- *Confidence in the employee.* Good feedback includes a statement that the manager has confidence that the employee will be able to improve her performance. It is important for the employee to hear this from the manager. This reinforces the idea that feedback is about performance and not the performer. Note, however, that this should be done only if the manager indeed believes the employee can improve her performance. In the case of a chronic poor performance, this type of information could be used out of context later if the employee is fired.
- *Advice and idea generation.* Feedback can include advice given by the supervisor on how to improve performance. In addition, however, the employee should play an active role in generating ideas on how to improve performance in the future.

Consider the following vignette in which Andrea, a supervisor, has observed a specific performance event and provides feedback to her subordinate. Andrea is the manager of a small retail store with approximately five employees. With a small staff Andrea looks for coaching opportunities on a weekly basis. Andrea is working with Matt today and she has just witnessed him complete a customer sale. Matt did not follow several steps, however, that should be included at each sale and, because the store is now empty, Andrea decides it is a perfect opportunity for a coaching session.

ANDREA:	Hey, Matt, that was great the way that you just assisted that customer in finding her correct size in the jeans. Thanks for taking the extra time to help her.
MATT:	Thanks, Andrea, not a problem.
ANDREA:	I would like to go over the sales transaction with you.
MATT:	Sure.
ANDREA:	After you helped the woman find her jeans, you promptly brought her over and rang her up. That was a good sale because those jeans were a full-priced item; however, you didn't complete all of the tasks associated with closing a sale. In the training last week, we discussed the importance of adding on additional sales, entering the customer's personal contact information in our computer, and letting them know about upcoming sales.
MATT:	Yes, I just remembered us talking about that. When customers seem in a hurry, I feel bad asking them additional questions.
ANDREA:	That's a very valid concern. Can we think of ways to increase the efficiency of adding these few steps into the sales transaction process so that you feel comfortable performing them in the future? I would like to help you do so, because increasing the number of items you sell during each transaction could help you win the upcoming sales contests.
MATT:	That would be great. I would really like some new ideas about talking with customers.
ANDREA:	No problem; I know that you are a very capable salesperson. You have great customer service skills, and I think that you can improve your sales and possibly win one of the upcoming contests.

Andrea and Matt then generate ideas on how to improve Matt's performance.

In this vignette, Andrea demonstrated several of the feedback behaviors listed in Table 9.5. She was specific about the behaviors and results, the information was verifiable, and it was timely because the behavior had just occurred. In addition, since Andrea

TABLE 9.5   What Most Effective Feedback Should Be
Timely
Frequent
Specific
Verifiable
Consistent
Private
Consequential
Descriptive first and evaluative second
Related to a performance continuum
Based on identifiable patterns of performance
A confidence builder for employees
A tool for generating advice and ideas

communicates her expectations on a weekly basis, the information she provides is consistent. Finally, she described the behavior first and then evaluated its effectiveness; she communicated confidence in Matt and she offered to help him generate ideas on how to improve his effectiveness. In spite of these positive features, however, there were also several things that Andrea left out when coaching Matt. First, she did not communicate the consequences of his behavior, for example, that his failure to follow the procedures could hurt sales for the entire store. Although the vignette does not describe the idea generation portion of the feedback session, she also did not describe small behaviors that Matt could demonstrate that would constitute an improvement in performance. Finally, Andrea did not communicate to Matt whether this behavior was a one-time incident or whether it was a pattern that was affecting his overall work performance.

Overall, if Andrea continues to look for coaching opportunities with her employees, her relationship with her employees and their performance in the store will continue to improve. However, to be more effective, she may need to work on communicating the patterns of behavior that lead to poor performance and the consequences of continued poor performance.

9.3.2.1 Praise

Good feedback includes information on both good and poor performance. Although most people are a lot more comfortable giving feedback on good performance than they are on poor performance, some guidelines must be followed when giving praise so that the feedback is useful in terms of future performance. First, praise should be sincere and given only when it is deserved. If praise is given repeatedly and when it is not deserved, employees are not able to see when a change in direction may be needed.[17] Second, praise should be about specific behaviors or results and be given within context so that employees know what they need to attempt to repeat in the future. For example, a manager can say the following:[18] "John, thanks for providing such excellent service to our client. Your efforts helped us renew our contract with them for another two years. It's these types of behaviors and results that our group needs to achieve our goal for this year. And, this is exactly what our company is all about: providing outstanding customer service." Third, in giving praise, managers should take their time and act pleased, rather than rushing through the information and looking embarrassed. Finally, avoid giving praise by referring to the absence of the negative, for example, "not bad" or "better than last time." Instead, praise should emphasize the positives and be phrased in terms of "I like the way you did that . . . " or "I admire how you did that . . . ".[19]

Consider the following vignette illustrating how a manager handles giving praise to his employee:

After the successful completion of a three-month project at a large telecommunications company, Ken, the manager, wants to congratulate Mike on a job well done. Ken calls Mike into his office one day after the project is completed.

KEN: Thanks for stopping by Mike, and thank you for all of your hard work over the past three months. I know that I may not have congratulated you on every milestone you reached along the way, but I wanted to take the time to congratulate you now. Your organizational skills and ability to successfully interact with multiple departments led to the successful completion of the project on time and within budget.

MIKE:　　　　　　　Thanks, Ken. I have really been putting extra effort into completing this project on time.

KEN:　　　　　　　It shows, Mike, and I appreciate all of your hard work and dedication to this team and our department. Thanks again and congratulations on a great end to a long three months.

In this vignette, Ken delivered praise to Mike successfully and followed the recommendations provided earlier. He was sincere and made sure not to praise Mike too often, so that when he did praise him, it was meaningful. He described how Mike's organizational and project management skills led to the successful completion of the project. Finally, Ken took his time in delivering the praise and made sure that Mike took the praise seriously.

9.3.2.2　Negative Feedback

Negative feedback includes information that performance has fallen short of accepted standards. The goal of providing negative feedback is to help employees improve their performance in the future; it is not to punish, embarrass, or chastise them. However, it is important to give negative feedback when this is warranted because the consequences of not doing so can be detrimental for the organization as a whole. For example, Francie Dalton, president of Dalton Alliances, Inc., noted, "In organizations where management imposes no consequences for poor performance, high achievers will leave because they don't want to be where mediocrity is tolerated. But mediocre performers will remain because they know they're safe. The entire organizational culture, along with its reputation in the marketplace, can be affected by poor performers."[20]

In spite of the need to address poor performance, managers are usually not very comfortable providing negative feedback. Why is this so? Consider the following reasons:

- *Negative reactions and consequences.*　Managers may fear that employees will react negatively. Negative reactions can include being defensive and even becoming angry at the information received. In addition, managers may fear that the working relationship, or even friendship, with their subordinates may be affected adversely and that giving negative feedback can introduce elements of mistrust and annoyance.
- *Negative experiences in the past.*　Many managers are likely to have received negative feedback at some point in their careers and they have experienced firsthand that this can hurt. Receiving negative feedback can be painful and upsetting; therefore, managers may not want to put their subordinates in such a situation.
- *Playing "god."*　Many managers may be reluctant to play a role of an all-knowing and judgmental god. They feel that giving negative feedback puts them in that position.
- *Need for irrefutable and conclusive evidence.*　Many managers may not want to provide negative feedback until they have been able to gather irrefutable and conclusive evidence about a performance problem. This task may be perceived as too onerous, so managers may choose to skip giving negative feedback altogether.

What happens when managers avoid giving negative feedback and employees avoid seeking it? A *feedback gap* results, in which managers and employees mutually instigate and reinforce lack of communication that creates a vacuum of meaningful exchanges about poor performance.[21] A typical consequence of a feedback gap is that, in the absence of information to the contrary, the manager gives the employee the message that performance is adequate. When performance problems exist, they are likely to become more intense over time. For example, clients may be so dissatisfied with the service they are receiving that they may eventually choose to close their accounts and work instead with the competition. At that time, it becomes impossible for the manager to overlook the performance problem and she has no choice but to deliver the negative feedback. At this stage of the process, however, feedback is delivered too late and often in a punitive fashion. Of course, feedback delivered so late in the process and in a punitive fashion is not likely to be helpful.

Alternatively, negative feedback is most useful when early coaching has been instrumental in identifying warning signs and the performance problem is still manageable. Negative feedback is also useful when it clarifies unwanted behaviors and consequences and focuses on behaviors that can be changed. There is no point in providing feedback on issues that are beyond the employee's control because there is not much she can do to improve the situation. In addition, employees are more likely to respond constructively to negative feedback when the manager is perceived as being trustworthy and making a genuine attempt to improve the employee's performance. In other words, the manager needs to be perceived as credible and also as instrumental in improving the employee's performance in the future.[22] Finally, negative feedback is most likely to be accepted when it is given by a source who uses straight talk and not subtle pressure and when it is supported by hard data. The supervisor must control her emotions and stay calm. If managers follow these suggestions, it is more likely that employees will benefit the most from negative feedback, even if employees are not particularly open to receiving it.[23] Following these suggestions leads to what has been labeled "actionable feedback," meaning that such feedback will allow employees to respond in constructive ways and lead to learning and performance improvement.[24]

Overall, regardless of whether the feedback session includes praise or a discussion of needed areas of improvement, it should provide answers to the following questions:[25]

1. How is your job going?
2. What can be done to improve your and your unit's/organization's job/products/services?
3. How can you better serve your internal and external customers?

9.4 PERFORMANCE REVIEW MEETINGS

Supervisors managing employee performance often feel uncomfortable in this role because managing performance requires that they be judges and coaches at the same time.[26] In other words, supervisors serve as judges by evaluating performance and allocating rewards. In addition, supervisors serve as coaches by helping employees solve performance problems, identify performance weaknesses, and design developmental plans that will be instrumental in future career development.

Not surprisingly, employees are usually not satisfied with their performance reviews. For example, a survey of Australian employees conducted by the Gallup organization found that less than 20% of employees reported that their performance reviews helped them improve their performance. Overall, the majority of respondents reported being dissatisfied with the level of feedback and frequency of performance reviews from managers.[27]

Because supervisors play these paradoxical roles, it is usually helpful to separate the various meetings related to performance. When meetings are separated, it is easier to separate the discussion of rewards from the discussion about future career development. This allows employees to give their full attention to each issue, one at a time.

Chapter 6 noted that performance management systems can have up to six formal meetings, including the following:

- *System inauguration.* The purpose of this meeting is to discuss how the performance management system works and which requirements and responsibilities rest primarily on the employee and which rest primarily on the supervisor.
- *Self-appraisal.* The purpose of this meeting is to discuss the self-appraisal prepared by the employee.
- *Classical performance review.* The purpose of this meeting is to discuss employee performance, including the perspectives of both the supervisor and the employee.
- *Merit/salary review.* The purpose of this meeting is to discuss what, if any, compensation changes will result as a consequence of the period's performance.
- *Developmental plan.* The purpose of this meeting is to discuss the employee's developmental needs and what steps will be taken so that performance will be improved during the following period.
- *Objective setting.* The purpose of this meeting is to set performance goals, both behavioral and results oriented, regarding the following review period.

Although these six types of meetings are possible, not all six take place as separate meetings. For example, the self-appraisal, classical performance review, merit/salary review, developmental plan, and objective setting meetings may all take place during one umbrella meeting, labeled "performance review meeting." However, as noted above, it is better to separate the various types of information discussed so that the employee and supervisor focus on each of the components separately. Note, however, that the conversation about compensation should be related to performance (i.e., employees must understand the direct link between performance and compensation decisions).

Regardless of the specific type of meeting, there are several steps that must be taken before the meeting takes place. Specifically, it is useful to give at least a two-week advance notice to the employee so she is informed of the purpose of the meeting and is prepared for it. Also, it is useful to block sufficient time for the meeting and arrange to meet in a private location without interruptions. Taking these steps sends a clear message that the meeting is important and that, consequently, performance management is important.

As noted above, most organizations merge several meetings into one labeled "performance review meeting." The typical sequence of events for such a meeting is the following:[28]

- *Explain the purpose of the meeting.* The first step includes a description of the purpose of the meeting and the topics to be discussed.
- *Self-appraisal.* The second step includes asking the employee to summarize her accomplishments during the review period. This is more easily accomplished

when the employee is given the appraisal form to be used by the supervisor before the meeting. This portion of the meeting allows the employee to provide her perspective regarding performance. The role of the supervisor is to listen to what the employee has to say and to summarize what he hears. This is not an appropriate time for the supervisor to disagree with what the employee says.

- *Share ratings and explain rationale.*   Next, the supervisor explains the rating he provided for each performance dimension and explains the reasons that led to each score. It is more effective to start with a discussion of the performance dimensions for which there is agreement between the employee's self-appraisal and the supervisor's appraisal. This is likely to reduce tension and to demonstrate to the employee that there is common ground and that the meeting is not confrontational. Also, it is better to start with a discussion of the performance dimensions for which the scores are highest and then move on to the dimensions for which the scores are lower. For areas for which there is disagreement between self- and supervisor ratings, the supervisor must take great care in discussing the reason for his rating and provide specific examples and evidence to support the score given. At this point, there should be an effort to resolve discrepancies and the supervisor should take extra care with sensitive areas. The employee should be provided with the opportunity to explain her viewpoint thoroughly. This is a very useful discussion because it leads to clarifying performance expectations. For dimensions for which the score is low, there should be a discussion of the possible causes for poor performance. For example, are the reasons related to lack of knowledge, lack of motivation, or contextual factors beyond the control of the employee?
- *Developmental discussion.*   Once the supervisor and employee agree on the scores given to each performance dimension, there should be a discussion of the developmental plan. At this point, the supervisor and the employee should discuss and agree on the developmental steps that will be taken to improve performance in the future.
- *Employee summary.*   Next, the employee should summarize, in her own words, the main conclusions of the meeting: what performance dimensions are satisfactory, which need improvement, and how improvement will be achieved. This is an important component of the meeting because it gives the supervisor an opportunity to learn if he and the employee are in accord.
- *Rewards discussion.*   The next step during the meeting includes discussing the relationship between performance and any reward allocation. The supervisor should explain the rules used to allocate rewards and how the employee would be able to reach higher reward levels as a consequence of future performance improvement.
- *Follow-up meeting.*   Before the meeting is over, it is important to schedule the next performance-related formal meeting. It is important that the employee sees that there will be a formal follow-up and that performance management is not just about meeting with the supervisor once a year. Usually, the next meeting will take place just a few weeks later to review whether the developmental plan is being implemented effectively.
- *Approval and appeals process discussion.*   Finally, the supervisor asks the employee to sign the form to attest that the evaluation has been discussed

with him. This is also an opportunity for the employee to add any comments or additional information she would like to see included on the form. In addition, if disagreements about ratings have not been resolved, the supervisor should remind the employee of the appeals process.

- *Final recap.* Finally, the supervisor should use the "past-present-future model." In other words, the supervisor summarizes what happened during the review period in terms of performance levels in the various dimensions, reviews how rewards will change based on this level of performance, and sums up what the employee will need to do in the next year to maintain and enhance performance.

Performance review discussions serve very important purposes. First, these discussions allow employees to improve their performance by identifying performance problems and solutions for overcoming them. Second, they help build a good relationship between the supervisor and the employee because the supervisor shows that she cares about the employee's ongoing growth and development and that she is willing to invest resources, including time, in helping the employee improve.

Unfortunately, these purposes are not always realized because employees may be defensive and many supervisors do not know how to deal with this attitude because they lack the necessary skills to conduct an effective performance review. How can we tell that an employee is being defensive? Typically, there are two patterns of behavior that indicate defensiveness.[29] First, employees may engage in a *fight response.* This includes blaming others for performance deficiencies, staring mutely at the supervisor, and other, more aggressive responses, such as raising her voice or even pounding the desk. Second, employees may engage in a *flight response.* This includes looking away, turning away, speaking softly, continually changing the subject, or quickly agreeing with what the supervisor is saying without basing the agreement on a thoughtful and thorough discussion about the issues at stake. When employees have a fight or flight response during the performance review discussion, it is unlikely that the meeting will lead to improved performance in the future. What can supervisors do to prevent defensive responses? Consider the following suggestions:

- *Establish and maintain rapport.* It is important that the meeting take place in a good climate. As noted earlier, this can be achieved by choosing a meeting place that is private and by not allowing interruptions to take place. Also, the supervisor should emphasize two-way communication and put the employee at ease as quickly as possible. This can be done by sitting next to the employee as opposed to across a desk, by saying his name, thanking him for coming, and initially engaging in small talk to reduce the initial tension. When good rapport is established, both the supervisor and the employee are at ease, relaxed, and comfortable. They can have a friendly conversation and neither is afraid to speak freely. Both are open-minded and can express disagreement without offending. On the other hand, when there is no good rapport, both participants may be nervous and anxious. The conversation is cold and formal and both may fear to speak openly. The supervisor and employee are likely to interrupt each other frequently and challenge what the other is saying.
- *Be empathetic.* It is important for the supervisor to put herself in the shoes of the employee. The supervisor needs to make an effort to understand why

the employee has performed at a certain level during the review period. This includes not making attributions that any employee success was caused by outside forces (e.g., a good economy) or that employee failures were caused by inside forces (e.g., employee incompetence).

- *Observe verbal and nonverbal cues.* The supervisor should be able to read verbal and nonverbal signals from the employee to determine if further clarification is necessary. The supervisor should be attentive to the employee's emotions and react accordingly. For example, if the employee becomes defensive, the supervisor should stop talking and allow the employee to express her point of view regarding the issue being discussed.
- *Minimize threats.* The performance review meeting should be framed as a meeting that will benefit the employee and not as a meeting that has as its goal employee punishment.
- *Encourage participation.* The employee needs to have her own conversational space to speak and express her views. The supervisor should not dominate the meeting; rather, she should listen without interrupting, and avoid confrontation and argument.

In spite of these suggestions, defensiveness may still be unavoidable in some situations. In such situations, supervisors need to recognize that employee defensiveness is inevitable and they need to allow it. Rather than ignoring the defensive attitude, supervisors need to deal with the situation head on. First, it is important to let the employee vent and to acknowledge the employee's feelings. To do this, the supervisor may want to pause to accept the employee's feelings. Then, the supervisor may want to ask the employee for additional information and clarification. If the situation is reaching a point that communication becomes impossible, the supervisor may want to suggest suspending the meeting until a later point.[30] For example, the supervisor may say, "I understand that you are angry, and that you believe you have been treated unfairly. It's important that I understand your perspective, but it's difficult for me to absorb the information when you are so upset. This is an important matter. Let's take a break, and get back together at 3:00 p.m. to continue our discussion." To be sure, if the relationship between the supervisor and the employee is not good, the performance review meeting is likely to expose these issues in a blatant and often painful way.

Consider the following vignette. Jason is the manager at a large accounting firm and Susan is one of the employees on his team. He chooses a conference room with privacy away from the other offices.

JASON:	Hi, Susan. I wanted to meet with you today to discuss your performance appraisal for this quarter. At any time, please offer your input and ask questions if you have any.
SUSAN:	OK.
JASON:	You did meet two important objectives that we set this quarter: sales and customer service. Thanks for your hard work.
SUSAN:	No problem.
JASON:	You did miss three of the other objectives.
SUSAN:	What? I worked as hard as I could! It wasn't *my* fault that the other people on the team did not carry their weight.

JASON:	Susan, I am not here to blame anyone or to attack you. I want to generate some ideas on what we can do to ensure that you meet your objectives and receive your bonus next quarter.
SUSAN,	*SITTING BACK WITH CROSSED ARMS:* I told you I worked as hard as I could.
JASON:	I know that you worked hard, Susan, and I know how hard it is to balance all of the objectives that we have in our department. When I first started, I had a hard time meeting all of the objectives as well.
SUSAN:	It is hard and I try my best.
JASON:	Susan, can you think of anything that we can work on together that would help you meet the last three objectives? Is there any additional training or resources that you need?
SUSAN:	I am having a hard time prioritizing all of my daily tasks. There is a class offered online on prioritizing, but I feel too busy to take it.
JASON:	That is good that you think the class will help. Take the class online, which will not disrupt your work schedule, and I will go to all of your meetings and followup with clients as needed.
SUSAN:	Thanks, Jason. I really appreciate your help.

How did Jason do in dealing with Susan's defensiveness? Overall, he did a good job. Jason was empathetic, he picked up on Susan's nonverbal behavior, he had her offer her input, he held the meeting in a comfortable, private location, and he emphasized that the meeting was to work on future performance and not to punish her. In the end, he was able to address Susan's defensiveness and turned a meeting that could have gone very poorly into a productive exchange of information and ideas.

SUMMARY POINTS

- Managers must possess several important skills to manage the performance of their employees effectively. Managers need to serve as coaches, to observe and document performance accurately, to give both positive and negative feedback, and to conduct performance review meetings.
- Coaching is an ongoing process in which the manager directs, motivates, and rewards employee behavior. Coaching includes several key functions, such as giving advice about what is expected about performance and how to perform well, giving employees guidance so employees know how to improve their performance, providing employees with support without being controlling, and enhancing employees' confidence and competence.

- Managers need to engage in a complex set of behaviors to perform the various coaching functions. These include the following: establish developmental objectives, communicate effectively, motivate employees, document performance, give feedback, diagnose performance problems, and develop employees.
- Managers' personalities and behavioral preferences determine their coaching style. Some managers prefer to be drivers and just tell employees what to do. Others prefer to be persuaders and try to sell what they want the employees to do. Yet others adopt an amiable style in which feelings take precedence and urge the employee to do what feels right or what the employee feels is the right way to do things. Finally, others prefer to be

analyzers and have a tendency to follow rules and procedures in recommending how to perform. None of these four styles is necessarily better than the others. The best coaches are able to change their styles and adapt to the needs of the employees.

- The coaching process is ongoing and cyclical and it includes the following five components: (1) setting developmental goals; (2) identifying resources and strategies needed to achieve the developmental goals (e.g., securing resources that will allow for engaging in activities to achieve the developmental goals); (3) implementing strategies (e.g., enrolling the employee in an online course); (4) observing and documenting developmental behaviors (i.e., the supervisor checks on the progress of the employee toward the attainment of the developmental goals); and (5) giving feedback (i.e., the supervisor provides information to the employee that helps adjust current developmental goals and guide future goals).

- Observing and documenting performance in general and performance regarding developmental goals in particular is not as easy as it may seem. Time constraints play a role, because managers may be too busy to gather performance information. Situational constraints may prevent managers from observing the employee directly. Finally, activity constraints may be a factor: when developmental activities are very unstructured, such as reading a book, the manager may have to wait until the activity is completed to assess whether any new skills and knowledge have been acquired.

- Observation and documentation of performance can be improved in several ways. Many of these issues were described in detail in Chapter 7 and include implementing a good communication plan that managers accept and the implementation of training programs that helps managers minimize rater errors (i.e., rater error training), share notions of what it means to successfully complete developmental activities (i.e., frame-of-reference training), observe performance more accurately (i.e., behavioral observation training), and become more confident managing employee performance (i.e., self-leadership training).

- Documenting an employee's progress toward achieving developmental goals and improving performance in general has several important benefits. These include the reduction of the manager's cognitive load, the enhancement of trust between the employee and the manager, the collection of important input to be used in planning development of activities in the future, and the development of a good line of defense in case of litigation.

- For documentation to be most useful, it must be specific, use adjectives and adverbs sparingly, balance positives with negatives, focus on job-related information, be comprehensive, be standardized across employees, and stated in behavioral terms.

- Feedback about performance in general and about developmental activities in particular serves several important purposes. These include helping build employee confidence, developing employee competence, and enhancing employee involvement with the unit and the organization as a whole.

- The mere presence of feedback does not mean that there will be positive effects on future performance. For feedback to be most useful, it must be timely, frequent, specific, verifiable, consistent over time and across employees, given in private, tied closely with consequences (e.g., rewards), address description first and evaluation second, discuss performance in terms of a continuum and not in terms of dichotomies (i.e., more and less and not all and nothing), address patterns of behavior and not isolated events, include a statement that the manager has confidence in the employee, and include the active participation of the employee in generating ideas on how to improve performance in the future.

- In general, managers do not feel comfortable giving negative feedback. This is because they fear that employees will react negatively, because they themselves have been given negative feedback in the past in a way that was not helpful and do not want to put their employees in the same situation, because they don't like playing god, and because they feel they need an onerous amount of information and evidence before giving negative feedback. However, when negative feedback is warranted and managers refuse to give it, poor performers may get the message that their performance is not that bad. Eventually, the situation may escalate to the point that the manager has no choice but to give negative feedback; the situation then becomes punitive and feedback is not likely to be useful. For negative feedback to be useful, it must be given early on when the performance problem is still manageable

- Supervisors play the paradoxical roles of judge and coach at the same time. These roles are assumed during the performance review meetings, which can include up to six separate formal meetings: system inauguration, self-appraisal, classical performance review, merit/salary review, developmental plan, and objective setting. In most organizations, these meetings are merged into just one or sometimes two. However, it is better to separate the meetings so that employees can focus on one issue at a time (e.g., supervisor's view on the employee's performance, rewards allocation, developmental plan).

- When all performance review meetings are merged into one, the components of such a meeting include the following: (1) explanation of the purpose of the meeting, (2) self-appraisal, (3) discussion of the supervisor's performance ratings and rationale and resolution of discrepancies with self-appraisal, (4) developmental discussion, (5) employee summary, (6) rewards discussion, (7) setting follow-up meeting, (8) approval and appeals process discussion, and (9) final recap.

- In meeting with the supervisor to discuss performance issues, employees may become defensive. Defensiveness is indicated by a fight or flight response. The supervisor can minimize defensiveness by: (1) establishing and maintaining rapport, (2) being empathetic, (3) observing verbal and nonverbal cues, (4) minimizing threats, and (5) encouraging employee participation.

- When defensiveness becomes unavoidable, the employee's attitude must be recognized and allowed expression. If the situation becomes intolerable, the meeting may be rescheduled for a later time.

Case Study 9.1 Was Robert Eaton a Good Coach?[1]

Robert Eaton was CEO and chairman of Chrysler from 1993 to 1998, replacing Lee Iacocca, who retired after serving in this capacity since 1978. Eaton then served as co-chairman of the newly merged DaimlerChrysler organization from 1998–2000. With 362,100 employees, Daimler-Chrysler achieved revenues of EUR 136.4 billion in 2003. DaimlerChrysler's passenger car brands include Maybach, Mercedes-Benz, Chrysler, Jeep, Dodge, and Smart. Commercial vehicle brands include Mercedes-Benz, Freightliner, Sterling, Western Star, and Setra.

From the beginning of his tenure as CEO, Eaton communicated with the people under him. He immediately shared his plans for the future with his top four executives, and then took the advice of his colleague, Bob Lutz, to look around the company before making any hasty decisions concerning the state of affairs at Chrysler. Eaton and Lutz found that Chrysler was employing the right staff and that they did not have to hire new people; they just had to lead them in a different manner, in a more participative style.

Eaton listened to everyone in the organization, including executives, suppliers, and assembly-line workers, to determine how to help the company succeed. Eaton also encouraged the employees at Chrysler to talk with one another. The atmosphere of collaboration and open-door communication (the two men sat across the hall from one another and never closed their doors) between Eaton and Lutz permeated throughout the organization. Eaton and Lutz's walk-around management style also showed employees that they were committed to and engaged in the organization. Furthermore, Eaton and Lutz held meetings with their executive team on a regular basis so that they could get together and exchange ideas and information from all areas of the organization.

Eaton even reorganized the way that Chrysler designed cars based on a study, previously disregarded by Iacocca, that had found that Chrysler had to be more flexible and its executives had to be in constant communication with the product design team. One employee is quoted as saying, "Bob Eaton does not shoot the messenger when he hears something he doesn't like or understand. He knows that not every idea is right. But Bob is off-the-wall himself. . . . He'll say something, and we'll tell him that it's a crazy idea. . . . He may not change his mind in the end, but he'll spend the time explaining to you what is behind his thought processes. Do you know what kind of confidence that inspires?" This type of open communication at the top proved extremely successful, as summed up by one designer: "It's a system that recognizes talent early and rewards it, and that creates a sense of enthusiasm for your work, and a sense of mission."

Another program that Eaton describes as empowering employees at Chrysler includes having all employees, including executives, participate in the process of building a new vehicle. Eaton explains that this shows all of the employees in the plant that executives are concerned about the

---

[1]Based on information provided by M. Puris, *Comeback: How Seven Straight-Shooting CEOs Turned Around Troubled Companies* (New York: Times Books, 1999) 80–118, Specifically chap. 4, "Robert Eaton and Robert Lutz; The Copilots."

proper functioning of new cars, and it also gives executives the opportunity to understand and solve problems at the factory level. Eaton states, "When we're done with our discussions, these guys know where we want to go and how we want to get there, and they go back and put the action plans together to do that. This goes for every single thing we do." He concludes, "Clearly at a company there has to be a shared vision, but we try to teach people to be a leader in their own area, to know where the company wants to go, to know how that affects their area, to benchmark the best in the world and then set goals and programs to go after it. We also encourage people not only to go after the business plan objectives, but to have stretch goals. And a stretch goal by definition is a fifty-percent increase. . . . If we go after fifty percent, something dramatic has to happen. You have to go outside of the box."

Based on the above description, please evaluate Bob Eaton's coaching skills using the accompanying table. If a certain coaching behavior or function is missing, please provide recommendations about what he could have done more effectively. ■

Major Functions	Present? (Y/N)	Comments/Recommendations
Give advice		
Provide guidance		
Give support		
Give confidence		
Promote greater competence		

Key Behaviors	Present? (Y/N)	Comments/Recommendations
Establish development objectives		
Communicate effectively		
Motivate employees		
Document performance		
Give feedback		
Diagnose performance problems		
Develop employees		

Case Study 9.2   What Is Your Coaching Style?[2]

Below are 15 rows of four words each. From each row, select and circle two words out of the four that best describe the way you see yourself. If all four words sound like you, select the two that are most like you. If none of the four sounds like you, select the two that are closest to the way you are. Then, total the number of words selected under each respective column.

[2]Coaching Guides. Available online at http://www.specialolympics.org/Special+Olympics+Public+Website/English/Coach/Coaching_Guides/Principles+of+Coaching/Developing+a+Picture+of+Your+Style.htm

	A	B	C	D
1	All-business/Organized	Bold	Personable	Deliberate
2	Listening	Telling	Courteous	Listening
3	Industrious	Independent	Companionable	Cooperative
4	No-nonsense	Decisive	Talkative	Reflective
5	Serious	Determined	Warm	Careful
6	To-the-point	Risk-taker	Amiable	Moderate
7	Practical	Aggressive	Empathetic	Nonassertive
8	Self-controlled	Authoritative	Shows emotions	Thorough
9	Goal-directed	Assertive	Friendly	Patient
10	Methodical	Unhesitating	Sincere	Prudent
11	Businesslike	Definite	Sociable	Precise
12	Diligent	Firm	Demonstrative	Particular
13	Systematic	Strong-minded	Sense of humor	Thinking
14	Formal	Confident	Expressive	Hesitative
15	Persevering	Forceful	Trusting	Restrained
Total				

Once you have totaled the number of words circled under each respective column, plot those numbers on their respective axes of the grid here. For example, if you circled six words in column A, mark the A axis next to the 6. Complete the same procedures for columns B, C, and D. Then extend the marks into each respective quadrant to create a rectangle. For example, consider the example of circling 7 words from the A list, 8 from the B list, 7 from the C list, and 8 from the D list. The rectangle would be the following:

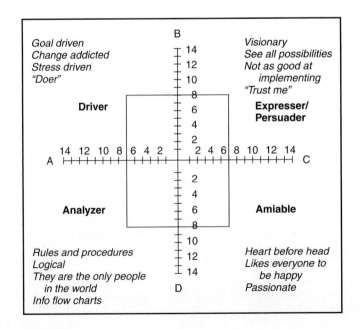

In this particular example, the area covered by the rectangle shows that that this person is predominantly a driver and an analyzer, but can also be a persuader and amiable. Now, create your own rectangle using your scores:

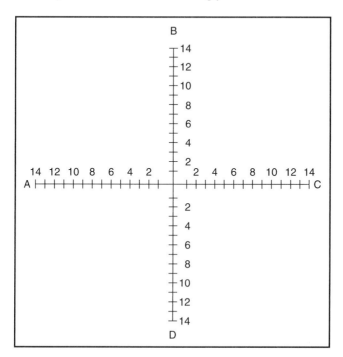

What is your coaching style? Is there a dominance of one style over the other three as indicated by an area predominantly covering one of the quadrants and not the others? If there is, what can you do to start using the other styles as well? ■

Case Study 9.3   Preventing Defensiveness

Spencer is Jeff's manager and needs to talk to him about his poor performance over the previous quarter. Jeff enters the room and sits across the desk from Spencer.

JEFF: Spencer, you wanted to talk to me?

SPENCER: Yes, Jeff, thanks for coming by. I wanted to talk about your performance last quarter. (*Spencer's phone rings and he answers it. Five minutes later Jeff is still waiting for Spencer. Jeff finally gets frustrated and Spencer notices Jeff looks at his watch several times.*) Sorry for the interruption Jeff, I know it is frustrating to be kept waiting.

JEFF: I am very busy. Can we get on with this?

SPENCER: Yes, absolutely. As you know you had some problems meeting all of your goals last quarter.

JEFF: Now wait a second, I met the most important goal.

SPENCER: Yes, you did, but you missed the other four.

JEFF: Just by a little and it wasn't my fault.

SPENCER: Jeff, you need to accept responsibility for your own performance and not push blame onto others. You need to meet your goals this

coming quarter or I will have to take more serious action.

JEFF: One bad quarter and you threaten to fire me? I can't believe this!

SPENCER: Just meet all of your goals and I won't have to take that action.

Given this vignette, what could Spencer have done to combat Jeff's defensiveness more effectively? ■

END NOTES

1. Allenbaugh, G. E. (1983). Coaching . . . A management tool for a more effective work performance. *Management Review, 72*, 21–26.
2. Hunt, J. M., & Weintraub, J. R. (2002). *The coaching manager: Developing top talent in business*. Thousand Oaks, CA: Sage.
3. Kiger, P. J. (2002, May). How performance management reversed NCCI's fortunes. *Workforce, 81*, 48–51
4. Byne, J. A. (1998, June 8). How Jack Welch runs GE. *Business Week*. Available online at http://www.businessweek.com/1998/23/b3581001. htm. Retrieval date: August 15, 2005.
5. Bacon, T. R., & Spear, K. I. (2003). *Adaptive coaching: The art and practice of a client-centered approach to performance improvement*. Palo Alto, CA: Davies-Black.
6. Foster, P. (2002). Performance documentation. *Business Communication Quarterly, 65*, 108–114.
7. Cleverly v. Western Electric Co., 594 F.2d 638 (8th Cir. 1979).
8. Walther, F., & Taylor, S. (1988). An active feedback program can spark performance. In A. D. Timpe (Ed.), *Performance: The art & science of business management* (pp. 293–299). New York: Facts on File Publications.
9. These quotes have circulated worldwide on the Internet. See, for example, http://www.cnenigeria.com/jokes/joke101.htm, http://www.teleweb.net/georgeeiben/Bossstories/FromActualEmployee Evaluations. htm, and http://www.avolites. org.uk/jokes/ appraisals.htm
10. Blake Jelley, R., & Goffin, R. D. (2001). Can performance-feedback accuracy be improved? Effects of rater priming and rating-scale format on rating accuracy. *Journal of Applied Psychology, 86*, 134–144.
11. Becker, T. E., & Klimoski, R. J. (1989). A field study of the relationship between the organizational feedback environment and performance, *Personnel Psychology, 42*, 343–358.
12. Silverman, S. B., Pogson, C. E., & Cober, A. B. (2005). When employees at work don't get it: A model for enhancing individual employee change in response to performance feedback. *Academy of Management Executive, 19*, 135–147.
13. Kluger, A. N., & DeNisi, A. S. (1996). The effects of feedback interventions on performance: Historical review, a meta-analysis, and a preliminary feedback intervention theory. *Psychological Bulletin, 119*, 254–284.
14. DeNisi, A. S., & Kluger, A. N. (2000). Feedback effectiveness: Can 360-degree appraisals be improved? *Academy of Management Executive, 14*, 129–139.
15. London, M. (2003). *Job feedback: Giving, seeking, and using feedback for performance improvement* (2nd ed.). Mahwah, NJ: Lawrence Erlbaum.
16. Goodman, J. S., Wood, R. E., & Hendrickx, M. (2004). Feedback specificity, exploration, and learning. *Journal of Applied Psychology, 89*, 248–262.

17. Audia, P. G., Locke, E. A., & Smith, K. G. (2000). The paradox of success: An archival and a laboratory study of strategic persistence following a radical environmental change. *Academy of Management Journal, 43*, 837–853.

18. Nelson, B. (1996). Providing a context for recognition. *Executive Edge Newsletter, 27*(11), 6.

19. Watkins, T. (2004). Have a heart. *New Zealand Management, 51*(2), 46–48.

20. Tyler, K. (2004). One bad apple: Before the whole bunch spoils, train managers to deal with poor performance. *HR Magazine, 49*(12), 79.

21. Moss, S. E., & Sanchez, J. I. (2004). Are your employees avoiding you? Managerial strategies for closing the feedback gap. *Academy of Management Executive, 18*, 32–44.

22. Kinicki, A. J., Prussia, G. E., Wu, B. J., & McKee-Ryan, F. M. (2004). A covariance structure analysis of employees' response to performance feedback. *Journal of Applied Psychology, 89*, 1057–1069.

23. Audia, P. G., & Locke, E. A. (2003). Benefiting from negative feedback. *Human Resource Management Review, 13*, 631–646.

24. Cannon, M. D., & Witherspoon, R. (2005). Actionable feedback: Unlocking the power of learning and performance improvement. *Academy of Management Executive, 19*, 120–134.

25. Laumeyer, J. A. (2002). *Performance management systems: What do we want to accomplish?* Alexandria, VA: Society for Human Resource Management.

26. McGregor, D. (1957). An uneasy look at performance appraisal. *Harvard Business Review, 35*(3), 89–94.

27. Moullakis, J. (2005, March 30). One in five workers "actively disengaged." *The Australian Financial Review*, 10.

28. Adapted from D. L. Kirkpatrick. *How to Improve Performance Through Appraisal and Coaching* (New York: AMACOM, 1982), 55–57.

29. Grote, D. (2002). *The performance appraisal question and answer book* (pp. 131–132). New York: AMACOM.

30. Showers, J. H. (2002). Managing the difficult employee. SHRH White Paper. *SHRM Online*. www.shrm.org/hrresources/whitepapers

C H A P T E R

10

Reward Systems and Legal Issues

You have to get rewarded in the soul and the wallet. The money isn't enough, but a plaque isn't enough either . . . you have to give both.

—JACK WELCH

Learning Objectives

By the end of this chapter, you will be able to do the following:

- Distinguish between traditional and contingent pay plans and know how each of these reward systems relates to the performance management system.

- Understand the reasons for the popularity of contingent pay plans.

- Describe how contingent pay plans can help improve employee motivation and performance.

- Be aware of the reasons contingent pay plans can fail.

- Design a contingent pay plan, taking into account key variables such as the organization's culture and strategic business objectives.

- Understand that pay is only one of many tools that can be used to motivate employees.

- Use rewards effectively so that they produce the effects intended.

- Know the principles of how to design an organization's pay structure, including how to conduct of a job evaluation.

- Understand the advantages of the broad-banding approach to designing a pay structure.

- Understand the role played by six legal principles in the implementation of performance management systems: employment at will, negligence, defamation, misrepresentation, and adverse impact.

- Identify the point at which a performance management system is allowing illegal discrimination.

■ Know what type of evidence employees need to provide to prove illegal discrimination and what type of evidence employers need to provide to prove lack of illegal discrimination.

■ Know the impact of key laws prohibiting discrimination based on race, sex, religion, age, disability status, and sexual orientation on the design and implementation of performance management systems.

■ Design a performance management system that is legally sound.

10.1 TRADITIONAL AND CONTINGENT PAY PLANS

A traditional approach in implementing reward systems is to reward employees for the positions they fill as indicated by their job descriptions and not necessarily based on how they do their work. In other words, employees are rewarded for filling a specific slot in the organizational hierarchy. In such traditional pay systems, one's job determines direct pay and indirectly determines benefits and incentives received. Typically, there is a pay range that determines minimum, midpoint, and maximum rates for each job. For example, a university may have five ranks for professors who are just hired:

1. instructor (pay range: $30,000–$45,000)
2. senior instructor (pay range: $40,000–$55,000)
3. assistant professor (pay range: $60,000–$90,000)
4. associate professor (pay range: $85,000–105,000)
5. professor (pay range: $100,000–$140,000)

As noted above, in a traditional reward system each of these positions would have a minimum, midpoint, and maximum salary. For the case of assistant professors, the minimum is $60,000 per year, the midpoint is $75,000, and the maximum is $90,000. Salary increases at the end of the year would be determined by seniority or a percentage of one's base salary (and the same percentage would be used for all workers). Rewards would not be based on teaching quality, as indicated by student teaching ratings, or research productivity, as indicated by number and quality of publications. If an assistant professor's base salary is $90,000, she cannot see an increase in her salary unless she is promoted to associate professor, because $90,000 is the maximum possible salary for this job title. In short, in traditional reward systems, the type of position and seniority are the determinants of salary and salary increases, and not performance. In such reward systems there is no relationship between performance management and rewards.

Contingent pay (CP), also called *pay for performance*, means that individuals are rewarded based on how well they perform on the job. Thus, employees receive increases in pay based wholly or partly on job performance. These increases can either be added to an employee's base salary or be a one-time bonus (Chapter 1 provided a description of different forms of compensation). When increases are not added to an employee's base salary, as in the case of one-time bonuses, they are called *variable pay*.

Originally, CP plans were used for top management only. Gradually, the use of CP plans extended to sales jobs. At present, however, CP plans have become more pervasive. For example, in 2001, 70% of workers in the United States were employed by organizations implementing some type of variable play plan, and many of these organizations tie variable pay (e.g., bonus, commission, cash award, lump sum) directly to performance. Similarly, a study of human resources (HR) practices worldwide found that organizations in Canada, Latin America, Taiwan, and the United States generally emphasize the link between performance and pay.[1]

Let's return to the example of salaries for university professors. When a CP plan is implemented, pay raises are determined in part or wholly based on performance. So, for example, two assistant professors may be hired at the same time at the same salary level (e.g., $75,000). However, if one of them outperforms the other year after year for several years, then eventually the better performing professor may make $110,000, which may be a higher level of pay than most associate professors make. This is because every year this assistant professor receives a substantial salary increase, part of which may be added to the base salary, based on her outstanding teaching and research performance. On the other hand, the other assistant professor may still be making the same amount, or close to the same amount, he was making when he was first hired. Under a traditional pay plan, an assistant professor would not receive a higher salary than most associate professors. Under such a plan, the assistant professor would have to be promoted to associate professor before she could receive a salary of $110,000, which is outside the traditional range for assistant professors.

10.2 REASONS FOR INTRODUCING CONTINGENT PAY PLANS

Why are organizations embracing CP plans? The results of a recent survey of Fortune 500 companies indicated that performance management systems are more effective when results are directly tied to the reward system.[2] This is because when the performance management system has a direct relationship with the reward system, performance measurement and performance improvement are taken more seriously. In other words, CP plans force organizations to clearly define effective performance and to determine what factors are likely to lead to effective performance. When a CP plan is implemented, organizations need to make clear what is expected of employees, what specific behaviors or results will be rewarded, and how employees can achieve these behaviors or results. This, in and of itself, serves an important communication goal, a because supervisors and employees are better able to understand what really matters. Also, high-achieving performers are attracted to organizations that reward high-level performance and high-level performers are typically in favor of CP plans.[3] Consequently, implementing CP plans can serve as a good tool to recruit and retain top performers. Finally, CP plans can project a good corporate image because the organization may be seen as implementing a system of rewards that is fair and based on clearly communicated expectations and standards.

Hicks Waldron, former CEO of cosmetics giant Avon, in an eloquent statement, explained why CP plans are becoming so popular: "It took me 30 years to figure out that people don't do what you ask them to do; they do what you pay them to do." How about organizations that are struggling financially? Can they still implement CP plans? Can they afford to give performance-based rewards to their employees? The answer is yes to both questions. Precisely, making sure that top performers are rewarded appropriately can help keep them motivated and prevent them from leaving the organization in difficult times. It is these top performers that are the organization's hope for recovery in the future. In fact, giving rewards to poor performers means that these rewards are taken away from high-level performers.[4] Consider the case of Corning, Inc., a fiber optic cable manufacturer (http://www.corning.com/). In 2002, sales were at an unprecedented low level and the stock price was just over $1, which is about 1% of its value in 2000. Corning had slashed more than 16,000 jobs in two years and had not been profitable since early 2001. Yet, they gave bonuses to employees who met performance goals during the year.[5]

Overall, CP plans help enhance employee motivation to accomplish goals that match organizational needs. More specifically, CP plans have the potential to help people change behavior and improve performance. For example, assume an organization is trying hard to improve customer satisfaction. Some units in this organization decide to implement a CP plan that awards cash to employees who improve their customer satisfaction ratings. In contrast, other units continue with a traditional pay plan in which there is no clear tie between performance levels and rewards. Who do you think will perform better—employees under the CP plan, or those under the traditional plan? Well, if all things are equal, it is likely that employees under the CP plan will improve the service they offer to customers.[6] In fact, a review of several studies concluded that using individual pay incentives increased productivity by an average of 30%.[7] However, this is just an average and productivity does not necessarily improve by 30% in every case. Recall our discussion in Chapter 4 regarding the determinants of performance. An employee's performance is determined by the joint effects of declarative knowledge, procedural knowledge, and motivation. CP plans address the motivational component. In other words, employees are likely to choose to expend effort, choose to expend a high level of effort, and choose to persist in this high level of expenditure of effort in the presence of financial incentives. But, the fact that employees are trying hard to provide good customer service does not mean that they will necessarily succeed. They still need the declarative and procedural knowledge to do so. If they do not know how to please customers, then they won't be able to satisfy them no matter how hard they try.

CP plans can help improve the motivation of employees when each of the following conditions is present:

1. Employees see a clear link between their efforts and resulting performance (expectancy).
2. Employees see a clear link between their performance level and the rewards received (instrumentality).
3. Employees value the rewards available (valence).

There is a multiplicative relationship among these three determinants of motivation so that

$$\text{Motivation} = \text{Expectancy} \times \text{Instrumentality} \times \text{Valence}$$

If the expectancy, instrumentality, or valence conditions are not met, then the CP plan is not likely to improve performance. For example, consider the situation in which the instrumentality condition is not present. Employees may value the rewards available and may want to get them (valence). They may also see that if they exert sufficient effort, they will be able to achieve the desired performance level (expectancy). But, they believe that the rewards received are not necessarily related to their performance level (i.e., no instrumentality). In this situation, employees are not likely to choose to exert effort because this will not get them the desired rewards.

CP plans and pay in general should not be seen as the Holy Grail of employee performance. First, pay can affect only the motivation aspect of performance. So, if an employee is not performing well, pay may not solve the problem if poor performance results from lack of declarative or procedural knowledge as opposed to lack of motivation. In addition, all three conditions must be present so that CP plans can have an impact on employee motivation. We should be aware that pay is not necessarily the perfect solution and that giving people more money will not automatically solve performance problems.

10.3 POSSIBLE PROBLEMS ASSOCIATED WITH CONTINGENT PAY PLANS

In spite of the potential positive impact of CP plans, we should be aware that not all CP plans work as intended. For example, in the 1990s, Hewlett Packard implemented CP plans in 13 separate sites. However, the plans were eventually abandoned in all but one. Hewlett Packard decided to abandon CP because the benefits did not outweigh the costs.[8] Why is it that CP plans may not succeed? Consider the following reasons:[9]

- *A poor performance management system is in place.*   What happens when a CP plan is paired with a poorly designed and implemented performance management system, which includes biased ratings and the measurement of performance dimensions that are not job related? This situation may lead some employees to challenge the CP legally. Also, rewarding behaviors and results that are not job related is likely to cause good performers to quit the organization. Finally, those who stay are not likely to be motivated to perform well.
- *There is the folly of rewarding A while hoping for B.*[10]   What happens when the system rewards results and behaviors that are not those that will help the organization succeed? Employees are likely to engage in these often counterproductive behaviors because this is what will get them the desired rewards. One such example is the hope that executives will focus on long term growth and environmental responsibility while in fact they are rewarded based on quarterly earnings. Given this situation, what are these executives likely to do? Will they think in the long term, or quarter by quarter? A second example is an organization that would like its employees to be more entrepreneurial and innovative, and yet does not reward employees who think creatively. What are employees likely to do? Will they be innovative and risk not getting rewards, or will they continue to do things the old way? A third example is an organization that would like employees to focus on teamwork and a one-for-all spirit and yet rewards employees based on individual results. This is the case of many professional sports teams. What are professional athletes likely to do? Will they pass the ball, or try to score themselves to improve individual statistics?
- *Rewards are not considered significant.*   What happens when a CP plan includes pay increases, and other rewards, that are so small that they don't differentiate between outstanding and poor performers? For example, what happens when the top performers receive a 5% pay increase and the average performer receives a 3% or 4% pay increase? In this context, rewards are not viewed as performance-based rewards and they do not make an impact. The message sent to employees is that performance is not something worth being

rewarded. For rewards to be meaningful, they need to be significant in the eyes of the employees. Usually, an increase of approximately 12%–15% of one's salary is seen as a meaningful reward and would motivate people to do things they would not do otherwise.

- *Managers are not accountable.* What happens when managers are not accountable regarding how they handle the performance and the performance evaluation of their employees? They are likely to inflate ratings so that employees receive what the manager thinks are appropriate rewards. Similarly, employees may set goals that are easily attainable so that performance ratings will lead to the highest possible level of reward. In other words, when managers are not held accountable, rewards may become the driver for the performance evaluation instead of the performance evaluation being the driver for the rewards.

- *There exists extrinsic motivation at the expense of intrinsic motivation.* What happens when there is so much, almost exclusive, emphasis on rewards? Employees may start to lose interest in their jobs, which in turn can decrease motivation. In some cases, the extrinsic value of doing one's job (i.e., rewards) can supersede the intrinsic value (i.e., doing the work because it is interesting and challenging). Sole emphasis on rewards can lead to ignoring the fact that employee motivation can be achieved not only by providing rewards but also by creating a more challenging and interesting work environment in which employees have control over what they do and how they do it.

- *Rewards for executives are disproportionately large compared to rewards for everyone else.* In many organizations, executive rewards are disproportionately large compared to the rewards received by everyone else in the organization. Consider the following information: a study conducted by Pearl Meyer & Partners in 2004 revealed that the average compensation received by CEOs in major U.S. corporations was US$9.84 million, compared to an average compensation for employees in nonsupervisory roles of $27,485. So, the compensation for these CEOs was over 360 times greater than that of their employees! Such a large difference, particularly when the performance of the organization is not stellar, can lead to serious morale problems. CEOs should be compensated according to their performance, and an important indicator of CEO performance is overall firm performance (e.g., stock price in the case of publicly traded organizations).

Table 10.1 summarizes reasons CP plans fail. Consider two examples of situations in which CP plans failed because of one or more of the reasons listed in this table.

TABLE 10.1   Reasons Contingent Pay Plans Fail

A poor performance management system is in place.

There is the folly of rewarding A while hoping for B.

Rewards are not significant.

Managers are not accountable.

There exists extrinsic motivation at the expense of intrinsic motivation.

Rewards for executives are disproportionately large compared to everyone else.

First, consider what happened at Green Giant, which is part of the General Mills global food conglomerate that includes such brands as Betty Crocker, Wheaties, and Bisquick. Green Giant implemented a bonus plan that rewarded employees for removing insects from vegetables. What was the result regarding performance? Initially, managers were pleased because employees were finding and removing a substantially higher number of insects. The initial enthusiasm disappeared, however, when managers found out that employees were bringing insects from home, putting them into vegetables, and removing them to get the bonus! A second example is the automotive division of Sears, a leading retailer of apparel, home, and automotive products and services, with annual revenues of more than US $40 billion. Their CP plan rewarded employees on the basis of parts and services sold to customers who brought cars in for repair. In California, a disproportionate number of Sears auto centers were making repairs. The California Consumer Affairs Commission conducted an 18-month investigation, and sent some of its members undercover posing as customers. What did they find? Sears employees were "finding" a lot of problems and making a lot of unnecessary repairs. Half of Sears' 72 auto-service centers in California routinely overcharged customers for repairs, and Sears mechanics also billed undercover agents for work that was never done on 34 of 38 undercover operations.[11]

10.4 SELECTING A CONTINGENT PAY PLAN

Assuming an organization wishes to implement a CP plan, what should the plan look like? Recall the discussion of various forms of compensation provided in Chapter 1. What considerations should be taken into account in choosing, for example, between offering employees group incentives, profit sharing, or individual sales commissions? A critical issue to consider is that of organizational culture. An organization's culture is defined by its unwritten rules and procedures. For example, is the organization fundamentally built around individual performance, or is teamwork the norm? Is the organization one in which high-level performers are seen as role models who should be emulated, or are they viewed as a threat to upper management?[12] Are we happy with the current culture, or do we wish to change it? CP plans are powerful tools that help solidify the current culture and that can be used to create a new type of culture. There should be a careful consideration of the culture of the organization before a specific type of CP plan is selected.

Consider the types of systems that can be implemented in cultures that we can label as traditional or involvement. Traditional cultures are characterized by top-down decision making, vertical communication, and clearly defined jobs. What type of plan should be implemented in organizations with this type of culture? An effective choice would be a plan that rewards specific and observable measures of performance, where that performance is clearly defined and directly linked to pay. Examples of such CP systems are the following:

- *Piece rate.*   Employees are paid based on the number of units produced or repaired. This is a system usually implemented in many manufacturing environments. In service organizations, this could also involve number of calls made or number of clients, or potential clients, contacted. This system is usually implemented in call centers.

- *Sales commissions.* Employees are paid based on a percentage of sales. This is a system usually implemented in car dealerships.
- *Group incentives.* Employees are paid based on extra group production based on results-oriented measures (e.g., sales volume for the group). This system is implemented frequently in the retail industry.

Involvement culture is different from a traditional culture. Organizations with involvement cultures are characterized by shared decision making, lateral communications, and loosely defined roles. Examples of systems that work well in organizations with involvement cultures are the following:

- *Profit sharing.* Employees are paid based on the performance of a group (e.g., team or unit) and on whether the group has exceeded a specific financial goal. This type of system is implemented in many large law firms.
- *Skill-based pay.* Employees are paid based on whether they acquire new knowledge and skills that are beneficial to the organization. This type of system is usually implemented in knowledge-based organizations such as software development companies.

In addition to the organization's culture, an important consideration in selecting a CP plan is the organization's strategic direction. Strategy is not only a key element in designing the performance management system, it is also a key element in designing a CP plan. Table 10.2 includes a selected list of strategic objectives and CP plans that are most conducive to achieving the objective.

Table 10.2 shows that if employee development is a key strategic priority, rewards should emphasize new skills acquired. If customer service is a priority, then rewards should emphasize competencies related to customer service and gain sharing. Gain sharing links individual and group pay to an organization's overall profitability. So, the greater the organization's overall profit, the greater the rewards given to individuals and teams in the organization. In this case, gain sharing would be based on whether customer service ratings improve during the review period. If the major goal of the CP

TABLE 10.2 CP Plans Recommended for Various Strategic Business Objectives	
Strategic Business Objective	*CP Plan*
Employee development	Skill-based pay
Customer service	Competency-based pay
	Gain sharing
Productivity: Individual	Piece rate
	Sales commissions
Productivity: Group	Gain sharing
	Group incentives
Teamwork	Team sales commissions
	Gain sharing
	Competency-based pay
Overall profit	Executive pay
	Profit or stock sharing

plan is to increase the organization's overall profit, choices include executive pay and profit or stock sharing. Executive pay includes cash bonuses that are given in response to successful organizational performance. Usually, however, executive pay includes company stock to ensure that executives' activities are consistent with the shareholders' interests and to encourage executives to tend to the long-term performance of the organization. This is also called profit sharing, although profit sharing is usually short term and focused on organizational goals while stock sharing and executive pay are more long term.

Stock sharing has caught media attention in recent years. In this type of plan, stock is distributed as a reward, or executives are given the option to buy company stock at a reduced rate per share. Unfortunately, this type of CP plan has led many executives to attempt to maximize their personal wealth by inflating the price of their personal stock, often through fraudulent means, and selling their stock before the public is aware of the situation. This is what happened in companies such as Enron and WorldCom, where thousands of investors lost their retirement funds. This is an example of the folly of rewarding A while hoping for B, described in the previous section.

10.5 PUTTING PAY IN CONTEXT

Is pay the main motivating factor driving people? For most of the twentieth century, the belief was that people go to work to collect a paycheck and money was the main, or even sole, motivator. In the twenty-first century, however, we now recognize that pay is not everything. For most people, money is an important motivator because it provides many things from fulfilling basic needs (e.g., food and shelter) to providing higher education for one's children and a means for retirement.[13] However, people seek more than just a paycheck when they go to work. People want to work in an environment of trust and respect, where they can have fun and develop relationships with others, and do meaningful and interesting work. People also want to balance their work and home lives. For example, a 2004 survey by the online job-searching site CareerBuilder.com showed that 42% of working fathers say they are willing to see a reduction in their pay if this means having a better balance between work and home.[14] In addition, people are looking for learning and developmental opportunities that may lead to better career opportunities in the future. Thus, managers must realize that pay is just one element in a set of management practices that can either improve or reduce employee commitment and satisfaction, teamwork, and performance. It is true that people do work for money and an organization's pay level and pay structure affect productivity.[15] But people also seek meaning in their lives and need leisure time to pursue nonwork interests. Organizations that believe that money is all that motivates people are basically bribing their employees and will eventually pay a high price in a lack of employee loyalty and commitment.[16]

So, when we think about rewards, we should think in broader terms than just pay. We can define a reward as something that increases the frequency of an employee action. In other words, when an employee is given a reward, we expect to increase the chances that specific results and behaviors will be repeated or the employee will engage in new behaviors and produce better results. If pay raises are not producing this result, because they are not meaningful or are given arbitrarily, then they should not be viewed as rewards. Praise and recognition for a job well done, without a monetary value attached, can be a powerful reward *if* such praise and recognition enhance the chances that specific results and behaviors will be repeated. Similarly, praise and recognition should not be seen as a reward if they do not motivate employees to perform well in the future.

What can organizations do to make sure actions intended to be rewards are actually seen as rewards? What can we do to make rewards work? Consider the following recommendations:[17]

- *Define and measure performance first, and then allocate rewards.* Before rewards are allocated, there must be a good performance management system in place that (1) defines performance and performance expectations, and (2) measures performance well. In many cases, organizations believe they have a rewards problem when in fact the problem is with the definition and measurement of performance.
- *Use only rewards that are available.* If the organization does not have financial rewards available, then employee expectations should be adjusted accordingly, and the focus should be on nonfinancial rewards. It makes no sense to discuss pay raises as an important component of a CP plan if existing budget constraints mean meager raises.
- *Make sure all employees are eligible.* In many organizations, top executives receive benefits such as profit sharing, stock options, executive life and liability insurance, invitations to meetings in attractive locations, and permission to fly first-class. But, are these truly rewards as we have defined them here? Do these incentives enhance motivation? In general, they seem to do so because they motivate lower-level employees to strive to become executives. However, what would happen if these types of incentives were extended to the lower ranks of an organization? What if nonexecutive members of the organizations were also eligible for such rewards based on their performance level? By making more employees eligible for the potential reward, there is a greater chance that more employees will strive to become top performers.
- *Make rewards visible.* Rewards should be visible to those who receive them. However, rewards should also be visible to others, together with information on what needs to happen for an employee to receive the reward in the future. This recommendation applies to both financial and nonfinancial rewards. Nonfinancial rewards in particular are usually more effective if they are made public. An exception to the visibility recommendation is that some individuals may prefer a nonvisible reward allocation to avoid being singled out for attention or to prevent disrupting group harmony.
- *Make rewards contingent.* Rewards should be tied to performance directly and exclusively. Imagine that an outsider is asked to guess the salary levels for various employees in an organization. Assume she can ask the following questions: *What* do people do (e.g., administrative assistant, mailroom clerk, VP for HR)? *How long* have they done it? and *How well* have they done it? If information based on the "How well?" question is not the most useful in guessing what salaries are, then the organization is not making rewards

contingent on performance. Unfortunately, this is the case in many organizations in which what people do and how long they've done it are far better predictors of their salaries than how well they perform. When rewards are not contingent on performance, organizations can alienate their best workers, precisely those who make the greatest contributions and can easily find employment elsewhere.

- *Make rewards timely.*   Rewards should be given soon after the result or behavior being rewarded. Experimental psychologists know that if a mouse in a cage pulls a lever and a lump of sugar appears 10 months later (on the mouse's anniversary date), then no learning will take place. This is why many organizations implement on-the-spot rewards.[18] For example, at Lake Federal Bank in Hamburg, Indiana, the president has an annual budget that he can use to give relatively small, spur-of-the-moment gifts to employees who are performing well. These spot bonuses do not have to be cash awards. They can be theater tickets, a prime parking space, or anything else targeting an employee's specific needs. How does he know what type of reward to give? The answer is simple: he gets to know his employees and watches what they do and how they spend their time when they have a chance to choose. If this does not work, then he simply asks them.

- *Make rewards reversible.*   Increasing an employee's base pay creates an annuity for the employee's tenure with the organization. If mistakes are made in the allocation of increases in base salary (especially upward), they are usually irreversible and can be very costly over time. This is why variable pay, which is not added to an employee's base salary, has become an attractive option to many organizations. Variable pay is consistent with the recommendations that rewards should be contingent and reversible. If high-quality performance occurs again, then the employee receives the additional compensation again. If high-quality performance does not occur, then the additional compensation is not given.

- *Use nonfinancial rewards.*   Unfortunately, many organizations underestimate the impact of nonfinancial rewards, including the following:

  - formal commendations and awards
  - favorable mention in company publications
  - private, informal recognition for jobs well done
  - public recognition, including praise, certificate of accomplishment, and letters of appreciation
  - status indicators, such as a new job title, larger work area, promotion, ability to supervise more people, and newer or more equipment
  - time, such as taking a longer break, leaving work earlier, and time off with or without pay
  - a more challenging work environment, responsibility, and freedom

This is likely why so many organizations use the phrase "rewards *and* recognition" to mean that rewards are financial and meaningful, whereas recognition is nonfinancial and not as meaningful. As noted above, we must put pay in context and understand that pay is important, but people go to work for other reasons as well. One advantage of nonfinancial rewards is that they are typically allocated following the recommendations provided here for making rewards work in general. That is, nonfinancial rewards are usually available (there is an unlimited supply of praise!); all employees are usually eligible; and nonfinancial rewards are visible and contingent, usually timely, and certainly reversible. But do they work? Fortunately, the answer is yes. For example, think about the following professions and what they have in common: teachers, soldiers, sailors, police officers, nurses, and volunteer workers in not-for-profit organizations. They all involve nonfinancial rewards including challenge, responsibility, and interesting and meaningful work. The financial rewards for doing these jobs are not very high or nonexistent. In spite of this, people in these professions tend to be highly motivated to do their jobs.

In sum, the concept of a reward is broader than just pay. Of course, money allows people to do a great many things. And, people do incredible things to get more and more of it. However, for rewards to be effective they must motivate employees to become, or continue to be, excellent performers. Pay can do this if it is allocated based on the recommendations listed in Table 10.3. We should not forget that people go to work for reasons other than money. If an organization is trying to solve performance problems by focusing on money only, one result is expected for sure: the organization will spend a lot of money. It is not always clear that anything will change unless rewards are given, taking into account the recommendations listed in Table 10.3.

We should also understand that providing nonfinancial rewards in meaningful ways can be a powerful motivator. Consider the example of the SAS Institute, the world's leader in business analytics software (www.sas.com). This company is legendary for having one of the lowest turnover rates in the software industry. Does SAS pay higher salaries than its competitors? Not really. What do SAS employees say about their organization? They say that they don't leave for other, perhaps more lucrative, jobs because SAS offers opportunities to work with the most up-to-date equipment, jobs have variety, other employees are congenial and smart, and the organization cares about its employees and appreciates their work.[19]

Think about your current job or the last job you had. How were rewards allocated? Which of the eight recommendations listed in Table 10.3 were followed in the process of allocating rewards? Based on this, how effective were the rewards that were given? Did they help improve employee motivation and performance?

TABLE 10.3 Recommendations for Making Rewards Work

Define and measure performance first, and then allocate rewards.

Use only rewards that are available.

Make sure all employees are eligible.

Make rewards visible.

Make rewards contingent.

Make rewards timely.

Make rewards reversible.

Use nonfinancial rewards.

10.6 PAY STRUCTURES

Regardless of whether an organization implements a reward system based on performance or not, they face the question of what salary to assign to *new* employees. An organization's pay structure classifies jobs into categories based on their relative worth. To return to the university example at the beginning of this chapter, how does this particular university assign salaries to new professors? Specifically, how does the university come up with the idea to create salary bands for each of five categories (i.e., instructor, senior instructor, assistant professor, associate professor, full professor)? How wide should these bands be? How many bands should be included in the system? Information to answer each of these questions is provided by what is called a *job evaluation*.

10.6.1 Job Evaluation

Job evaluation is a process of data collection through which an organization can understand the worth of the various jobs and, as a result, can create a pay structure. Job evaluation includes a consideration of what skills, knowledge, and abilities are required for each job, how valuable the job is for the organization, and how much pay other organizations allocate to these jobs. There are several job evaluation methods available, but the most popular are ranking, classification, and point.[20]

Of the three, the *ranking method* is the fastest and simplest to implement. It consists of two steps. First, a job description is created for each job. As described in Chapter 2, a job description results from a job analysis and summarizes the job duties, needed knowledge, skills, and abilities (KSAs), and working conditions for each job. Second, job descriptions are compared to each other in terms of how valuable each job is for the organization. As a result of these comparisons, jobs are ranked from most to least valuable. The most valuable job will be given the highest pay, followed by the second most valuable job, and so forth. The ranking method requires little time, and minimal effort is needed in administering it. On the other hand, it has some drawbacks. First, the criteria for ranking may not be understood clearly. That is, evaluators may not share the same views regarding which criteria should be used to rank the various positions in terms of relative worth to the organization. Second, the distance between each rank is not necessarily equal. That is, the distance between the job ranked number 1 and the job ranked number 2 may not be the same as the distance between the number 2 job and the number 3 job. These unequal distances may not be reflected in the resulting differences in pay between the jobs.

The *classification method* also consists of two steps. First, a series of classes or job families are created. Each job class, sometimes referred to as a "grade," has a unique label and includes a sufficiently detailed description of the work performed so that it will be easy to classify all individual jobs within one class. Second, each individual job is placed within a job class. The end result is a set of classes, each including several jobs. For example, the U.S. federal government has a pay structure that includes 18 classes. Each class includes several jobs. For example, class 1 includes all jobs that are performed under immediate supervision, such as routine work in office, business, and fiscal operations and the elementary work of a technical character in a professional, scientific, or technical field. This class, in turn, includes a number of jobs considered equal in terms of the contribution they make to the organization and, therefore, should be paid equally. Jobs falling in different classes are considered differently and also are compensated differently. The classification method has several advantages, including the fact that jobs can be quickly slotted into the structure. In addition, classification levels are readily accepted by employees because they seem to be valid. On the other hand, the classification method requires extensive time and effort to be administered and, similar to the ranking method, differences between classification levels may not be equal.

The *point method* is the most time-consuming of the three, but it is the one that provides the most accurate results in terms of the pay scale for each job compared to all other jobs in the organization. The first step includes identifying *compensable factors*. Compensable factors are characteristics of jobs that add value to the organization and for which the organization is willing to pay. For example, an organization may decide that there are four factors that are important: skills, experience required, responsibility, and working conditions. Specifically, the more the skills, experience required, and responsibility, and the worse the working conditions, the more the job is worth to the organization. Second, factors are scaled. For example, a five-point scale may be used for each factor ranging from 1 (i.e., very little is needed for this position) to 5 (i.e., a great deal is needed for this position). For example, for the factor "responsibility," an entry-level job would receive a score of 1 and a managerial job a score of 4. It is important that each score be associated with a narrative description of what each number means; otherwise, evaluators may not understand the meaning and differences between the various scores. For "responsibility," a score of 1 could be "is mainly responsible for one's own job performance," whereas a score of 3 could be "is responsible for the performance of a work unit of at least 20 individuals." Third, each factor is assigned a weight so that the sum of weights for all factors should be 100%. For example, "skills" may receive a weight of 35%, "experience required" 15%, "responsibility" 40%, and "working conditions" 10%. Returning to our university example, the job evaluation form for the job of instructor may be as follows:[21]

Job Evaluation Form				
Position: Instructor				
Compensable Factors	Degree ×	Weight	=	Points
Skills	1	35		35
Experience required	2	15		30
Responsibility	1	40		40
Working conditions	2	10		20
			Total	125

The evaluation for the position of associate professor may be as follows:

Job Evaluation Form				
Position: Associate Professor				
Compensable Factors	Degree ×	Weight	=	Points
Skills	3	35		105
Experience required	4	15		60
Responsibility	4	40		160
Working conditions	2	10		20
			Total	325

As a result of the point system, each job is assigned a specific number of points that can then be translated into specific monetary figures. For example, each point may be worth $300, so the median salary for instructors would be $125 \times \$300 = \$37,500$ and the median salary for associate professors would be $325 \times \$300 = \$97,500$. How does the organization determine the amount of money to be allocated to each point? This is usually done through the collection of market compensation data. In other words, the university gathers information on how much other universities pay to instructors, senior instructors, and so forth. In the case of business schools, this is done annually by the Association to Advance Collegiate Schools of Business (AACSB). Other organizations can design their own surveys, or rely on organizations that do this on a regular basis (e.g., http://www.salary.com, http://www.haypaynet.com). Then, this information is used to adjust the monetary value given to each point so that the resulting pay ranges for the various types of jobs are comparable to those of the organization's competitors.

When compensation surveys are conducted, they include not only information on base pay, but also information on all types of compensation (e.g., bonuses) and on benefits (e.g., allowances, income protection). Ultimately, the consideration of what salaries are assigned to the various jobs or types of jobs is dependent on information obtained through compensation surveys. The important issue to recognize is that the relative difference in pay between the various positions has been established through an internally consistent method, regardless of the monetary value assigned to each point. The point system helps establish the worth of each job *relative to all other jobs* within the organization.

The point method has two notable advantages. First, it involves a comprehensive measurement of the relative worth of each job for the organization. Second, ranking jobs is easy to do once the total points for each job are known. On the other hand, it requires extensive time and effort to administer.

A study of different job evaluation systems that considered over 16,000 jobs found that the resultant ranking of jobs was similar, regardless of which job evaluation method is used.[22] This suggests that, given that different methods produced the same end result, the ranking method should be used because it is the most advantageous from a practical standpoint (i.e., it requires less time and effort to administer). However, this same study found that pay grade classification was very much affected by the type of system used. That is, small changes in total job worth scores had a profound impact on the resulting pay structure. Thus, this result argues in support of using the point method because it is more precise and accurate regarding the computation of total job worth scores. Regardless of which job evaluation method is used, fairness is an important issue to consider. Thus, evaluators should be seen as impartial and objective. In most cases, evaluators include supervisors and job evaluation analysts who are hired from outside of the organization (i.e., from a consulting firm).

10.6.2 Broad Banding

In recent years, many organizations have chosen to collapse job classes into fewer categories, usually about five. Each of these broader pay categories is called a *band*. In the case of our university example, one band may include the two instructor positions (which do not require a research component as part of the job), and a second band may include the three professor jobs (which require research as well as administrative duties as part of the job). Alternatively, one band may include all five teaching categories. Other bands within the university pay structure could include administrators and staff, for a total of not more than five bands that would include all jobs, from security guards to professors to university president.

Broad banding has become increasingly popular worldwide. For example, a survey distributed to 193 organizations by the Institute of Personnel and Development (IPD) showed that broad banding is the most common pay structure.[23] This same survey indicated that the number 1 reason broad banding is implemented is that it provides more flexibility in rewarding people. Other reasons include the need to reflect changes in organizational structure, to provide a better base for rewarding growth in competence, to devolve more responsibility for pay decisions to managers, and to provide a better basis for rewarding career progression.

The fact that so many organizations are embracing broad banding to design their pay structures is reflective of changes in the nature of work. Because of the democratization of information produced by the Internet, workers can gather data on what other organizations are paying employees with similar skills and experience. Those workers who believe that they are underpaid can try to find work elsewhere. Organizations cannot afford to lose their most competent workers, and having a pay structure based on broad banding allows for salary increases for individuals based on merit that do not require a change in job classification or even job title. In addition, organizations are becoming flatter and less hierarchical, and broad banding reflects these organizational changes. Because of this, the IPD report concluded that "whatever the many forms broad banding takes, it seems to be here to stay."

So far, this chapter has discussed the relationship between performance management and reward systems. Next, we turn to a different topic: the relationship between performance management and the law.

10.7 PERFORMANCE MANAGEMENT AND THE LAW[24]

Although we have not discussed legal issues in depth, several chapters touched upon how to design and implement performance management systems to be fair and acceptable. Usually performance management systems that are fair and acceptable to employees are also legally sound. A basic principle that guides the design of a fair system is that procedures are standardized and that the same procedures are used with all employees. In other words, when the rules and procedures are known by everyone and they are applied in the same way to everyone, the system is likely to be seen as fair. This is also the basic principle underlying the implementation of performance management systems that are legally sound. Legislation and court cases in the United States, the United Kingdom, and many other countries around the world indicate that discriminatory effects of a performance management system can be minimized by applying this basic principle: treat everyone in exactly the same way.

10.8 SOME LEGAL PRINCIPLES AFFECTING PERFORMANCE MANAGEMENT

There are six important concepts that often come into play in the case of litigation related to the implementation of a performance management system: employment at will, negligence, defamation, misrepresentation, adverse impact, and illegal discrimination.

- *Employment at will.* In employment at will, the employer or employee can end the employment relationship at any time. This type of employment relationship gives employers considerable latitude in determining whether, when, and how to measure and reward performance. Thus, an employer could potentially end the employment relationship without documenting any performance problems. However, there are two exceptions regarding an organization's ability to terminate an employee under these circumstances. First, there may be an implied contract derived from conversations with others in the organization or from information found in the company's documentation (e.g., employee handbook) indicating that employees would be terminated for just cause only. Second, decisions about terminating an employee should consider a potential violation of public policy. A 1995 case decided by the Supreme Court of Hawaii illustrates the implied contract exception to the employment at will doctrine.[25] Harry Michael Mathewson was a pilot for Aloha Airlines and was fired just two weeks before a one-year at-will probationary period would have expired. The termination was based on supposed poor peer performance ratings. However, it turned out that Mathewson had been blacklisted by the pilots' union for having worked as a scab for another airline during a strike, and he received negative reviews based on that fact, and not on his performance at Aloha. The airline violated an implied contract to provide fair and unbiased evaluations, which was based in part on the company's employee handbook. This case illustrates the benefits of basing termination decisions on information from a good performance management system, even under employment at will.

- *Negligence.* Many organizations outline a performance management system in their employee manual, employment contract, or other materials. When the system is described in such documents and not implemented as described, legal problems can arise. For example, there may be a description of how frequently appraisals take place, or how frequently supervisors and employees are to meet formally to discuss performance issues. If an employee receives what she believes is an unfair performance evaluation and the system has not been implemented as was expected, she may be able to challenge the system based on negligence on the part of the organization.

- *Defamation.* Defamation is the disclosure of untrue, unfavorable performance information that damages an employee's reputation. An employee can argue that the organization defamed her if the employer states false and libelous information during the course of the performance evaluation, or negligently or intentionally communicates these statements to a third party such as a potential future employer, thus subjecting the employee to harm or loss of reputation. Note that the definition of *defamation* includes the disclosure of *untrue* information. Defamation can take place when an employee is evaluated based on behaviors that are irrelevant and not job related, when an evaluator does not include information that would explain or justify poor performance, or when an evaluator revises a prior evaluation in an attempt to justify subsequent adverse action taken against the employee. However, defamation does not exist when information regarding poor performance is clearly documented.

- *Misrepresentation.* Whereas defamation is about disclosing untrue unfavorable information, misrepresentation is about disclosing untrue *favorable* performance and this information causes risk or harm to others. When a past employer provides a glowing recommendation for a former employee who was actually terminated due to poor performance, that employer is guilty of misrepresentation. As an example, consider a case decided by Supreme Court of California.[26] Randi W., a 13-year-old female student enrolled in a middle school, accused her school vice-principal, Robert Gadams, of sexual molestation. Gadams had glowing letters of recommendation from other school districts (i.e., his former employers), who recommended him without reservation. For example, one letter of recommendation stated, "I wouldn't hesitate to recommend [the vice-principal] for any position!" However, the former employers knew that Gadams had performance problems that included hugging female students and making sexual overtures to them. In fact, he had been pressured to resign because of such behavior. The Supreme Court of California ruled that employers can be held liable for negligent misrepresentation or fraud when an employer fails to use reasonable care in recommending former employees without disclosing material information that has a bearing on their performance.

- *Adverse impact.* Adverse impact, also called *unintentional discrimination*, occurs when the performance management system has an unintentional impact on a protected class. This can happen when women receive consistently lower performance ratings than do men. For example, adverse impact can take place for the position of firefighter if a performance dimension deals with physical strength. If members of a protected class receive consistently lower performance ratings, then the employer must be able to demonstrate that the performance dimension measured is an important part of the job. In this case, the fire department should demonstrate that physical strength is a key KSA for the job of firefighter and, based on the argument of business necessity, an appropriate measure should be included as part of the performance evaluation and every employee should be evaluated in the same fashion. As a precautionary measure, data should be gathered on an ongoing basis regarding performance scores obtained by members of various groups, broken down by the categories indicated by the law (e.g., sex, ethnicity). A periodic review of these data can help detect the presence of adverse impact and the organization can take corrective action if necessary.

- *Illegal discrimination.* Illegal discrimination, also called disparate treatment, means that raters assign scores differentially to various employees based on factors that are not performance related, such as race, nationality, color, or ethnic and national origin. As a consequence of such ratings, some employees receive more training, feedback, or rewards, than do others. This definition of illegal discrimination is given, for example, in the Race Relations Act of 1976 in the United Kingdom and in Title VII of the Civil Rights Act of 1964 in the United States. Illegal discrimination is usually referred to as *disparate treatment* because employees claim they were intentionally treated differently because of their sex, race, ethnicity, national origin, age, disability status, or other status protected under the law.

The majority of cases involving performance management systems involve a claim of disparate treatment. What can an employee do if, for example, she feels she was given unfairly low performance scores and skipped over for promotion because she is a woman? To make such a claim, an employee can present direct evidence of discrimination such as a supervisor making sexist comments that may have influenced the performance management process. Alternatively, she needs to provide evidence regarding the following issues:

- She is a member of a protected class.
- She suffered an adverse employment decision as a result of a performance evaluation (i.e., was skipped over for promotion).
- She should not have been skipped over for promotion because her performance level deserved the promotion.
- The promotion was not given to anyone, or it was given to an employee who is not a member of the same protected class (i.e., another woman).

If an employee provides this kind of evidence, the employer must then articulate a legitimate and nondiscriminatory reason for not having given the promotion to this female employee. Usually this involves a reason that is clearly performance related. This is the point at which employers benefit from having designed and implemented a system that is used consistently with all employees. Such a system is legally defensible and any decisions that resulted from the system, such as promotion decisions, are also defensible.

We must distinguish *illegal* discrimination from *legal* discrimination. A good performance management system is able to discriminate among employees based on their level of performance, and this is legal discrimination. A system that does not do this is not very useful. However, a good performance management system does not discriminate illegally. Illegal discrimination is based on variables not related to performance such as sex, national origin, and ethnicity.

10.9 LAWS AFFECTING PERFORMANCE MANAGEMENT

In the past few decades, several countries have passed laws prohibiting discrimination based on race, ethnicity, national origin, sex, religion, age, disability status, and sexual orientation. For example, the following laws have been passed in the United Kingdom:

- *Equal Pay Act of 1970.*   Aims to give individuals the right to the same contractual pay and benefits as a person of the opposite sex in the same employment.
- *Race Relations Act of 1976.*   Makes it illegal to discriminate against someone on the grounds of nationality and color, or ethnic, racial, or national group.
- *Sex Discrimination Act of 1975.*   Makes it illegal to discriminate on the grounds of sex, marital status, and gender reassignment in a limited manner.
- *Disability Discrimination Act of 1995.*   Makes it illegal to discriminate on the grounds of disability status.
- *Employment Equality (Sexual Orientation) Regulations 2003.*   Makes it illegal to discriminate on the grounds of sexual orientation.

- *Employment Equality (Religion or Belief) Regulations 2003.* Makes it illegal to discriminate on the grounds of religion and belief.

Similarly, the following laws have been passed in the United States:

- *Equal Pay Act of 1963.* Prohibits sex discrimination in the payment of wages.
- *Civil Rights Act of 1964 (as amended by the Equal Employment Opportunity Act of 1972).* Prohibits discrimination on the basis of race, color, religion, sex, or national origin.
- *Age Discrimination in Employment Act of 1967 (as amended in 1986).* Prohibits discrimination on the basis of age.
- *Americans with Disabilities Act of 1990.* Makes it illegal to discriminate against people with disabilities.

Taken together, these laws, which have similar counterparts in other countries, aim at forcing organizations to implement performance management systems that are applied consistently to all employees, regardless of demographic characteristics. Although these laws are not enforced to the same degree throughout the world, their collective goal is that performance management systems focus on measuring performance by assessing job-related factors and not personal, individual characteristics.

Designing a system that is legally defensible is not a difficult goal to achieve and it is a natural consequence of implementing a system following the recommendations offered in this course. To summarize some of the key issues that have been discussed throughout this course, Table 10.4 lists key recommendations on how to implement a performance management system that is legally sound.

Two researchers from the United Stated reviewed 295 different U.S. circuit court decisions regarding litigation involving performance management systems.[28] The goal of their study was to understand the factors carrying the most weight in the decisions

---

TABLE 10.4 Characteristics of Legally Sound Performance Management Systems[27]

Performance dimensions and standards are clearly defined and explained to the employee, job related, and within the control of the employee.

Procedures are standardized and uniform for all employees within a job group.

The system is formally explained and communicated to all employees.

Employees are given timely information on performance deficiencies and opportunities to correct them.

Employees are given a voice in the review process and are treated with courtesy and civility throughout the process.

The system includes a formal appeals process.

Performance information is gathered from multiple, diverse, and unbiased raters.

Supervisors are provided with formal training and information on how to manage the performance of their employees.

The system includes thorough and consistent documentation, including specific examples of performance based on firsthand knowledge.

The system includes procedures to detect potentially discriminatory effects or biases and abuses in the system.

reached by the court. They investigated various features of the performance management systems that were challenged in court, including many of the characteristics listed
in Table 10.4. What was their conclusion? They found that systems that emphasized the
measurement of job-related performance dimensions, provided written instructions to
raters, and allowed employees to review appraisal results were more likely to with-
stand legal challenge. Overall, these researchers concluded that employees' perceptions of whether the system was fair and employees were given due process were the
most salient issues considered by the courts. This conclusion reinforces the recommendation offered throughout this course: to allow employees to participate in the design
and implementation of the system because employee participation leads to the design
of systems viewed as fair.

SUMMARY POINTS

- Traditional pay plans do not have a link with the performance management system. Instead, pay and other rewards are allocated based on position and seniority. In contrast, contingent pay plans, also called pay for performance plans, allocate rewards wholly or partly based on job performance. When rewards given in the context of contingent pay plans are not added to an employee's base pay, they are called variable pay.

- Contingent pay plans are increasingly popular because, when they are in place, performance measurement and performance improvement are taken more seriously. Specifically, these plans force organizations to define effective performance and to determine what factors are likely to lead to effective performance. In addition, implementing these plans can serve as a good tool to recruit and retain top performers because they are attracted to organizations that reward high-level performance.

- Contingent pay plans also enhance employee motivation to accomplish goals that match organizational needs. But, for contingent pay plans to affect motivation positively, there needs to be a clear link between employee effort and employee performance (expectancy) and between employee performance and the rewards

received (instrumentality), and employees need to value the rewards available (valence).

- Contingent pay plans often fail for several reasons. First, they may be tied to a poor performance management system in which the performance dimensions measured are not relevant to organizational success. Second, the system may be rewarding behaviors and results that are counter to the needs of the organization, such as rewarding executives for short-term results as opposed to long-term growth and environmental responsibility. Third, employees may not see rewards as valuable, for example, when the difference between the rewards received by the best and the worst performers is not really meaningful. Fourth, managers may not be accountable for the system and implement it ineffectively. Finally, there may be a sole focus on extrinsic rewards, such as pay and other tangible compensation, instead of also focusing on intrinsic rewards, such as a challenging and interesting work environment in which employees have control over what they do and how they do it.

- There are many choices in the design of a contingent pay plan. It is important that the plan be congruent with the culture of the organization. People in organizations that have a traditional or an involvement culture are likely to feel more comfortable with different types of plans. For example, organizations with a traditional culture involving top-down decision making and clearly defined jobs are likely to find that a system including piece rate, sales commissions, and group incentives works well. On the other hand, organizations with an involvement culture including shared decision making and loosely defined jobs would benefit most from a system that includes profit sharing and skill-based pay. In addition to an organization's culture, the strategic business objectives also determine which type of system would work best. For example, if an organization prioritizes customer service, then competency-based pay would work well, whereas an organization prioritizing teamwork would benefit most from a plan including teams sales and gain sharing. In sum, decisions about how rewards are allocated and what types of rewards are given need to be made based on the organization's culture and strategic business objectives.

- Pay is not the only factor that motivates people. People want more out of a job than a paycheck. People seek an environment based on trust and respect, where they can have fun and develop relationships with others, and engage in meaningful and interesting work. Reward systems that focus on pay and other monetary rewards exclusively at the expense of nonfinancial rewards are basically bribing their employees and eventually pay a high price in a lack of employee loyalty and commitment. Rewards systems must go beyond pay and consider as rewards anything that increases the chances that specific behaviors and results will be repeated, or that employees will engage in desirable behaviors and produce desirable results in the future. Defined this way, rewards can include the following:
  - formal commendations and awards
  - favorable mention in company publications
  - private, informal recognition for jobs well done
  - public recognition, including praise, certificates of accomplishment, and letters of appreciation
  - status indicators, such as a new job title, larger work area, promotion, ability to supervise more people, and newer or more equipment
  - time, such as taking a longer break, leaving work earlier, and time off with or without pay
  - a more challenging work environment, responsibility, and freedom

- Several recommendations must be followed for rewards to work as intended. First, performance must be defined clearly and measured well before rewards are allocated. Second, if financial rewards are not available, employee expectations should be adjusted accordingly and the focus should be on nonfinancial rewards only. Third, all employees must be potentially eligible to receive the rewards. Fourth, rewards must be visible. Fifth, rewards must be contingent on performance and received only if the desired behaviors are displayed and the desired results are produced. Sixth, rewards must be timely and given soon after the result or behavior being rewarded has taken place. Seventh, rewards must be reversible so that employees do not feel entitled, and continue to be motivated by the desire to obtain again the reward in the future. Finally, rewards should be both financial and nonfinancial.

- An organization's pay structure classifies jobs into categories based on their relative worth. There are three popular job evaluation methods that allow organizations to design a pay structure: ranking, classification, and point. The ranking method consists of comparing job descriptions and ranking jobs based on overall relative worth. The classification method consists of first creating classes or categories of jobs (based on relative worth), and then placing all jobs into an appropriate category. The point method consists of identifying compensable factors and assigning scores to all jobs based on their standing regarding each compensable factor. The point method is the most accurate of the three, but is also the most time-consuming and difficult to administer. Ultimately, the consideration of what salaries are assigned to the various jobs or types of jobs is dependent on information obtained through compensation surveys.
- Broad banding is a type of pay structure that collapses all job classes into few categories, usually about five. Broad banding has become very popular because it gives organizations flexibility in rewarding people. In addition, broad banding reflects changes in organizational structure, provides a better base for rewarding growth in competence, gives more responsibility for pay decisions to managers, and provides a better basis for rewarding career progression.
- One or more of six legal principles are usually involved in cases of litigation regarding performance management systems. First, employment at will implies that the employer can end the relationship at any time and gives employers latitude in determining whether, when, and how to measure and reward performance. However, even in employment at will relationships, organizations benefit from having a

well-designed and implemented performance management system to guide decisions because other principles, such as implied contract and violation of public policy, may take precedence over employment at will. Second, employers can be accused of negligence if they do not follow performance management practices outlined in training manuals, employee handbooks, or other official documents. Third, employers can be accused of defamation if they make false statements during the course of the performance evaluation, negligently or intentionally communicate these statements to a third party such as a potential future employer, and thus subject employees to harm or loss of reputation. Employers can be accused of misrepresentation if they disclose untrue, favorable performance information that causes risk or harm to others. Fourth, employers can be accused of adverse impact, also called unintentional discrimination, if the performance management system has an unintentional impact on members of a protected class (e.g., women) and they receive consistently lower performance evaluations than do members of other classes (e.g., men). Finally, employers can be accused of illegal discrimination, also called disparate treatment, when evaluators assign scores differentially to various employees based on factors that are not performance related, such as race, nationality, color, or ethic and national origin.

In the context of performance management, an employee alleging illegal discrimination needs to show he or she is a member of a protected class, suffered an adverse employment decision as a result of a performance evaluation, should not have suffered this adverse impact because he or she performed adequately, and any rewards he or she deserved (e.g., promotion) were not given to anyone or were not given to an employee who is not a member of the same protected class (e.g., religious minority, ethnic minority, women). On the other hand, if an organization receives a legal challenge, it needs to provide evidence that the decision made was based on a legitimate and nondiscriminatory reason that was clearly performance related. In contrast to *illegal* discrimination, *legal* discrimination, an essential characteristic of a good performance management system, differentiates among employees based on performance-related factors.

- Several countries, such as the United Kingdom and the United States, have passed laws prohibiting discrimination based on race, sex, religion, age, disability status, and sexual orientation. Although the enforcement of these laws is uneven across countries, these laws have as their goal that organizations implement performance management systems that are applied consistently to all employees, regardless of demographic or other personal characteristics that are not job related.

- Designing and implementing a performance management system that is legally sound is not a difficult goal. This simply involves creating a system following the best practice recommendations described throughout this text. Specifically, performance dimensions and standards should be clearly defined and explained, job related, and within the control of the employee. Procedures should be standardized, used uniformly, and communicated to all employees. Employees should be given timely information on performance deficiencies and opportunities to correct them. Employees should be given a voice in the review process and treated with courtesy and civility throughout the process. The system should include a formal appeals process and performance information should be gathered from multiple, diverse, and unbiased raters. Supervisors should be provided with formal training; the system should include consistent and thorough documentation as well as procedures to detect potentially discriminatory effects or biases and abuses.

Case Study 10.1   Making the Case for a CP Plan at Architects, Inc.

Architects, Inc., is a large commercial architectural firm that specializes in the design of small to medium sized structures such as churches, private schools, and business offices. The company employs commercial architects and engineers with various levels of education, credentials, and experience. The current performance management system utilizes a traditional pay system that uses seniority for the basis of pay ranges and increases. The company currently has three ranks for architects and engineers. Each of these pay ranges determines minimum, midpoint, and maximum rates. The following outlines the three ranks:

1. Entry-level architect/engineer (pay range $35,000 – $50,000)
2. Junior architect/engineer (pay range $45,000 – $75,000)

3. Senior architect/engineer (pay range $55,000 – $100,000)

Seniority and a percentage of the base salary determine salary increases at the end of the year, and the same percentage is used for all employees. Rewards are not based on the quality of work performed, new design innovations, productivity, or customer satisfaction. Therefore, if a junior architect/engineer reaches a base salary of $75,000, he or she cannot see a salary increase unless this employee is promoted to a senior architect/engineer position because the maximum salary for a junior architect/engineer is $75,000.

You believe implementing a CP plan is a good idea. Please write a one-page memo to the president of the company describing the potential benefits of doing so to gain approval for implementing the new CP plan. ■

Case Study 10.2   Selecting a CP Plan at Dow AgroSciences[1]

Dow AgroSciences LLC, based in Indianapolis, Indiana, is a global leader in providing pest management and biotechnology products that improve the quality and quantity of the earth's food supply and contribute to the health and quality of life of the world's growing population. Dow AgroSciences has approximately 6,000 people in over 50 countries dedicated to its business, and has worldwide sales of approx-

imately US$3 billion. Dow AgroSciences is a wholly owned subsidiary of the Dow Chemical Company.

Consider the following information about Dow AgroSciences:

Mission. Dow AgroSciences delivers innovative technology that exceeds market needs and improves the quality of life of the world's growing population.

---

[1]This case study is based, in part, on information available online at http://www.dowagro.com/about. Retrieval date: August 15, 2005.

We do this through responsible pest control, aiding the production of an abundant, nutritious food supply, and the use of plants as a renewable agricultural resource to produce new and improved agricultural outputs.

Vision.   We are a premier company applying chemical, biochemical, and genetic solutions to agricultural and specialty market needs.

Core Values.   To ensure the prosperity and well-being of Dow AgroSciences employees, customers, and shareholders, cumulative long-term profit growth is essential. How we achieve this objective is as important as the objective itself. Fundamental to our success are our core values we believe in and practice:

- Employees are the source of Dow AgroSciences' success. We communicate openly, treat each other with respect, promote teamwork, and encourage personal initiative and growth. Excellence in performance is sought and rewarded.
- Customers receive our strongest commitment to meet their needs with high-quality products and superior service.
- Products are based on innovative technology, continuous improvement, and added value for our customers and end users.
- Our conduct demonstrates a deep concern for human safety and environmental stewardship, while embracing the highest standards of ethics and citizenship.

In light of the Dow AgroSciences' mission, vision, and core values, what do you think is a type of CP plan that is likely to be successful? Explain the rationale behind your choice. ■

Case Study 10.3   Possible Illegal Discrimination at Tractors, Inc.

Tractors, Inc., is a family-owned heavy equipment (excavators, tractors, paving equipment, etc.) company that has been in business for over 25 years. Over the past several years, the company has experienced rapid growth, going from 100 employees to 500 employees. Tractors, Inc., is beginning to realize that it needs to change or enhance its current performance management system. The company currently uses the same performance management system it implemented over 10 years ago.

The current performance management system consists of the following documented process:

- Performance reviews are to be conducted on a yearly basis (at the time of the employee's anniversary date with the company). One month prior to the employee's anniversary date, the supervisor/manager is to complete the standard performance appraisal form and pay increase form (if applicable), which should then be reviewed by the supervisor's manager prior to the supervisor's meeting with the employee. There are no set guidelines about how to complete the form or rate the employee's actual job performance—this is left to the reviewing supervisor's discretion.

- Once approvals have been secured, the supervisor schedules a formal meeting with the employee to discuss the appraisal.
- During the meeting, the manager reviews the ratings with the employee, including any comments that the manager may have made, opportunities for improvement and development are discussed, and the employee receives information on his or her change in pay (if applicable). At that time, the employee is given the opportunity to add any additional comments and sign the form for official submittal the human resources department. The company's unwritten policy is that employees are not permitted to keep a copy of their performance review; however, they can go to the human resources department at any time to request permission to review their past performance appraisals. Employee performance reviews are kept on file in the human resources department during the employee's tenure at the organization.

In recent months, the company has received several complaints from female employees regarding the performance management system. The complaints received are as follows:

- The employee does not have the opportunity to provide input into her performance evaluation prior to the actual meeting.
- Managers do not complete performance reviews in a timely manner. For instance, several employees have complained that they received their review three to six months after their actual anniversary date.
- Two female employees have complained that they were passed up for promotions for reasons other than performance issues. One employee cited the example of her rating in the "attendance" category as follows: "Overall Sue's attendance is acceptable and she works the hours necessary to complete her job; however, if she were to make better arrangements for handling her children's after-school activities, she would be available to work longer hours." Sue felt that, because she is a single mother, men in her department with less experience and job knowledge are promoted because they either do not have families or have stay-at-home wives to take care of their children.

Consider Tractors, Inc.'s performance management system in light of what we have discussed as an ideal system and how a company can ensure that its system is legally sound. As the new human resources manager, you have been asked to identify those areas of the current performance management system that could face a legal challenge. Please develop a one-page summation, identifying the potentially illegal aspects of the current system and your suggestions for making the current system more legally sound. ∎

END NOTES

1. Milliman, J., Nason, S., Zhu, C., & De Cieri, H. (2002). An exploratory assessment of the purposes of performance appraisals in North and Central America and the Pacific Rim. *Human Resource Management, 41*, 87–102.

2. Lawler III, E. E. (2003). Reward practices and performance management system effectiveness. *Organizational Dynamics, 32*, 396–404.

3. Trevor, C. O., Gerhart, S. L, & Boudreau, J. W. (1997). Voluntary turnover and job performance: Curvilinearity and the moderating influences of salary growth and promotions. *Journal of Applied Psychology, 82*, 44–61.

4. Wells, S. J. (2005). No results, no raise. *HR Magazine, 50*(5), 76–80.

5. Bates, S. (2003). Top pay for best performance. *HR Magazine, 48*(1), 30–38.

6. Heneman, R. L. (2002). *Strategic reward management: Design, implementation, and evaluation.* Greenwich, CT: Information Age.

7. Locke, E. A., Feren, D. B., McCaleb, V. M., Shaw, K. N., & Denny, A. T. (1980). The relative effectiveness of four methods of motivating employee performance. In K. D. Duncan, M. M. Gruenberg, and D. Wallis (Eds.), *Changes in working life* (pp. 363–388). New York: Wiley.

8. Beer, M., & Cannon, M. D. (2004). Promise and peril in implementing pay-for-performance. *Human Resource Management, 43*, 3–48.

9. Adapted from D. Grote, *The Complete Guide to Performance Appraisal.* New York: AMACOM, 1996, chap. 14.

10. Kerr, S. (1975). On the folly of rewarding A while hoping for B. *Academy of Management Journal, 18*, 769–783.

11. "Systematic Looting:" In an undercover sting, Sears' auto-repair service gets nailed. (1992, June 22) *Time*. Available online at http://www.time.com/time/archive/preview/0,10987,1101920622-159901,00.html

12. Risher, H. (2002). Pay-for performance: The keys to making it work. *Public Personnel Management, 31*, 317–332.

13. Rynes, S. L., Gerhart, B., & Minette, K. A. (2004). The importance of pay in employee motivation: Discrepancies between what people say and what they do. *Human Resource Management, 43*, 381–394.

14. Singletary, M. (2004, June 20). Divorced fathers need to be more than cash machines. *The Denver Post*, 1. K13.

15. Brown, M. P., Sturman, M. C., & Simmering, M. J. (2003). Compensation policy and organizational performance: The efficiency, operational, and financial implications of pay levels and pay structure. *Academy of Management Journal, 46*, 752–762.

16. Pfeffer, J. (1998). Six dangerous myths about pay. *Harvard Business Review, 76*(3), 109–111.

17. These recommendations are adapted from S. Kerr. "Organizational rewards: Practical, Cost Neutral Alternatives That You May Know, But Don't Practice," *Organizational Dynamics 28*(1999): 61–70.

18. Taylor, C. (2004). On-the-spot incentives. *HR Magazine, 49*(5), 80–84.

19. Pfeffer, J. (1998). Six dangerous myths about pay. *Harvard Business Review, 76*(3), 109–111.

20. The description of job evaluation methods is drawn from G. T. Milkovich and J. M. Newman. *Compensation Management*, 7th ed. (New York: McGraw-Hill, 2002) and R. L. Heneman, Job and Work Evaluation: A Literature Review, *Public Personnel Management 32*(2003): 47–71.

21. These job evaluation forms are adapted from G. T. Milkovich and J. M. Newman. *Compensation Management*, 7th ed. (New York: McGraw-Hill, 2002), 140.

22. Van Sliedregt, T., Voskuijl, O. F. & Thierry, H. (2001). Job evaluation systems and pay grade structures: Do they match? *International Journal of Human Resource Management, 12*, 1313–1324

23. IPD Survey Report 11 (2000). *Study of broad-banded and job family pay structures.* Institute of Personnel and Development. London, UK: Author.

24. This section draws heavily from S. B. Malos, "Current Legal Issues in Performance Appraisal," in, *Performance Appraisal: State of the Art in Practice*, ed. J. W. Smither, 49–94 (San Francisco: Jossey-Bass, 1998).

25. Mathewson v. Aloha Airlines, Inc., 82 Haw. 57, 919 P.2d 969 (1996).

26. Randi W. v. Muroc Joint Unified School District, 14 Cal. 4th 1066, 60 Cal.Rptr.2d 263 (1997).

27. Adapted from Exhibits 2.2 and 2.3 S. B. Malos, "Current Legal Issues in Performance Appraisal," in *Performance Appraisal: State of the Art in Practice*, ed. J. W. Smither, 49–94 (San Francisco: Jossey-Bass; 1998).

28. Werner, J. M., & Bolino, M. C. (1997). Explaining U.S. courts of appeals decisions involving performance appraisal: Accuracy, fairness, and validation. *Personnel Psychology, 50*, 1–24.

11

Managing Team Performance

The greater the loyalty of a group toward the group, the greater is the motivation among the members to achieve the goals of the group, and the greater the probability that the group will achieve its goals.

—RENSIS LIKERT

Learning Objectives

By the end of this chapter, you will be able to do the following:

■ Know the definition of a team and understand why teams are so pervasive in organizations worldwide.

■ Understand the importance of managing team performance in addition to individual performance.

■ Understand the various types of teams and how different types of teams may require different types of performance measurement.

■ Be aware of challenges associated with the design and implementation of performance management systems that include a team component.

■ Extend guidelines on how to design performance management systems that consider individual performance to systems that include both individual and team performance components.

■ Design and implement a performance management system that focuses on (1) individual performance, (2) individual performance that contributes to team performance, and (3) team performance.

■ Extend principles regarding how to reward individual performance to how to reward team performance.

11.1 DEFINITION AND IMPORTANCE OF TEAMS

Thus far, this book has focused mainly on the measurement of employees working individually and not in teams. Although the book has referred to individual and team performance, the emphasis until this point has been on individual performance. However, the discussion of team performance is important and deserves its own chapter given the increasing pervasiveness of teams in organizations world wide. It is virtually impossible to think of an organization that does not organize its functions at least in part based on teams.[1] Evidence of this is a recent survey of Fortune 1,000 companies that found that these companies considered teamwork and how to make the most out of teams their number one priority.[2]

A team is in place when *two or more people interact dynamically and interdependently and share a common and valued goal, objective, or mission.*[3] Examples of teams range from a group of top managers working together face-to-face on an ongoing basis toward the achievement of corporate goals to programmers in India and the United States writing programming code that will eventually be put together as one software program. Teams do not have to be permanent and team members do not have to be in the same geographic location. In fact, team members do not need to have met in person to be members of the same team. As long as they work together, they need each other, and they share common goals, they are considered to be members of the same team. Numerous organizations are structured around teams, including teams called autonomous work groups, process teams, or self-managing work teams. When autonomous work groups are in place, members have the authority to manage their own tasks and interpersonal processes as they carry out their work.

Why are teams so popular? First, businesses are facing increased pressures, including global competition, and they see the use of teams as a possible way to improve products and services and increase productivity. Also, meeting the needs of global customers often requires teams with members from different parts of the world. Second, many organizations have gone through downsizing and restructuring, which has led them to become flatter and to reduce the number of hierarchical levels. Using teams provides greater flexibility for these organizations. Third, products and services are becoming very complex and this requires that many people contribute their diverse talents to the same project. In most cases, no one individual can surpass the combined talent of an entire group. Finally, rapidly changing business environments are also responsible for the popularity of teams because teams are able to respond more quickly and more effectively to changes than can individuals working alone.

Although many organizations choose to structure around autonomous work teams, and teams in general, team-based organizations do not necessarily outperform organizations that are not structured around teams.[4] In other words, team performance often does not fulfill its promise. Therefore, it makes sense for performance management systems to go beyond focusing on individual performance. Specifically, the system should target not only (1) individual performance, but also (2) an individual's contribution to the performance of his or her team(s), and (3) the performance of teams as a whole. An organization that includes any type of teams would therefore benefit from managing the performance of both individuals *and* teams.

Including team performance as part of a performance management system is a natural extension of a system that had focused on individual performance only.

The general principles that we have discussed in this book thus far still apply. For example, we are still trying to design and implement the best possible system. Specifically, the system should have strategic congruence, be thorough, practical, meaningful, reliable, acceptable, ethical, and so forth (see Section 1.6 in Chapter 1). In addition, a system including team performance should also consider the possible dangers of a poorly implemented system, such as the use of false or misleading information, wasting time and money, damaging relationships, and so forth (see Section 1.3 in Chapter 1). A consideration of team performance adds a layer of complexity to any performance management system, but the fundamental principles guiding the design and implementation of the system discussed throughout this book remain the same.

It is important to note that some conditions are necessary for team performance management to lead to improved team performance. Three important conditions are the following:[5]

- The processes involved in the performance of the team are relatively unconstrained by other requirements of the task or the organization. For example, the organization should not constrain the amount of effort and skill that the team members can invest in a particular team-based project. An example of a constraint may be individual and team goals that compete against each other.
- The team is designed well and the organizational context supports team performance. In other words, there are elements in the organization that support team performance (e.g., reward systems, training systems).
- Performance feedback focuses on team processes that are under the control of team members. There is no point in providing feedback on aspects of performance that are beyond the control of the team.

11.2 TYPES OF TEAMS AND IMPLICATIONS FOR PERFORMANCE MANAGEMENT

Teams can be classified based on the complexity of the task (from routine to non-routine tasks) and membership configuration (from static to dynamic).[6] Routine tasks are well defined, there are few deviations in how the work is done, and outcomes are easily assessed once the task is completed. In contrast, non-routine tasks are not defined well, there are no clear specifications on how to do the work, and outcomes are usually very long term and difficult to assess. Membership configuration includes how long the team is expected to work together and the stability of its membership. Figure 11.1 shows that there are three main types of teams based on the task complexity and membership configuration dimensions.

- *Work or service teams.* These are intact teams engaged in routine tasks, including manufacturing or service tasks. An example is a group of people working at the assembly line in a car manufacturing plant such as Saturn or Saab. The work or service team includes people who have worked together for some time and know each other well. Most members share a similar set of skills.
- *Project teams.* These are teams assembled for a specific purpose and expected to disband once their specific tasks are completed. The tasks are outside the core production or service of the organization and are therefore not as routine as

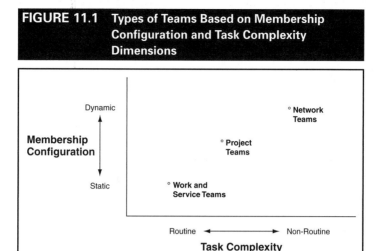

FIGURE 11.1   Types of Teams Based on Membership Configuration and Task Complexity Dimensions

Adapted from Scott, S. G., and Einstein, W. O. (2001). Strategic performance appraisal in team-based organizations: One size does not fit all. Academy of Management Executive, 15, 107–116, Figure 1. p. 110.

those of work or service teams. Examples are the team that developed IBM's first personal computer and the team that developed the original Taurus/Sable at Ford. Project teams include members from different functional areas who don't know each others' specialties and, therefore, are highly dependent on one another's high level of specific knowledge and usually sophisticated skill sets.

* *Network teams.*   These teams include membership that is not constrained by time or space and membership that is not limited by organizational boundaries. Usually, team members are geographically dispersed and stay in touch via telecommunications technology such as e-mail and video-conferencing, and of course telephone. Their work is extremely non-routine. Network teams usually include a combination of temporary and full-time workers, customers, vendors, and even consultants. An example is the group of Russian and U.S. astronauts and scientists who communicated and worked together during months of training using telecommunications technology, each from their respective countries, before some of them actually worked face-to-face in the Mir space station.

Team performance management must consider the type of team in question before performance measures are put in place. Different performance measurement methods are particularly appropriate depending on the type of team being evaluated. Work and service teams can clearly benefit from peer ratings because members observe one another's performance on a daily basis. In addition, because team members have similar responsibilities, everyone is familiar with the competencies needed to do the job. Project teams do not stay together for long periods of time and, therefore, the measure of results at the end of a project may not benefit the team's development, because the team is likely to disband once the project is over. Instead, measurements should be taken periodically as the team works on the project so corrective action can be taken as necessary, before the project is completed. This is precisely the type of measurement system Hewlett-Packard uses with its project teams in charge of product development. Network teams are transitory and engage in unique tasks on an as-needed basis. It is difficult to measure specific outcomes. Instead, performance management of network teams emphasizes the future instead of the past and focuses on developing individual competencies, such as the team members' capacity to innovate, adapt, be flexible, and solve problems.

11.3 PURPOSES AND CHALLENGES OF TEAM PERFORMANCE MANAGEMENT

Regardless of the extent to which a performance management system is concerned with individual, team performance, or both, the goals of the system are the same as those discussed in Chapter 1: strategic, administrative, informational, developmental, organizational maintenance, and documentational. In the specific case of a system concerned with team performance, one additional goal is to make all team members accountable and to motivate them to have a stake in team performance.

Many organizations have become more team based, but they have not changed their performance management systems to accommodate this new organizational reality. This presents a unique challenge. If the organization is based on teams but performance is still measured and rewarded at the individual level, team performance will suffer. In fact, some of the individual rewards may motivate people *not* to contribute to team performance and, instead, to focus on individual performance only.

In general, organizations that choose to include a team component in their performance management system must ask the following questions:

- *How do we assess relative individual contribution?* How do we know the extent to which particular individuals have contributed to team results? How much has one member contributed in relation to the other members? Are there any slackers or free riders on the team? Is everyone contributing to the same extent, or are some members covering up for the lack of contribution of others?
- *How do we balance individual and team performance?* How can we motivate team members so that they support a collective mission and collective goals? In addition, how do we motivate team members to be accountable and responsible individually? In other words, how do we achieve a good balance between measuring and rewarding individual in relation to team performance?
- *How do we identify individual and team measures of performance?* How can we identify measures of performance that indicate individual performance versus measures of performance that indicate team performance? Where does individual performance end and team performance begin? And, based on these measures, how do we allocate rewards to individuals versus teams?

The remainder of this chapter discusses how to include a team component in a performance management system. In doing so, we consider how organizations can address each of these questions.

11.4 INCLUDING TEAM PERFORMANCE IN THE PERFORMANCE MANAGEMENT SYSTEM

Although the questions asked may seem difficult to address, designing a performance management system that includes team performance is not difficult if we follow some basic principles. Specifically, recall the basic components of the performance management process as shown in Figure 11.2. You may recall this is the same figure used in Chapter 2. Now, let's consider each of the components of the process when we design a system that includes team performance.

11.4.1 Prerequisites

The first component of the performance management process involves two prerequisites. First, there is a need to have good knowledge of the organization's mission. This prerequisite is present regardless of whether there is an emphasis on team performance or not. This knowledge, combined with knowledge regarding the mission of the team's unit, allows employees to make contributions that will have a positive impact on the unit and organization as a whole. Second, there is a need to have good knowledge of the job in question. In the case of individual jobs, a job analysis is conducted to allow for the determination of the key components of a particular job: what tasks need to be done, how, and what knowledge, skills, and abilities (KSAs) are needed. Similarly, if we have good information regarding what a *team* is supposed to do and how, then it is easier to establish criteria for team success.

In addition to considering the team as a whole, we also need to identify KSAs that will allow individuals to make a positive contribution to the team. These include not only KSAs related directly to the task at hand such as a programmer who needs to have knowledge of the programming language. These are KSAs that are especially conducive to team performance. Examples are the following:[7]

- *Communication.* Giving and receiving constructive feedback, listening, and sharing information and ideas.
- *Decision making.* Helping the team make decisions.
- *Collaboration.* Dealing with conflict effectively, committing to the team and its goals, valuing the diversity and experience of other team members, and sharing accountability.

You will probably recognize these KSAs because they are closely related to our discussion in Chapter 4 of what we labeled contextual performance, prosocial behaviors, or organizational citizenship behaviors. Contextual and task performance must be considered separately because they are not necessarily parallel. An employee can be highly proficient at her task, but be an underperformer regarding contextual performance. In other words, an employee can be an excellent performer when working individually, but a substandard performer when working with others.

Consider how the prerequisites component in Figure 11.2 is implemented at the University of California at San Diego (UCSD).[8] This university, as are many others around the world, is structured around academic and administrative units called departments. Each of these departments can be considered a team. In terms of the prerequisites component, individual departments at UCSD develop a mission

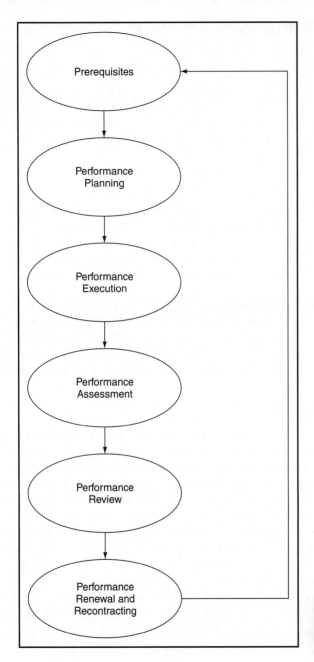

FIGURE 11.2   Performance Management Process

statement that is clearly related to the overall university's mission. This process allows each member of the team to become knowledgeable regarding the university's overall mission. Then, once the department's mission is created, individual job descriptions are discussed and directly linked to both the mission of the university and the department. Job descriptions include KSAs needed for both individual and department performance.

11.4.2 Performance Planning

The second component of the performance management process involves performance planning. Performance planning includes the consideration of results and behavior. In addition, performance planning involves the creation of a developmental plan. Each of these issues needs to be considered at the team level: results expected of the team, behaviors expected of team members, and developmental objectives to be achieved by the team and its members. A discussion of results needs to include key team accountabilities, specific objectives for each key accountability (i.e., goals to be reached), and performance standards (i.e., what are acceptable and unacceptable levels of performance). A discussion of behaviors needs to include competencies (i.e., clusters of KSAs). Finally, the developmental plan includes a description of areas that need improving and goals to be achieved in each area. The plan includes goals not only for the team as a whole, but it also includes developmental objectives for individual performance that will benefit team performance. For example, the team may have as its goal to improve its internal decision-making processes, and some team members may have the individual goal to improve listening skills, which would help improve the team's decision-making processes.

Consider how the planning component is played out at Duke University in Durham, North Carolina.[9] Duke considers planning to be the foundation of its performance management system, which creates the groundwork for what the supervisor and team expects of the individual throughout the performance year. The process at Duke consists of two parts: (1) understanding the behaviors that are expected and (2) defining the expected job results.

11.4.3 Performance Execution

The third component of the performance management process involves performance execution. Autonomous teams are solely responsible for performance execution. However, when a team has a supervisor, then both the team and the supervisor share responsibilities regarding performance execution. For example, team members need to be committed to goal achievement and should take a proactive role in seeking feedback from one another as well as from the supervisor (if there is one). The burden is on the team to communicate openly and regularly with its supervisor. Also, team members are responsible for being prepared for the performance review by conducting regular and realistic peer appraisals. In this way, team members have solid information regarding their performance as perceived by other team members before they meet with the supervisor. The supervisor also has important responsibilities, including observing and documenting team performance and the relative contribution of the team members, updating the team on any changes in the goals of the organization, and providing resources and reinforcement so that team members can be motivated to succeed.

11.4.4 Performance Assessment

The fourth component of the performance management process is performance assessment. All team members must evaluate one another's performance as well as the performance of the team overall. Peer evaluations are a key component of the assessment stage because they lead to higher levels of workload sharing, cooperation, and performance.[10] Also, team coordination and feedback improve when peers monitor the performance of all other members in the team. This, in turn, leads to the recognition of errors and to taking subsequent actions to correct these errors quickly.[11] Peer evaluations can also include team members nominating someone else as the review period's most valuable performer (MVP). In addition, the supervisor evaluates the performance of each team member as well as the team as a whole. Finally, members from other teams also evaluate the performance of the team. This would apply only if members of other teams have firsthand experience with the performance of the team in question.

Involvement of each team member in the evaluation process increases their ownership and commitment to the system. Self-appraisals also provide important information to be discussed during the performance review. In the absence of self-appraisals, it is often not clear to supervisors if the team and its members have a real understanding of what is expected of them.

In short, three types of performance need to be assessed: (1) individual performance or task performance, which refers to the specific activities required by one's individual job, such as a programmer's ability write quality code; (2) individual performance or contextual performance, which refers to specific activities that contribute to team performance, such as team members cooperating with each other; and (3) team performance as a whole. Although the saying goes, "There is no 'I' in team," this just isn't so, because teams consist of individuals with their individual motivation, needs, and talents. The system should include a good combination of both "me" and "we" considerations.[12] Thus far, this book has addressed the "me" side of the equation by focusing on individual performance management. This includes both task and contextual performance (see Chapter 4).

How can we assess the "we" side of performance? As in the case of measures of individual performance, measures of team performance should include both results and behaviors. Team performance as a whole can be measured using the following four performance dimensions:[13]

1. *Effectiveness.* This is the degree to which results satisfy team stakeholders, including both internal and external customers. Results could be the same as those that are measured to evaluate individual performance. Specifically, these can include measures of quality, quantity, cost, and time.
2. *Efficiency.* This is the degree to which internal team processes support the achievement of results, team growth, and team member satisfaction. This can include measures of communication, coordination, collaboration, and decision making.
3. *Learning and growth.* This is the degree to which the team is able to learn new skills and improve performance over time. Specific measures can include innovation, documented learning, best practices, and process improvements.
4. *Team member satisfaction.* This is the degree to which team members are satisfied with their team membership. Specific measures can include team members' perceptions regarding the extent to which teamwork contributes to their growth and personal well-being.

In total, there should not be more than about 15 measures of overall team performance.[14] Otherwise, team members may spend too much time collecting information and monitoring their activities and not sufficient time working on their assigned tasks. In addition, when the team has a meeting to assess its own overall performance, it is helpful to include a person from outside the team as part of the performance discussion. This helps team members be as objective as possible when they evaluate their performance.

11.4.5 Performance Review

The fifth component of the performance management process is the performance review. This is when the team members meet with the supervisor or manager to discuss how they have been working. In organizations that are structured around autonomous teams, there may not be a supervisor or manager. In that case, a team leader or representative would meet with a performance review board, which includes representatives of all teams.

At least two meetings are needed. First, the supervisor meets with all members of the team together. The focus of this meeting is to discuss overall team performance including results achieved by the team as a whole. Information for this meeting comes from team members evaluating their collective performance, other teams evaluating the team in question, and the supervisor's evaluation. Second, the supervisor meets with each team member individually. The focus of this meting is to discuss how the individual's behaviors contributed to team performance. Information for this meeting comes from individuals evaluating their own performance, peer ratings of the individual's performance, and the supervisor's evaluation.

Both meetings emphasize the past, the present, and the future. The past involves a discussion of performance during the review period. The present involves any changes in compensation depending on results obtained. The future involves a discussion of goals and developmental plans the team and its members will be expected to achieve during the next review period.

11.4.6 Performance Renewal and Recontracting

The final component of the performance management process involves performance renewal and recontracting. Essentially, this component is identical to the performance planning stage. However, performance renewal and recontracting uses information gathered during the review period to make adjustments as needed. For example, some new key accountabilities and competencies may be included. Conversely, some goals may have to be adjusted either upward or downward.

In short, including team performance as part of the performance management system includes the same basic components that are included in individual performance. An important difference is that, in addition to individual performance, the system includes individual performance as it affects the functioning of the team, as well as the performance of the team as a whole.

11.5 REWARDING TEAM PERFORMANCE

Teams are a pervasive fact of organizational life. Because of this, organizations that implement performance management systems that include team performance also redesign their rewards system to reward team performance. For example, about 59% of

Fortune 1,000 companies had a team-based reward system in 1990, but this number rose to 80% in 1999.[15] This number needs to be qualified because it does not mean that the entire organization rewards team performance. The results from this survey suggest that at least some units within these organizations reward team performance. Nevertheless, this statistic provides evidence regarding the increasing number of organizations that have some kind of team-based reward system. As an illustration, teams of workers in the production line at Motorola's plant in Tianjin, China, receive additional compensation if they keep the percentage of errors under a prespecified threshold.

Organizations can reward team performance in ways similar to those in which they reward individual performance. For example, consider the case of Phelps Dodge Mining Company (http://www.phelpsdodge.com/index-pdmc.html). Recently, it implemented a team-based reward system involving over 4,200 employees in six locations throughout North America. The company moved from being unionized to being nonunionized in the 1980s, and a key strategic objective was to help employees to move away from working for an hourly wage to understand how to work as a salaried workforce. To do so, team performance was measured and rewarded accordingly. For example, a team goal in a truck maintenance shop was to shorten the time that trucks were off-line for maintenance. Goals are set through the active participation of all team members. Then, employees are given additional compensation depending on whether they hit team-based goals.

Team-based rewards are effective if they are implemented following the same principles used for individual rewards discussed in Chapter 10 (see Table 10.3). For example, all employees should be eligible, and rewards should be visible, contingent, and reversible. Also, in implementing team rewards, we need to be aware of the factors that make rewards fail (see Table 10.1). For example, rewards given to team members based on the extent to which they cooperate with each other are likely to enhance accuracy, but not necessarily speed.[16] If the goal of the reward is to motivate employees to work faster, giving rewards for cooperation may be yet another example of the "folly of rewarding A while hoping for B."

An organization can have a variable pay system in which an individual is eligible for a bonus if his or her team achieves specific results. This reward would be in addition to any performance-based rewards allocated according to individual performance (either task performance or contextual performance). The amount of the bonus could also be controlled by the team: teams that are able to generate savings that result from controlling cost and improving efficiency may see some of this money back in the form of bonuses. In this case, the rewards are called *self-funded*. In other cases, the bonus can come from a company-wide pool that varies each year, based on overall organizational performance.

SUMMARY POINTS

- A team is in place when two or more people interact dynamically and interdependently and share a common and valued goal, objective, or mission. Individuals can be members of the same team even if they work in different organizations and different geographic

locations. Teams are pervasive in today's organizations and it would be difficult to find an organization with some type of work not done by teams.

- Because teams are so pervasive, it is important that the performance management system focus not only on individuals but also on teams. Organizations should take proactive steps to make sure teams perform well, that their performance improves on an ongoing basis, and that individuals are active and motivated contributors to their teams.

- Including team performance as part of the performance management system is a natural extension of a system that focuses on individual performance only. The general principles that we have discussed in this book thus far still apply. However, teams differ based on the tasks they perform (from routine to non-routine) and based on membership configuration (from static to dynamic). Measures of team performance need to take into account the type of team being evaluated.

- Including a team component in the performance management system has some unique challenges. The system needs to achieve a good balance between individual and team performance measurement and reward. In other words, it is not sufficient to measure and reward overall team performance. There also needs to be a way to measure and reward the contribution that each individual makes to the team. In this way, individuals are held accountable for contributing to team performance.

- A performance management system that includes a team component needs to focus on three types of performance: (1) individual performance, (2) individual performance that contributes to team performance, and (3) team performance. All three are necessary for a system to be successful.

- The performance management process of a system including a team performance component is similar to the process of a system including individual performance only. The components of the process include (1) prerequisites, (2) performance planning, (3) performance execution, (4) performance assessment, (5) performance review, and (6) performance renewal and recontracting. Although the inclusion of a team component adds a layer of complexity to the process, the fundamental principles guiding the design and implementation of the system discussed throughout this book remain the same.

- If the performance management system includes the measurement of individuals' contribution to team performance and overall team performance, it also needs to reward these types of performance. The principles guiding the allocation of rewards in systems including a team component are the same as those guiding the allocation of rewards in systems including individual performance only. For example, rewards should be visible, contingent, and reversible.

Case Study 11.1   Not All Teams Are Created Equal[1]

Public Service Works is a large public service organization. The company's performance management system reflects the focus placed on results, the need for creativity and imagination, and the need for continuous improvement. Under its current framework, the system links individual performance with that of the team or department, as well as the organization. Therefore,

- Department business plan goals link to the business plan and business priorities.
- Performance goals and measures grow out of a department's business plan.
- Employee performance measures align with those of the organization.
- The department, teams, and individuals are rewarded and recognized on the basis of these measures.

The organization's team structure consists primarily of *work or service teams*, which align with the company's departments. However, because of the close relationship with local government entities, the organization also utilizes *network teams* that focus on government regulatory needs as they relate to public service providers and *project teams* that are assembled on an as-needed basis to work on various projects that come from the *network teams*.

Here are the elements of the current performance management system:

Organizational performance.
Organizational performance measurement is a continuous process to assess the department's performance — efficiency,

effectiveness, and client satisfaction — in relation to the vision and business plan. The steps in the process include

1. *Business plan goals and strategies.* Identify the desired outcomes that the organization is seeking to achieve and outline how the goals will be realized.
2. *Human resources department plan.* Outline the key strategies the department will undertake to address identified human resources issues to meet its business plan, within the context of the vision, values, government business plan, and the HR plan.
3. *Performance measures.* Identify specific criteria to monitor progress toward the goals.
4. *Targets.* Describe specific performance levels to achieve the desired outcome.
5. *Learning supports.* Identify practices, policies, and initiatives that provide incentive and encouragement to employees to develop new skills, knowledge, and abilities.

Employee performance. Employee performance can be enhanced through a continuous and interactive process to help departments and teams achieve business goals and to help employees continually improve. The steps in the process include

1. *Performance plans.* Link employee performance to that of the organization and identify and set measures for desired outcomes.

---

[1]This case is based, in part, on actual information. The name Public Service Works was created to protect the identity of the actual firm.

2. *Orientation.* Provide information for employees regarding their new job and the organization to enhance understanding and effectiveness.

3. *Learning and developmental plans.* Identify competency development required for employees to carry out the performance plan.

4. *Performance coaching.* Provide ongoing performance feedback and assistance to employees from managers, supervisors, and other key individuals.

5. *Performance assessment.* Provide a summary of feedback received throughout the performance period and analyze what employees have achieved relative to the desired outcomes set out in their performance and learning plans and handle the subject of performance pay increases.

Public Service Works' current performance recognition (pay) plan supports and reinforces desired performance for both the organization and employee as follows:

- *Performance pay.* This is compensation for employees that links pay with individual performance. It consists of a market-driven base pay and a market-driven increase system that provides the ability to address cost-of-living increases and a bonus based on achievement of department and individual and team goals.
- *Special programs.* The company also has two recognition programs for outstanding performance: (1) Award of Excellence, which can be applied for and awarded to team leaders and (2) Executive Excellence Recognition, which is a unique program that recognizes teams that achieve measurable enhancements in the service they provide. Each of these programs requires an application process and the award is then determined by a committee.

Consider the performance management process (see Figure 11.2) as it is applied in implementing team-based systems. Then, please answer the following questions:

1. How is Public Service Works implementing each of the components of the performance management process?
2. Consider how Public Service Works assesses performance. Which aspects of the measurement system are appropriate and which are not, given its goal of enhancing team performance?
3. What additions or revisions should be made to each of the components of the performance management process to make the system more effective from a team performance point of view? ■

Case Study 11.2 Team Performance Management at Duke University Health Systems[2]

At Duke University Health Systems (DUHS) in Durham, North Carolina, managing performance is an ongoing process based on four principles. The following outlines the current team performance management system:

---

[2]This case is based, in part, on information available online at http://www.hr.duke.edu/compensation.

Planning. Planning is the foundation of the performance management process. It lays the groundwork for what the supervisor and team expect of the individual. There are two parts to the planning process: (1) understanding the behavior that is expected and (2) defining the job results expected.

- *Understanding behavior.* Five categories of behavior have been established for all DUHS employees (including senior administrators and new employees): customer focus, teamwork, creative problem solving, continuous learning, and diversity. Those supervising other employees are also expected to demonstrate two additional behaviors: strategic communication and performance management.
- *Defining job results.* The supervisor and individual establish expected job results as part of the planning stage. These expected job results are based on the goals of the department and the individual's job description.

Feedback and coaching. Feedback should be given often during the performance management process, so that there are no unexpected surprises at the end of the year. The feedback process involves

- *Ongoing feedback and coaching.* Throughout the year the supervisor should call attention to both good behaviors and those that need improvement.
- *An interim review.* Around the middle of the performance cycle, the employee and supervisor will meet to discuss performance and expected job results that need to be modified. During this time, improvement opportunities for the remainder of the year will be identified.
- *Obtaining and documenting feedback.* The supervisor will document the individual's performance based on feedback from a variety of sources, including (1) his or her own direct observation; (2) third-party reports from customers, peers, direct reports (if any), and managers whom the employee interacts with; and (3) the employee's own self-assessment.

Evaluation. This is the formal documentation of the performance results for the year. Evaluation and development link individual performance expectations (established at the beginning of the year) with department, entity, and broad organizational goals. This part of the performance process includes

- *Assessing individual performance.* The employee and supervisor assess performance during the year based on the job results and behavior expected.
- *Assigning overall performance rating.* Fifty percent of the rating is based on job results and 50% is based on behaviors.
- *Conducting the formal performance review.* The formal meeting gives the employee time to discuss past performance and areas for continued growth.
- *Performance rating standards.* These ratings are the following: Below Expectations (significant improvement is needed), Achieved Expectations (consistently demonstrated expected and effective behaviors), and Exceeded Expectations (consistently demonstrated role model behaviors and exceeded expected job results).

Reward. The final step of the performance management system is the reward. Pay and performance are designed to reward those who contribute to the success of the Health System, so employees are evaluated at the end of the fiscal year. The success of the Health System is measured in terms of the goals in the DUHS balanced scorecard, which consists of (1) Clinical Quality/Internal Business, (2) Customer Service, (3) Work Culture, and (4) Finances. The individual's merit increase is based on two factors: (1) the organizational success and (2) individual and team contribution to that success, as reflected in the individual's overall performance.

Consider the performance management process (see Figure 11.2) from a team point of view. Using the table here, describe whether each of the components in the process is implemented at Duke University. In some cases, a component may be partially present or present, but under a different name. Please indicate this when appropriate. ∎

Process Component	Present at Duke University? (with comments if appropriate)
Prerequisites	
Performance planning	
Performance execution	
Performance assessment	
Performance review	
Performance renewal and recontracting	
Rewarding team performance	

Case Study 11.3   Team-Based Rewards for the State of Georgia[3]

In 2001, the state of Georgia's Department of Human Resources (DHR) updated its performance management system. The performance management process is used for all employees who are to receive performance evaluations. The following outlines the basic process of this system:

- *Manager training.* Prior to utilizing the system, all managers receive training in how the system works and how to implement each phase of the system.

- *Performance planning.* This is the first step of the performance management system process and is used to create the employee's performance plan. Developing a performance plan involves identifying job and individual responsibilities and performance expectations. It is the primary responsibility of the manager to develop this plan using input from the employee that he or she may want included in the performance plan.

---

[3]This case is based, in part, on information available online at http://www2.state.ga.us/departments/dhr/pmpguide.pdf.

- *Performance coaching.* Coaching is the key supervisory activity during a performance period. It involves ongoing communication, both formal and informal, that motivates employees by letting them know where they stand in meeting expectations and carrying out responsibilities. The three steps to performance coaching are (1) observing performance; (2) providing regular performance feedback, based on information gathered through personal observation, team input, and input from the employee; and (3) documenting performance.
- *Performance evaluation.* This phase culminates with a meeting between the evaluating supervisor and the employee to rate performance and discuss appropriate salary increases and developmental planning for the employee.
- *Performance development.* Supervisors should discuss performance development with each employee. A developmental plan *must* be developed for each employee who is rated "does not meet expectations" or "needs improvement" in the area of Employment Terms and Conditions. The structured approach of the developmental plan has three objectives: (1) to enhance employee strengths, (2) to decrease employee areas that need improvements, and (3) to meet organizational and team needs.
- *Salary increase.* Salary increases are awarded annually to each eligible employee. To be eligible for a performance-based salary increase, employees must

- Receive an overall rating for Job and Individual Responsibilities of at least "met expectations."
- Receive an overall rating for Terms and Conditions of Employment of at least "needs improvement."
- Salary increases for each evaluation period for employees who "met or exceeded expectations" are restricted to the following guidelines:
  - An overall rating of "met expectations" will receive a standard increase, based on the amount identified for the evaluation period.
  - An overall rating of "exceeded expectations" will receive a standard increase as noted above, along with a lump sum identified for the evaluation period.
  - Each year a specified amount of money is set aside for salary increases. Because funds are limited, the salary increase amounts may be reduced if the department exceeds the allocated funds. If the salary increase amounts must be reduced, the reduction percentage will be the same for all employees.
  - Unless otherwise authorized, employees at or above pay grade are not eligible for a performance-based salary increase, and employees who are near the pay grade maximum will be granted an increase to the pay grade maximum only.

Please answer the following questions:
1. Based on the features of a good reward system as described in the chapter, what are the positive aspects of the state of Georgia's reward system?

2. Based on the features of a good reward system, what are the negative aspects of the state of Georgia's reward system?

3. Based on your answers to questions 2 and 3, what recommendations would you have for the state of Georgia for improving its current reward system? ■

END NOTES

1. Naquin, C. E., & Tynan, R. O. (2003). The team halo effect: Why teams are not blamed for their failures. *Journal of Applied Psychology, 88*, 332–340.

2. Roomkin, M. Rosen, S., & Dubbs, N. (1998). *Human resources practices survey.* New York: Deloitte & Touche.

3. Reilly, R. R., & McGourty, J. (1998). Performance appraisal in team settings. In J. W. Smither (Ed.), *Performance appraisal: State of the art in practice* (pp. 245–277). San Francisco: Jossey-Bass.

4. Hackman, J. R. (1998). Why teams don't work. In S. R. Tindale & L. Heath (Eds.), *Theory and research on small groups* (pp. 245–265). New York: Plenum.

5. Hackman, J. R., & Wageman, R. (2005). A theory of team coaching. *Academy of Management Review, 30*, 269–287.

6. Scott, S. G., & Einstein, W. O. (2001). Strategic performance appraisal in team-based organizations: One size does not fit all. *Academy of Management Executive, 15*, 107–116.

7. Reilly, R. R., & McGourty, J. (1998). Performance appraisal in team settings. In J. W. Smither (Ed.), *Performance appraisal: State of the art in practice* (pp. 245–277). San Francisco: Jossey-Bass.

8. University of California, San Diego, HR Department. *Guide to performance management.* Available online at http://www.hr.ucsd.edu/~staffeducation/guide/teams.html. Retrieval date: August 28, 2005.

9. Duke University Health System. *Duke HR performance management process.* Available online at http://www.hr.duke.edu/payperformance/about_performance/planning.html. Retrieval date: August 28, 2005.

10. Erez, A., Lepine, J. A., & Elms, H. (2002). Effects of rotated leadership and peer evaluation on the functioning of effectiveness of self-managed teams: A quasi-experiment. *Personnel Psychology, 55*, 929–948

11. Marks, M. A., & Panzer, F. J. (2004). The influence of team monitoring on team processes and performance. *Human Performance, 17*, 25–41.

12. Brumback, G. B. (2003). Blending "we/me" in performance management. *Team Performance Management: An International Journal, 9*, 167–173.

13. MacBryde, J., & Mendibil, K. (2003). Designing performance measurement systems for teams: Theory and practice. *Management Decision, 41*, 722–733.

14. Meyer, C. (1994). How the right measures help teams excel. *Harvard Business Review, 72*, 95–101.

15. Garvey, C. (2002). Steer teams with the right pay. *HR Magazine, 47* (5), 70–78.

16. Beersma, B., Hollenbeck, J. R., Humphrey, S. E., Moon, H., Conlon, D. E., & Ilgen, D. R. (2003). Cooperation, competition, and team performance: Toward a contingency approach. *Academy of Management Journal, 46*, 572–590

Name Index

Note: Page entries followed by *t* refer to tables; entries followed by *f* refer to figures; entries followed by *b* refer to boxes.

A

Adams, Scott, 28
Accenture, 78
Accounting, Inc., 168, 169
Alexandria, Virginia, 32
Aloha Airlines, 243
Architects, Inc., 251
Association to Advance Collegiate
    Schools of Business
    (AACSB), 241
Aurora, Colorado, 137
Avon, 229

B

Balme Library, 45, 46
Bankers Life and Casualty, 67, 68
Berube, Edward M., 67
Bisquick, 233
Bleustein, Jeffrey L., 61
Bristol-Myers Squibb (BMS), 87
Bush, George W., 150

C

California Consumer Affairs
    Commission, 233
Canada, 229
Canadian military
  Behavioral observation (BO)
    training, 160
  Frame of Reference (FOR)
    training, 159
Cardiolite, 87
CareerBuilder.com, 235
Center for Creative
    Learning, 181*t*
Chrysler, 220
CIPD, 176
Civilian Personnel Management
    Service (U.S. Department of
    Defense), 31*b*, 64*b*

Cleverly, John E., 204
Coca-Cola Company, 58
Corning, 230
Crocker, Betty, 233
Crosby, Philip, 196

D

DaimlerChrysler, 220
Dalton Alliance, Inc., 211
Dasani, 58
Deaconess Hospital, 35
Delaware, job analysis
    questionnaire, 32
Delaware, state of, 32
Dell
  employee rating supervisors, 130
  performance management, 66
Dell, Michael, 130
Denver International Airport, 54
Department of Justice, 148, 149
Department of Transportation, 110
Developmental Dimensions
    International, 181*t*
Dilbert, 72
Disney Consumer Products, 108
Dodge, 220
Dow AgroSciences, LLC, 252
Drucker, Peter F., 1
Dublin (Ireland), 81
Duke University, 263
Duke University Health
    Systems, 269

E

Eaton, Robert, 220, 221
Enron, 235

F

Federal Express, 131, 132
Flaubert, Gustave, 194

Fortune 500 companies, 131, 229
Fortune Magazine, 130
Freightliner, 220
Frontier, 54, 55, 73

G

Gadams, Robert, 244
Gallup, 212
General Mills, 233
General Electric
  coaching, 199
  forced distribution, 99
Georgia Department of Human
    Resources, 272
Green Giant, 233
Greif, 59, 60

H

Harley-Davidson, Inc.
  goals, 61
  vision and mission statements,
    71, 72
Hewlett-Packard, 231, 260
HR-survey.com, 75

I

Iacocca, Lee, 220
IBM, 259
  environmental analysis, 56, 57
  performance management, 6
Information Technology (IT)
    Project Manager, 96, 111
Institute of Personnel and
    Development (IPD), 242
Internet, 224, 242
Interstate Commerce Commission
    (ICC), 33*b*
IRI Consultants to Management,
    181*t*
Irving, Texas, 104

Subject Index

Note: Page entries followed by *t* refer to tables; entries followed by *f* refer to figures; entries followed by *b* refer to boxes.

Author Index